"Palmer applies philosophy and relig.... .... what it means to hold a belief, show why beliefs often divide us, and argue that divergent beliefs conflict less than we realize."
— BlueInk

"It comes to the convincing, timely, and valuable conclusion that if a person's beliefs lead to living a happy, moral, and productive life, then those beliefs are justified."
— Foreword Reviews

"This book is well argued and broadly researched. It has challenged me to think more carefully about the basis of my beliefs. That is the best measure of its success."
— William DiPuccio, Ph.D.

"I got a kick out of the chapter on Spinoza. It's quite a feat how the book bridges the gap between the ancients and the moderns. This one book could easily absorb an entire year of teaching at college."
— Lindy Hayes, Attorney-at-Law

"If enough of us read it, it might lead us to be more kind and understanding of our fellow human beings."
— Jim Grey, software engineer

"Weaves together history, biology, philosophy, religion, and politics ... Using a dash of humor and an accessible style of writing, this book will delight fans of books like Yuval Harari's Sapiens. Highly Recommended."
— Amazon reviewer

WHY SANE PEOPLE BELIEVE

CRAZY THINGS

How Belief Can Help
or Hurt Social Peace

www.WhySanePeopleBelieveCrazyThings.com

N.S. Palmer

Consilience Publishing, LLC

5868 E. 71st Street E226

Indianapolis, IN 46220

www.consilience-publishing.com

Cover design by Darlene Swanson / Van-Garde.com

Why Sane People Believe Crazy Things by N.S. Palmer —1st edition

ISBN 978-0-692-15155-6 (paperback)

ISBN 978-0-692-17123-3 (eBook)

Dedicated to my father:
May the memory of the righteous be a blessing.

Table of Contents

Acknowledgments

PAUL DE ANGELIS, MY EDITOR, was the best coach and critic for whom a writer could wish. He encouraged me generously when I did it right and nagged me mercilessly when I did it wrong. He has my deepest gratitude.

Dan Buckley at the Indiana University Department of Philosophy reviewed an earlier version of the manuscript and made many helpful suggestions.

Barry Mesch at Hebrew College reviewed some of the material about belief. Melinda Nearhoof at Hebrew College also reviewed the manuscript and made helpful suggestions from a religious-studies perspective. John Buisson provided very helpful criticisms of Chapters 15 and 16.

The late Brand Blanshard at Yale was my philosophical mentor and, second only to my father, was my personal role model. His ideas provide much of the foundation for this book, though he would disagree with some of what I've written.

My family patiently endured my incessant updates about the progress of "the book" and will be glad to see it in print. My friends and colleagues likewise provided support and encouragement.

Preface

"It was the best of times,
it was the worst of times,
it was the age of wisdom,
it was the age of foolishness,
it was the epoch of belief,
it was the epoch of incredulity,
it was the season of Light,
it was the season of Darkness,
it was the spring of hope,
it was the winter of despair.

We had everything before us, we had nothing before us, we were all going direct to Heaven, we were all going direct the other way— in short, the period was so far like the present period ..."

-- Charles Dickens, A Tale of Two Cities

YOU'VE GOT AN UNCLE FRANK. EVERYONE DOES. He watches Fox News and reads Breitbart. He thinks that capitalism is great, taxes are terrible, and welfare is for freeloaders.

You've also got an Aunt Sally. Everyone does. She watches CNN and reads *The New York Times*. She thinks that socialism is great, taxes are too low, and police are thugs with badges.

Both Uncle Frank and Aunt Sally are basically good people. They're honest and considerate. They're sincere. They're intelligent and educated. But God help you if they're seated next to each other at your wedding. You'll have to recite your vows loudly enough to be heard over the acrimonious argument that's emanating from the pews.

Uncle Frank and Aunt Sally are sane, but they believe crazy things. They believe those things with a fervor and fanaticism that make them seem even crazier.

Multiply that situation by a few hundred million cases, and you've got America in 2020. You've also got Great Britain, France, Germany, and other countries that are tearing themselves apart.

Both Uncle Frank and Aunt Sally think that the world is going to hell.

But what they don't know is that *they* are the ones driving it there.

They're not doing it on purpose, but they're doing it. Why? And how can they stop doing it? How can they -- and we -- return to some version of sanity?

That's why you have this book. It's not magic. It can't solve the problem by itself. But it provides some of the answers. Solving the problem depends on you.

People like Uncle Frank and Aunt Sally often have real, substantive disagreements that they could resolve. The problem isn't simply that they disagree. They disagree about a lot of things without getting angry.

But some issues make them feel that disagreement marks a line between "us" and "them." Someone who belongs to them is an enemy, enemies are evil people, and evil people must be defeated or destroyed -- before they destroy us.

Of course, Uncle Frank and Aunt Sally aren't actually crazy, so they don't consciously believe those things about each other. Even so, in the heat of an argument, it's how they feel. Those feelings can spill over into their normal lives. They won't shoot at each other, but they might not speak to each other for 10 years. And when the feelings occur in people who really *are* crazy or in the grip of mob hysteria, they cause hatred and violence. Lives are destroyed: sometimes figuratively, often literally. Peaceful societies disintegrate into warring tribes.

What can we do about it?

We can't fix the problem completely because it comes from human nature. We can only reduce the damage and minimize the risks. That depends on seeing the big picture.

There's a story about three blind men examining an elephant. The first man grabs one of its legs and says that an elephant is like a tree. The second grabs its tail and says that an elephant is like a rope. The third grabs one of its ears and says that an elephant is like a leaf. Meanwhile, the elephant is not amused by all that inappropriate touching, so it stomps the men into mush.

If the men had been able to see the entire elephant, they would have proceeded with greater caution. Sadly, each of them could perceive only a small part of the situation. Result: mush.

Most books about social discord focus on a single topic in a single way. Many of the books are excellent. However, they're like the three blind men examining an elephant. Their narrow focus prevents them from seeing how different problems connect to each other. This book shows the connections, including:

- How beliefs divide "us" from "them."
- How biology biases our judgment about us, them, and about our beliefs.
- How beliefs can unite societies instead of dividing them.
- Why beliefs that seem to conflict often don't really conflict.
- What history shows about the problems and their solutions.
- What we can do about the problems -- and what we *can't* do.

Nobody can "fix" the world completely or permanently. But you can make it better. Don't worry about what you can't do. Just do what you can: "even the angels can do no more."

Chapter 1:
How to Explain Anything

"Explaining metaphysics to the nation;
I wish he would explain his explanation."

-- Lord Byron (18th-century English poet)

THIS BOOK BEGINS WITH A MYSTERY: "Why do sane people believe crazy things?"

"Fair enough," you might think. "But what does that have to do with explaining things?"

The connection is this: the mystery arises from an unhelpful way of explaining belief. This book tries to persuade you that a new way of explaining belief can solve the mystery. And you need some reasonable way to decide if my new explanation works better than the old one.

Explanations solve mysteries

Many people believe things that seem crazy to us. Their beliefs seem crazy for one or more of three reasons:

- There's not much evidence *for* the beliefs.
- There's plenty of evidence *against* the beliefs.
- The beliefs themselves seem unclear.

If such beliefs were held only by the ignorant, the stupid, or the insane, it wouldn't worry us too much. Holding crazy beliefs is part of their job description. But many "crazy" beliefs are held by people who are educated, intelligent, and who seem as sane as any of us. How can that be? It's a mystery.

Of course, which beliefs are "crazy" depends on who you ask. Some people think it's crazy to believe that God exists:

> *"God? Seriously? A kindly old man in a white robe who lives in the sky, protects you from harm, and gives you stuff when you pray for it? Can you say 'fantasy father figure'? Does the ghost of Elvis talk to you, too? Science can explain everything. We don't need God."*

To other people, the evidence of God's existence seems so strong that atheism is an incomprehensible choice:

> *"If you see a watch, you know there's a watchmaker. The universe is far more complex and beautiful than a watch. It couldn't have happened by chance. It was designed and built by an intelligent Creator who ordained the laws of physics. That's why science works: God."*

Other beliefs seem less crazy but make it just as difficult to reach agreement. Raise taxes? On whom? Why? How much? Will taking extra vitamins improve your health? Is country X a threat that requires military action? Is President X a maniac or a hero? Did Movie X deserve to win an Academy Award for Best Picture?

Global warming is a prime example. Some people believe in it and call anyone who doubts it a "global warming denier." Others believe that global warming talk is a socialist conspiracy. They argue incessantly but neither side can convince the other. Ironically, it's usually because neither side knows what it's talking about.

Think about that for a second. Do most people know anything about climate science? Do you? We all have *beliefs* about global warming, but we can't back up our beliefs with any reasons worthy of the name. The vast majority of people rely on magazines or websites that they trust. Most people who write for those magazines don't know anything, either. They're just regurgitating what *they* read, or what they heard from someone with a Ph.D. and a lab coat.

I went to the trouble of reading a book about climate science. It didn't convince me one way or the other about global warming -- though the author clearly believed in it -- so I fell back on expert opinion. A friend of mine was a climate scientist at NASA. He doubted global warming in the 1990s, but since then he got religion about it. Now he thinks we'd better fix the problem *fast* or we'll be in terrible trouble. So my opinion is based on what he said. The difference between me and most people is that I relied on a person instead of a website. If our expert sources are wrong about global warming, then so are we.

By the way, if a person holds belief X and calls non-believers "X deniers," it's a sure sign that the person regards X as a sacred belief, not to be doubted or questioned. You can think of your own examples: there are lots of them in the news. A sacred belief might be true or it might be false. What makes it sacred is the attitude of the believers, not the belief itself.

But the mystery remains: You, I, and our acquaintances are not crazy people, but we all hold beliefs that -- when not outright crazy -- are at least vague and short on evidence. Sometimes, we hold the beliefs with religious fervor, and the less evidence there is, the more intensely and insistently we believe; the more inclined we are to scream at our particular "deniers."

Why?

The answer lies in how we explain belief. If we don't explain it or we explain it wrong, then the mystery stays mysterious. If we explain it right, the mystery disappears.

Explanations provide understanding

Ever since the first stirrings of intelligence in our distant ancestors, we have wondered and asked questions: Who are we? What are we? Why are we here? What kind of world is this? Why do we suffer and die? How can we live and be happy?

To answer those questions, we've told stories that begin with mysteries and end with beliefs that solve the mysteries. Telling stories is how we understand the world. Explanations are stories.

On its face, that seems like an odd suggestion. Should we look to a book like *The Cat in the Hat* for scientific explanations? What does telling stories have to do with understanding the world?

The answer becomes clear when you think about what it means to understand things. You already have an intuitive grasp of what it means, but you've probably never thought about it or tried to put it into words. Let's try something simple:

"Why are you reading this book?"

It might be because your spouse liked the book and wants to discuss it. You might be waiting on your flight at the airport and the book seemed more interesting than watching people argue with the gate attendants. But you understand why you're doing it. That means something simple:

If you understand something, then you can give an explanation of why it's true.[1]

Notice an important point:

How you explain it depends on your purpose.

Our minds did not evolve to explain things in the abstract. They evolved to achieve specific purposes such as surviving, prospering, and passing on our genes to the next generation. As a result, our purposes always affect the explanations we give. If you're waiting on your flight at the airport but you're reading the book because your spouse liked it, then you wouldn't mention the airport in your explanation, and vice versa.

Let's consider the relation between understanding and explanation. Here are examples of things we can understand:

- The speed of light is 186,282 miles per second.

---

[1] Note that when you understand or explain something, you *connect it* to something else. The more you connect it, the better you understand it. This will be relevant in later chapters about the nature of meaning and truth.

- You can get to the store by going north on Ditch Road.

- The internal angles of a triangle add up to 180 degrees.

- It's usually wrong to break promises.

You know many things like those. Understanding them is more than just knowing them. It means you can also explain why you think they're true. Your explanation might be more or less detailed and include more or less evidence, but you can give one. You might say, for example:

- My physics textbook said that the speed of light is 186,282 miles per second. If my physics textbook says something about physics, it's true. Therefore, the speed of light is 186,282 miles per second.

- My uncle said that he got to the store by going north on Ditch Road. I went north on Ditch Road and I arrived at the store. Therefore, you can get to the store by going north on Ditch Road.

- My geometry textbook gave a proof that the internal angles of a triangle add up to 180 degrees. I didn't understand a word of it, but my teacher will mark that answer right if I give it on the test. Therefore, the internal angles of a triangle add up to 180 degrees.

- The Bible says "Thou shalt not lie," and it's lying to make a promise but then break it. When people break promises to me, it makes me feel bad. Therefore, it's usually wrong to break promises.

Explanations are stories with purposes

Notice that almost all of these stories are about people: what they did, saw, felt, or produced. The stories begin with a question, stated or implied, such as "What's the speed of light?" or "How can I get to the store?" They describe how someone answered the question, then they give a belief as the answer.

The most abstract story is the first one, about the physics textbook. However, if you ask how the answer got into your textbook, you get stories -- all the way back to the story of the Danish astronomer Olaus Roemer, who in 1676 first measured the speed of light by observing the moons of the planet Jupiter. That story produced a belief about the speed of light.

But stories contain more than beliefs: feelings, memories, images, customs, and behavior also form part of the stories' meaning. They provide context for our fundamental beliefs, sense of self, and ways of dealing with life. Often, they also provide a guide for action.

Ancient people believed that earth, water, and sky were separate because God divided them, or because the Mesopotamian god Marduk defeated the sea goddess Tiamat and split her body; or, later, because gravity made matter form into planets. Even the last explanation, impersonal as it seems, included stories about people doing things: Copernicus, Kepler, and Newton, for instance. And though gods aren't people in the human sense, they have thoughts, goals, and motivations like human people.

What about purpose? We tell different kinds of stories for different purposes. The stories both include and imply beliefs. Some have practical impact and others don't. For example:

- **National-origin stories** make us believe that our nations are good and their government is legitimate. That motivates us to cooperate for the common good, obey the law, and fight to defend our nations in war. Stories of King David support Israel's legitimacy, just as stories of the Founders and the American Revolution do the same for the United States.

- **Practical stories** tell us how to do things. If Uncle Joe says he found a grocery store by driving two miles north on Ditch Road, we believe that if we follow the same steps as in the story, we will get to the grocery store.

- **Moral stories** tell us about certain kinds of situations, then try to make us feel positively about one way of acting (the "moral" choice) and negatively about others.

- **Philosophical stories** tell us about different ways of looking at the world, and ask if they make sense to us. They try to get us to adopt particular "big picture" views of the world. Sometimes the stories have practical implications, but often they don't. One such story denies the reality of space and time. However, even people who tell that story plan to drive home after work. They *say* they don't believe in space and time, but they sure *act* like they believe in them.

We verify the stories and their beliefs in different ways, depending on the type of story and the purpose for which it's told.

To verify national-origin stories, we look at historical evidence: critically for other countries, credulously for our own country because we *want* that story to be true. For practical stories, we either follow the steps in the story or ask someone who's done it. For moral stories, we imagine the situation and how we'd feel if it happened to us. For philosophical stories, we consult our common-sense view of the world. We ask if the story makes sense to us and explains a lot.

Stories can serve more than one purpose. For example, national-origin stories can provide historical information even though it's not their main purpose. The American Revolution was launched officially by the Declaration of Independence, whose signers risked their "lives, fortunes, and sacred honor" by signing it. American Founder John Hancock signed first. The British had already issued a death warrant for him, so he made his signature extra large in defiance of the edict. Notice how the national-origin story of the United States combines historical fact (the Declaration of Independence) with an inspiring but less certain story about Hancock's signature.

Likewise, even a simple practical story about how to get to the store can serve other purposes. It might help someone evaluate a particular neighborhood as a place to live, since it tells how far residents must travel to get their groceries.

Telling a story about belief

This book tells a story about belief: what it is, why it is that way, and what it does for us and society. The story explains how beliefs can be harmful by sparking hatred and conflict. It also explains how beliefs can be helpful by promoting goodwill and cooperation.

It's a *philosophical* story because it argues for a specific way to define belief. It argues that if you adopt the definition, it's easier to understand human society, morals, and politics: that's the purpose of the story. However, you can't test it like you can test a story about how to get to the store. There's no physical procedure you can perform that shows the definition is true or false. Nor are there historical records to back it up. You're unlikely to have strong moral feelings about the correctness of a definition. And if you have a different purpose, such as studying the relation between beliefs and brain events, then you might tell a different story that's more helpful for your particular purpose.

Definitions are a special kind of story

So how can you know if the definition is true?

The first step is to be careful about that word "true." In the abstract, definitions are neither true nor false. You can define things any way you want. For specific purposes, a definition might be more or less *useful*. And if your purposes change, your definitions might change as well. You might define belief in one way to understand society and politics, but define it in a different way to understand logic or human religious experience. Each definition would focus on aspects of belief that were relevant to your purpose, but without denying the other aspects. The purpose determines the focus.

Being useful is definitions' practical role in our lives, but some work better than others. In addition to being useful, they can fit well or poorly with the rest of our definitions, beliefs, and practices. That kind of "fit" is how definitions can be true or false.

For example, I could define the word "cow" as "four cars standing side by side." A single car would then be one-fourth of a cow.

However, the definition doesn't fit our other definitions and our normal beliefs, so nobody would understand what I was saying. It's also not useful, since "cow" would refer to what we'd usually consider four things and "car" to one-fourth of a thing.

Defining a cow as four cars affects our description of the world. Under that description, you can't get milk from a cow. The connection runs both ways: the definition implies a description, and the description implies the definition.

Our normal description of the world defines cows as female bovine animals. It includes beliefs that you *can* get milk from a cow. Therefore, defining "cow" as four cars is fine in the abstract, but is wrong relative to our normal description of the world. It's also not useful to us.

So there are two ways we can evaluate definitions:

- **Truth:** A word's definition is "true" if it matches the ordinary meaning of the word for our particular linguistic group. That's what truth means as applied to definitions.

- **Usefulness:** A word's definition is useful if it helps us achieve a particular goal, such as explaining specific observations or predicting future events. Note that the same definition might *not* be useful for other goals.

Ideally, we'd like our definitions to satisfy both criteria. But even if they don't, it's not a problem as long as we remember that we're using a special definition for a specific purpose. Happily, the definition of belief in this book does satisfy both criteria.

By the way, a common tactic in philosophy is to use special definitions in a kind of "bait and switch." For example, some writers define "knowledge" in a way that makes it impossible to know anything. Then they draw the startling conclusion that knowledge is impossible

– forgetting that it's only impossible if we accept their special definition.

How to know if a story is true

When we hear stories about the world, we start with four questions:

- What do they mean?

- Are they true?

- What's the justification for believing them?

- What actions and attitudes should we take?

As already noted, a definition of belief isn't right or wrong in the abstract. We can define it any way we like. This book offers a definition that it claims is "correct" in the sense of being more useful for social and political analysis than alternative definitions. How can we decide if it's a good, useful definition?

Let's apply the criteria from the previous section: truth and usefulness.

The first criterion is "truth" – that is, consistency with what we mean by belief in everyday life. Does the definition identify the same things as we do by "belief" -- *i.e.*, does it have the same meaning? It should satisfy:

- **Requirement 1:** Pick out *all* the cases we'd ordinarily call "belief." If we would say that "Joe believes X," then the definition should apply to that case.

- **Requirement 2:** Pick out *only* the cases we'd ordinarily call "belief." If we would not say that "Joe believes X," then the definition should not apply to that case.

Now this first criterion comes with a disclaimer. We might unreflectively think of belief in a certain way, but after careful consideration, we might amend our unreflective idea. So our ordinary sense of belief is a starting point, not the final word on the subject.

It's also important to realize that the first criterion is not just about words.[2] The reason we want our definition to correspond to the ordinary meaning of "belief" is that we want it to be about what we think it's about. If the definition picks out all and only the same things as our ordinary idea of belief, then we have reasonable assurance that we're talking about the right thing.

The second criterion is usefulness for achieving our purpose. Does our definition of belief help us to improve our lives, our social relationships, and our world? That's a high standard to meet. Most philosophical stories don't achieve it, nor does anyone expect them to achieve it.

How could the story be useful? Here's one way. Too often, beliefs divide us from our fellow human beings. They provide an excuse for hatred, persecution, and bloodshed. But it doesn't have to be that way. We can do better.

"Doing better" requires us to understand how and why beliefs can unite us or divide us. If a new way of looking at belief can help us do that, then it's useful for that purpose. One more criterion is explanatory power. If our definition of belief only makes sense under certain conditions, and doesn't help us to understand anything else, then it doesn't satisfy our second criterion. But if it applies to widely different situations and if puzzling cases suddenly "make sense" in the light of our definition, then it has explanatory power.

Our purpose in these early chapters is to find a definition of belief that helps us understand human society, morals, and politics. In the later chapters that deal with the nature of truth, meaning, and our experience of the transcendent, we'll assume a definition that's more helpful for those purposes. The definitions don't conflict, but they have different purposes and focus on different aspects of belief.

If our stories about belief are consistent with the way we identify beliefs, are useful for our purpose, and explain a lot of things, then they're good philosophical stories. We should accept them.

---

[2] Confusion on this point was almost the entire inspiration for 20th-century "ordinary-language philosophy."

Our quest will take us on a surprising journey through religion, philosophy, linguistics, neuroscience, psychology, sociology, history, and biology.

If everything "fits together" at the end, then we've got a winner.

Chapter 2:
What Belief Isn't

"Belief is the affirmation that what has been represented is outside the mind just as it has been represented in the mind."

--Maimonides, The Guide of the Perplexed, Chapter 50.

JUDAH HALEVI WAS A POET. Saadia Gaon and Moses Maimonides were philosophers. On the surface, their approaches to belief seem completely different: Halevi celebrated experience while Saadia and Maimonides followed logic.

But at a higher level, they agreed almost completely on one point: "Why believe?" And their agreement stemmed from two mistakes: mistakes about what belief is.

Two historical mistakes about belief

Halevi (1086-1145 CE) is today best known for *The Kuzari*[3], which presents a fictional dialogue between a king and a Jewish sage. The king dreams that an angel told him his actions were not pleasing to God, so he asks a philosopher, a Christian, and a Muslim for advice.

---

[3] Though usually referred to as *The Kuzari*, the book's formal title is *The Book of Refutation and Proof on Behalf of the Despised Religion*.

The philosopher responds with airy abstractions. He says that God is beyond our understanding and cannot be pleased or displeased. He gives logical arguments but dismisses the king's main concern: What should he do to please God?

The Christian and the Muslim are more sympathetic, but they fail to offer adequate evidence for their religious claims. Both of them recognize the validity of the Torah (the first five books of the Bible), so the king finally turns to a Jewish sage -- a representative of "the despised religion." What are his arguments?

The sage says simply that he believes in the God of Abraham, who revealed Himself to the entire Jewish nation at Sinai and proved Himself by miracles that they also witnessed. He argues that because God revealed himself publicly to a vast number of people, His existence and revelation are undeniable, as is His choice of the Jewish people as "the pick of mankind." The sage says that by converting to Judaism, the king could make his actions pleasing to God.

Halevi was deeply distrustful of our ability to find religious truth by reason. He justified his conclusions by reference to the belief of Jewish people in his time that their ancestors had encountered an anthropomorphic God at Sinai.

On the other hand, both Saadia (882-942 CE) and Maimonides (1135-1204 CE) thought that reason could find any religious truth, at least any we could understand. In the Prolegomena to his *Book of Beliefs and Opinions* (also known as *Book of Doctrines and Beliefs*), Saadia wrote:

> *"There exist three sources of knowledge: The knowledge given by sense perception; the knowledge given by reason; and inferential knowledge."*

Saadia thought we could get most of our knowledge, including religious knowledge, from those sources. He considered prophecy to be only a shortcut to knowledge that we could acquire more slowly by reason. He later added "authentic tradition" as a fourth source, but unlike Halevi, did not mainly rely on it.

In his "Letter on Astrology," Maimonides wrote similarly about the three grounds of knowledge:

"The first is a thing for which there is a clear proof deriving from man's reasoning ... The second is a thing that a man perceives through one of the five senses ... The third is a thing that a man receives from the prophets or from the righteous."

Like Saadia, Maimonides recognized the validity of tradition because he believed in rabbinic Judaism, but he put tradition in last place. Most of his ideas about God are highly abstract and based on philosophical reasoning.

If Saadia and Maimonides both emphasized reason, but Halevi denied that reason was a reliable guide in religion, then how did they agree "almost completely"?

They agreed in assuming that beliefs could only be justified by looking *backward*.

For Halevi, Jews looked backward at their tradition about Sinai. For Saadia and Maimonides, they looked backward at empirical evidence and logical arguments. We had to look backward at the *reasons* for the beliefs, not forward at the *results* of the beliefs. We had to look at what led to the beliefs, not where the beliefs themselves led.

They failed to consider the results of beliefs because all three of them -- in common with most thinkers throughout history -- took the idea of belief for granted. They didn't seriously consider what belief is, what it does, or what it means for beliefs to be true in different contexts.

As a result, all three of them were only vaguely aware that beliefs do a lot more than make assertions. They had made two crucial mistakes about belief:

- They assumed that beliefs were entirely mental.

- They assumed that beliefs' only job was to assert things about the world.

The first mistake led to the second. If beliefs are entirely mental, then the only person who knows for sure about them is the believer. As a result, beliefs by themselves could have no other jobs besides asserting things. They had no social impact. Normal moral rules did not apply to them. The only rules about beliefs that mattered were rules of proof: backward-looking rules about logic and evidence.

At least in some ways, the second assumption is obviously wrong. Beliefs also perform moral, psychological, spiritual, and social functions. They help us to lead decent, happy lives in stable and harmonious societies. Saadia and Maimonides acted like they knew it, even though it did not fit in their philosophies. The closest Maimonides came to recognizing other functions of belief was in Book 3, Chapter 28 of his *Guide for the Perplexed*. He argued that certain beliefs are "necessary" for successful social life. A later chapter here discusses necessary beliefs.

Centuries later, the German Jewish philosopher Moses Mendelssohn observed in his "Letter to Lavater" that even incorrect beliefs could have good results we should consider:

> *"Whoever cares more for the welfare of mankind than for his own renown will keep a rein on his opinions concerning [dubious beliefs] ... I am obliged to remain silent if these errors are accidentally connected to the promotion of the good."*

We'll return to Mendelssohn's view in Chapter 6, but the point is clear: logic, evidence, and tradition are all valid justifications of belief -- but *results* are also important.

To understand why, we must identify what belief actually is – and what it isn't. We will venture outside of religion and philosophy to look at the question of why people have beliefs at all.

Why is "believing" something that human beings do? Evolutionary psychology will provide some context, as will sociology, mathematics, and the history of science. We will look at how these ideas apply to some traditional religious beliefs. Finally, we will examine how the ideas can help us increase religious and social tolerance in our often bloody and hate-drenched world.

A historically influential example

To set the stage, let's look at a belief that's had enormous influence in Western history. Unsurprisingly, it's from the Bible: the belief that "God gave the Torah to Moses at Sinai." We could just as easily use other religious or secular beliefs, for example, about Jesus, or about string theory in physics. However, the belief about Sinai illustrates all of the important points.

In the beginning of the Jewish faith, just as for most theistic religions, people thought of God anthropomorphically. They thought He had a physical body, was finite, powerful but not omnipotent, and lived in the universe but hadn't created it. Biblical scholar Yochanan Muffs describes the situation in his book *The Personhood of God*:

> "Both Christians and Jews, each in their own way, have even accepted God's physical attributes without much care ... Pre-philosophical Jews and Christians accepted both psychic and somatic anthropomorphism as a root principle of their faith."

Now, I apologize for Professor Muffs if his statement is a little obscure. He's a smart man but he's writing for other academics who are fluent in jargon. "Pre-philosophical" simply means that ancient Jews and Christians didn't think of religion in philosophical terms. Except for ancient Athenians, hardly anyone *did* think that way.

Jews and Christians finally got started with philosophical reasoning in the 6th century CE[4] when they first encountered the newly-translated works of Plato and Aristotle. Before that, few people ever thought to ask what kind of being God was. It was enough simply to study the Bible and what it said about God.

If the Bible said that God got angry, walked around the Garden of Eden, or talked to Moses, people took the statements at face value without thinking about them too much. Getting angry suggested that God had emotions like humans did, and walking around the garden suggested He had a physical body. Hence, it seemed that God was like humans, just bigger, more powerful, and immortal. That's what Muffs means by "psychic and somatic anthropomorphism."

Given that understanding of God, the belief that God gave the Torah to Moses at Sinai is relatively unproblematic -- at least on the level

---

[4] A few earlier Jewish and Christian writers dabbled with philosophical ideas, and even the Bible includes them. However, the ideas weren't developed systematically until later. Philo of Alexandia (25 BCE - 50 CE) came the closest to doing it but didn't go all the way. As Hans Lewy writes in *3 Jewish Philosophers*, Philo's "main work is an exegesis of the Bible and not a working out of first principles. Consequently his philosophical concepts lie scattered throughout his writings ..."

of meaning if not on the level of historical and archaeological evidence. A finite, visible anthropomorphic being, who lives in the universe but did not create it and did not transcend it, gave (dictated) a book to a man. You can visualize Moses sitting on a rock, taking notes while a glorious, shining Being floats in the air above him.

However, as the centuries passed, the ancient Israelites changed their idea of God. Instead of being an anthropomorphic mountain god who was similar to other national gods of the Ancient Near East, He became the *Creator ex nihilo* (Creator from nothing) of the universe: infinite, transcendent, incomprehensible, and utterly "other."

That coincided with the Israelites' religious change from *monolatry* (worship of one God and belief that other gods exist) to *monotheism* (worship of one God and denial that any other gods exist).

The change from a human-like to a transcendent God had philosophical merit, but it made the traditional belief as incomprehensible as the God to whom it referred, who Muffs writes had:

> "... been reduced—or elevated, according to one's own personal taste—to an impersonal principle: Omniscient, Omnipotent, All-Good, Infinite, and so on ... Philosophy has lost its radical doubt (God is still affirmed as a person), while myth has lost its fire (God is not much of a person)."

Making God transcendent and incomprehensible makes the statement that "God gave the Torah to Moses at Sinai" into nonsense, because the subject is unknown and unknowable, while the verb is, according to Maimonides (*The Guide to the Perplexed*, Part I, Chapter 56) equally unknowable:

> "His essential attributes, may He be exalted, in the existence of which they believe, must not be like the attributes of other beings ... Similarly, the terms 'knowledge,' 'power,' 'will,' and 'life,' as applied to Him, may He be exalted, and to all those possessing knowledge, power, will, and life, are purely equivocal, so that their meaning when they are predicated of Him is in no way like their meaning in other applications."

In spite of that, people say that the belief does have meaning and they make it an important part of their lives. The people who say it are sane, educated, and employed. They have families. They pay taxes.

They obey the law. If you engage them in conversation, they're perfectly lucid.

If they say the belief has meaning for them, we must presume that they're right, even if we don't quite see what the meaning is. It must be doing something for them. What can that be? If the belief is logically meaningless, then it's not asserting anything, at least not anything we would ordinarily consider a fact.

Moreover, the belief is immune to empirical falsification. The parts of the belief that have meaning ("... the Torah to Moses at Sinai") have historical and archaeological implications. Those are either not fulfilled or actively contradicted by the evidence we have; and yet, believers in the Biblical account continue to insist on it.

It's a belief that, considered as a whole, seems logically meaningless. To the extent that it does have meaning, people believe it in the face of absent or contrary empirical evidence. *Whatever* it is, it's not a straightforward belief like "Joe gave the book to Sarah." ·

So there seem to be different kinds of beliefs. Some make factual claims and are factually verifiable. Others also seem to make claims, but they have no obvious connection to what we normally think of as evidence. If we now consider that belief is expressed in various forms of behavior, then a hypothesis begins to take shape: whatever they are, beliefs do things.

What beliefs *do* depends on the context and the type of belief; different types of justification are relevant to producing different types of results. A good story about belief should explain all the different things that beliefs do.

Theories of belief

Most people hold a rather naive and unreflective view of belief. To believe something, they think, is to consider and mentally affirm a specific statement, such as "2 + 2 = 4," "There is an elephant in the living room," "My spouse loves me," or "God loves me."

This is the traditional "mental act" view of belief, as stated by the Jewish philosopher Maimonides in the quote that begins this chapter. A more recent view is the "dispositional" theory of belief, which holds that beliefs are learned tendencies to act in certain ways. Another current view is the neuroscientific view, which in various ways reduces beliefs to brain events.

Contemporary academic philosophers use lots of different terminology but address the same issues. Their most popular view is representationalism, which combines elements of all three views, as do dispositionalism, interpretationism, functionalism, and various "eliminative" theories. Each of the theories has its merits and defects, but all of them boil down in one way or another to the three basic views we'll discuss here. Let's take a look at those ways of explaining belief, to see if they satisfy the two basic requirements from Chapter 1:

- **Requirement #1:** Pick out *all* the cases we'd ordinarily call "belief." If we would say that "Joe believes X," then the definition should apply to that case.

- **Requirement #2:** Pick out *only* the cases we'd ordinarily call "belief." If we would not say that "Joe believes X," then the definition should not apply to that case.

Beliefs are not mental states

The oldest view is the mental-act theory. The theory combines two things: a mental state of considering a statement and a mental state ("mental act") of affirming the same statement. Here, we'll refer to it more generally as the mental-state theory.

As you'd expect of a theory endorsed by Maimonides, it has a lot of truth. On this view, when a person believes something, he or she:

- Thinks of the words forming the statement.
- Thinks of associated images, memories, actions, or feelings:
  - ✓ An arithmetic problem: Writing out the steps on paper.
  - ✓ A loving spouse: The spouse behaving in loving ways.
  - ✓ A benevolent God: Whatever images the believer associates with the term "God," as well as feelings of love, benevolence, and security.

- Mentally affirms (in a mental act) that the statement and its associations correspond in some manner to a reality viewed as separate from the affirming mental state.

Maimonides says "outside the mind" instead of "separate from the affirming mental state." However, that doesn't quite work. Someone might have a belief about his or her own mental states: *e.g.*, "I believe that I believe in the mental-state theory." So we'll say "separate from the mental state" instead of "outside the mind."

The believer does not need to vocalize the belief or act in ways consistent with it. It's all internal. Nobody else needs to know about it, and that's actually a problem for this theory of belief.

Under the mental-state view, belief occurs at a particular time and place in the mind of a particular person. For example, if I recall and affirm my belief that Hillsdale College is a fine educational institution, my act of belief occurred at my desk on October 15.

There's no doubt that sometimes, the mental-state view applies. When we think of a proposition and mentally affirm it, we perform what we can reasonably call a mental act of belief.

We perform mental acts of belief mainly to assert facts, though we can have side-purposes as well. For example, we might mentally believe that:

- Belief 1: Dogs are mammals.
- Belief 2: Two plus two equals four.
- Belief 3: There is an elephant in my living room.
- Belief 4: I should set a good example for my children.
- Belief 5: America is the greatest country in the world.

We can mentally believe all of those things because whether or not they're true, we can understand them. They refer to things we can see, touch, or explain in terms of everyday experience.

Note, however, that the beliefs differ from each other in important ways. Beliefs 1, 2, and 3 are purely factual assertions about dogs, numbers, and an elephant. Under normal circumstances, they would not affect how you feel or how you see the world. Their impact on your behavior is limited to a few specific situations. They differ in other ways: the first is based on definition, the second on calculation, and the third on observation. However, those differences do not affect how we react to having the beliefs.

Beliefs 4 and 5 are not factual beliefs; instead, they evaluate things and behaviors, implying the believer's commitment to act in certain ways.

Problems with the Mental-State Theory

In spite of its common-sense plausibility, the mental-state view of belief has three problems:

- It ignores the public functions of beliefs.
- It implies that beliefs are dateable.
- It implies that nobody can know what anyone else believes.

Problem #1: Beliefs Have Public Functions

It's with belief 4 ("I should set a good example for my children") that we start to run into problems. It asserts a moral fact, and that's a plausible subject of a mental state. However, it does a lot more than that. It also entails:

- Making (or at least considering) a commitment to behavior that the speaker considers morally good.
- Visualizing instances of the behavior.
- Strengthening the believer's emotional readiness to engage in the behavior.
- Actually engaging in the behavior when possible and appropriate, at least a little.

Those are not unintended side-effects. They are an essential part of having such a belief. There would be no point in considering such a belief (or stating it out loud) unless one were interested in doing the other things as well. If belief were just a mental state, it couldn't do those things. If someone claimed to have the belief but never acted on it when he or she had the chance, we'd say that he or she didn't really believe it at all.

Belief 5 ("America is the greatest country in the world") is an evaluation that implies some factual statements: in particular, that America is better than other countries.

However, if you ask someone who holds belief 5 to tell you exactly how America is best, you're likely to get a blank stare. Facts are largely irrelevant to such beliefs. Moreover, such beliefs are seldom if ever merely "thought." Instead, believers proclaim them loudly and enthusiastically in the presence of other people. They perform three main functions:

- They encourage the believers and their hearers to defend America (however they conceive it) against attacks.

- They express (to self and others) the believers' membership in the group called "Americans."

- They express (to self and others) the believers' loyalty to the group called "Americans."

Like belief 4 ("I should set a good example for my children"), belief 5 involves making a commitment, as well as trying to strengthen certain kinds of feelings and behavior. However, belief 5 is mainly expressive, signifying believers' membership in the group "Americans," their pride in the group, and their commitment to support the group in conflicts with other groups. As with belief 4, the connected behavior is crucial. If a person failed to behave in ways consistent with the belief, we'd say that he or she didn't really believe it at all.

When an utterance expresses a belief rather than states it, the words used might have little or no connection to the belief it expresses. In such a case, the words are less important than the behavior itself. And any purely "mental" acts hardly matter at all.

If members of a group of people all say "God bless America" or "Vive la France," they do not assert any beliefs corresponding to the words they use. Instead, they express beliefs and signify attitudes associated with the verbal formulas they uttered. They express belief that the countries have good features, and usually that they are citizens of those countries. To themselves and others, they express their warm feelings about the countries, they indicate their membership in the national groups, and they signify loyalty to those groups.

Problem #2: Beliefs Are Not Dateable

Another problem of viewing beliefs as mental states is that it makes beliefs "dateable." Because belief requires a mental act of affirmation, beliefs occur at specific times and places.

That consequence is not entirely false. Suppose I consider the proposition that "The sky is blue" and mentally affirm it. Then I believe it. At a specific time and place, I have engaged in a mental act of belief (whatever experience that mental act is for me).

But what about when I'm not thinking of the belief? Do I stop believing "the sky is blue" as soon as I think about something else? If to believe things is to affirm them in a mental act, then we believe them only while we are doing it. All other times, we do not believe them.

Problem #3: We Can Know What Other People Believe

A third problem is that if belief is a mental state, we can never know what other people believe. But we *can* know what other people believe. Therefore, belief is not a mental state, or at least not only that.

Is this just a trivial complaint about our lack of mind-reading ability? If we can't read other people's minds, then of course we can't directly know what they believe in the privacy of their own minds. You might argue that it's a silly objection: We can't read other people's minds, but on the basis of their statements and behavior, we can infer what they believe.

However, that's not the problem. The problem is this: We can never know what another person's mental states are. If belief is a mental state, private to the person who has it, then we can never know what another person believes.

Suppose you and I agree that it's healthful to follow a vegan diet. I say it, and you voice your agreement. I observe that you follow a vegan diet and that you urge other people to do the same. On that basis, can I infer what your mental state of belief is?

This is a tough point to grasp. Suppose that when I believe "It's healthful to follow a vegan diet," I mentally imagine hearing the words corresponding to my belief. Suppose that when you have the same belief, you imagine hearing the chimes of Big Ben. However, both of us say and act consistently in following a vegan diet and uttering statements in support of it.

Do I know how you act? Yes. Do you know how I act? Yes. Does either of us know what private mental state the other has? Absolutely not -- and it doesn't even matter. Everyone could have different mental states of belief and we'd not only never know, but wouldn't see it as significant. If someone says X, never denies it, and acts consistently with it, then the person believes X. We don't need to know what his or her private mental experiences are, whether they're of words or of a duck quacking.

If beliefs were mental states, then that wouldn't be true. But we in fact can know what other people believe. Therefore, beliefs are not mental states.

The fact that our mental states are private is crucial. If any theory depends on people knowing what other people privately experience, then the theory is false. That will affect how we define belief, meaning, and communication in general.

Frankly, of the three problems, I see problem #3 as the clincher argument. Beliefs are not mental states, or at least not only mental states. Mental states are involved as necessary conditions for belief (as is consciousness), but they're not the same thing as the beliefs themselves.

Therefore, the view that beliefs are mental states fails both requirements: It fails to identify all the cases we'd call belief, and it fails to identify only the cases we'd call belief. It's definitely part of the story, but It leaves out a lot of things that we need to understand belief.

Beliefs are not dispositions

Problems with the mental-state theory led to a different theory: the dispositional theory. On this view, to hold a belief is to have a disposition to behave in certain ways in certain situations.

If the idea of dispositions is unfamiliar, don't worry: it's quite simple. If you have a disposition to do something, it just means that in the right situation, you'll probably do it. For example, I have a disposition to eat chocolate donuts. If you put chocolate donuts in front of me, I will probably eat them. That's why I stay out of donut shops. As the fictional movie detective Dirty Harry said, "A man's got to know his limitations."

If I believe that one plus one equals two, or that Albany is the capital of New York state, common sense asserts that I continue to believe them even when I'm not thinking of them. What belief means in that instance is one or more of three things:

- **Mental state:** If I were to consider the statements that "one plus one equals two" and "Albany is the capital of New York," I would mentally affirm them.

- **Statement:** In certain circumstances, I would say that "one plus one equals two" and "Albany is the capital of New York." Psychologists call this "verbal behavior." It makes no difference which language I use to say these things. I could just as easily have said "eins und eins ist zwei" or "un plus un égale deux."

- **Behavior:** In certain circumstances, I would act as if those statements are true. If I want two lumps of sugar in my tea, I will not take one lump and then three lumps as if that made two lumps: instead, I'll take one and then another one. If I want to see the state legislature of New York, I will not drive to Buffalo: instead, I'll get out the map and look for the shortest route to Albany. This is non-verbal behavior.

Notice that all of those examples begin with some variation of an "if" clause: *if* I considered some statements, *if* someone asked me a question, or *if* I were doing certain things.

The dispositional theory of belief includes the mental-state view but puts the emphasis elsewhere, on what the believer would say or do if certain things were true. It's kind of a new, improved version of the mental-state theory that fixes some of its problems. If beliefs are dispositions to think or behave in certain ways, then:

- Beliefs can have public effects through public speech and behavior.

- Beliefs don't disappear when we're not thinking of them.

- Because beliefs can have public effects, we can know what other people believe.

However, dispositions are if-then statements. They describe not what is, but what probably *would* be if believers were in certain situations. They do not assert, for example:

Sam says that dogs are mammals.

What they *do* assert is that if certain things happened, then Sam would do certain things:

If asked whether or not dogs are mammals, Sam replies "Yes, dogs are mammals."

As a result, dispositions have the same problem as mental states: they're invisible. All we can ever observe are the statements and behaviors. We base our reactions and our own behavior on those, not on how people would behave in situations that don't currently exist. We can never observe dispositions.

Dispositions also can't explain beliefs held in the past. Yesterday, nobody asked Sam if dogs were mammals. Did he believe it anyway? We might say that if someone had asked him, then he would have said dogs are mammals, but notice what that is: it's a prediction we are making about something that didn't happen. Especially in that kind of case, the disposition has nothing to do with Sam: it's a prediction that we might or might not make. It's all ours. Sam almost has nothing to do with it.

Let's give credit to the dispositional theory: it explains a lot. Just like the mental-state theory, it accurately reflects how we sometimes think about belief. But its flaw as an overall view of belief is that it's about what *might* happen, not what *does* happen. It's part of the story, but only part of it.

To sum up, let's look at a different kind of example. On earth's moon, in an area called the Sea of Tranquility, sits a rectangular piece of metal that's the high-water mark of human civilization. It has squiggles on its surface that look like this:

HERE MEN FROM THE PLANET EARTH

FIRST SET FOOT UPON THE MOON

JULY 1969, A.D.

WE CAME IN PEACE FOR ALL MANKIND

Sitting there undisturbed, in the silence of an airless moon, the squiggles do nothing. Do they have a disposition to do anything?

The answer depends on what happens. If a human who understood English once again stood in front of the metal plate, then the squiggles would say words corresponding to their shapes in English. In that situation, they have a disposition to say something in English.

But consider another case. Suppose that an alien from another star system stood in front of the plate. The alien doesn't understand English. His sensory organs differ from those of humans, so he perceives the squiggles in a way we can only guess. They remind the alien of his favorite pasta dish at a restaurant on the other side of the galaxy. In that situation, the squiggles have a disposition to remind someone of a pasta dish that you can only get far, far out in space.

You can think of other cases, but the point is obvious. What the squiggles have a disposition to do depends not on the squiggles themselves, but on other things that happen in their vicinity. The squiggles "have" an infinite number of possible dispositions, but the dispositions aren't properties of the piece of metal. The dispositions are possibilities that something will happen around it. If a particular thing doesn't happen, then the corresponding disposition doesn't exist.

And that's the other point. The disposition itself never happens. What happens, or not, is that a human stands in front of the plate and sees English text; an alien stands in front of the plate and thinks of his favorite pasta dish; or any of countless other possible if-then situations.

Something that never happens, can't be seen, and can be almost anything is not an adequate explanation of belief. The view that beliefs are dispositions fails both requirements #1 and #2. We'll have to look elsewhere.

Beliefs are not brain events

The newest view of belief is the neuroscientific view. With variations and many different names, it holds that beliefs are patterns of brain activity or are reducible to them.

Though it's stated in terms of recent scientific research, it's not really new. It is in fact an updated version of an ancient theory called "materialism." It's now called "physicalism."

Physicalists say that nothing exists but matter, energy, and patterns of matter and energy that they confusingly call "information." That's how they explain rocks, stars, the human body, and -- less convincingly -- consciousness. As far as they're concerned, the human mind is just a brain with delusions of grandeur. It's all physical in the end.

That might seem kind of nuts, but physicalists have their reasons. Most important is that they think science can answer all of our questions: not just about friction, atomic theory, or planetary orbits, but about the human soul and its problems. Love, justice, beauty, meaning, and belief: to physicalists, they can all be explained in terms of matter and energy. If physical science can study something, then it's real; otherwise, it's imaginary, and imagination itself is also physical. But physicalists have a more substantive reason, too.

Physicalism is a response to the problems of another theory called "dualism." Dualism says that mind and body are radically different kinds of things. Mind is a mental thing, not subject to physical laws, more or less independent of our bodies, and having no particular location in time and space: "conceived as a peculiar, perhaps immaterial, substance distinct from the brain."[5]

On the other hand, our bodies -- including our brains -- are physical things. They are subject to physical laws. They exist at particular locations in time and space.

This raises two challenging problems. First, how can a non-physical thing (the mind) interact with physical things (the brain and the body)? If I decide to hold up two fingers, then absent some disease or disability, my hand goes up and extends two fingers: a mental event caused a physical event. If someone is offended by my gesture and kicks me in the shin, then I feel a pain in my leg: a physical event caused a mental event.

We know, or at least think we know, what it means for an event to cause another event of the same kind. If I think of my grandfather, that's a mental event. It causes me to recall his book-lined study and the smell of his pipe: my act of remembering is another mental event. I know the experience of having one thought lead to another. Likewise, if one billiard ball strikes another, that's a physical event. Its impact exerts a force on the second ball that causes it to move: that's another physical event. No problem.

But as for how a mental event causes a physical event or vice versa, we haven't a clue. If you decide to put your hand in front of a moving billiard ball, then your hand moves as you decided. How did the mental experience of deciding to move your hand cause the physical hand to move? When the ball hits your hand, the physical impact causes you to feel something that corresponds to the impact. How did we get from the impact to the feeling? To say it's because of sensory nerves in your hand only moves the problem back a step: how does the disturbance of physical nerves in your hand cause a mental experience? Dualism has no good answer for such questions.

The second problem is even more troubling. If the brain and body are physical things and are subject to physical laws, then their operation will be consistent with those laws. In particular, that seems to rule

---

[5] Bennett, M. and Hacker, P., "Selections from *Philosophical Foundations of Neuroscience*," in Bennett (2003), p. 6.

out non-physical causes of physical events. The movements of my hand must be entirely determined by antecedent physical causes. To suggest that a mental event can cause my hand to move is tantamount to saying that the law of cause and effect doesn't always apply in the physical universe. It's like saying that even if the first ball doesn't hit it, the second ball can decide by itself to start moving.

Physicalists, including supporters of the neuroscientific view, solve the problem by insisting that mental events are physical events. In its essentials, their argument is the same as it was over 2,000 years ago when the poet Lucretius wrote in *De Rerum Natura*:

All nature, as it is in itself,

Of two things: there are bodies and there is void

In which these bodies are and through which they move ...

Impossible without body, must we not

Admit that mind and spirit are bodily?

Today, we have many more details to add. Lucretius didn't know about neurons, action potentials, Broca's area, or any of the scientific discoveries in which modern physicalists couch their accounts of mind. But the argument still boils down to this:

1. Only physical things exist.
2. But consciousness exists.
3. *What?!* There goes our theory ...
4. Therefore, consciousness must be physical.

The problem is that premise 1 (only physical things exist) is contradicted by a common-sense interpretation of premise 2 (consciousness exists). Both cannot be true. We can either abandon the belief that only physical things exist or we reinterpret consciousness as a physical thing. Physicalists choose the latter as a matter of faith, though they are by their own admission not conscious of doing so.

The existence of consciousness is the paramount challenge to a purely physical account of belief, but it's not the only one. However accurate in scientific details, a description of brain processes is plainly not a description of belief as it has always been understood.

Let's look at muscular strength for an analogy. We now know that muscles contain filaments of actin and myosin that contract. Our muscles break down fats and carbohydrates to get energy. That's how this happened in the Bible's Book of Judges:

> *28 Then Samson called to the LORD, "O Lord GOD! Please remember me, and give me strength just this once, O God, to take revenge of the Philistines, if only for one of my two eyes."*
>
> *29 He embraced the two middle pillars the temple rested upon, one with his right arm and one with his left, and leaned against them;*
>
> *30 Samson cried, "Let me die with the Philistines!" and he pulled with all his might. The temple came crashing down on the lords and on all the people in it. Those who were slain by him as he died.*

Was Samson's strength the same thing as the muscle fibers and chemical reactions that made it possible? Did the Biblical writers think about fats, carbohydrates, and muscle fibers? To ask those questions is to answer them. The same applies to statements about belief and, more generally, to those about consciousness.

Supporters of the neuroscientific explanation are certainly talking about *something*, perhaps even something important, but they are not talking about belief or consciousness. They have *changed the subject* to one with which they feel more comfortable.

If someone stated a belief in X, and behaved consistently with it, we would say he believed X even if neuroscientists found no corresponding brain processes. The view of beliefs as brain processes fails requirement #1: it does not identify all the things we'd call belief.

If neuroscientists found that a person had brain processes corresponding to belief X, but she neither stated belief in X nor behaved consistently with it, we would say that she did not actually believe X. The view of beliefs as brain processes fails requirement #2: it does not identify only those things we would call belief.

Beliefs are not brain events, even if -- just like mental states -- brain events are normally involved in having beliefs. We must look elsewhere.

Chapter 3:
What Belief Is

"No one really knows how beliefs are represented in our brains ... it seems reasonable to think of them as sentences -- constrained by the language we use to construct sentences."

-- Nils J. Nillson, Understanding Beliefs

BY NOW, WE KNOW WHAT BELIEF IS NOT. It's not a mental state, it's not a disposition, and it's not a brain process. Those things are part of the story, but none of them is helpful for the purpose of analyzing human society, morals, and politics. That purpose determines where we should focus.

Beliefs do many things

So where should a definition focus for our current purpose? Let's consider an example. Suppose that I stand up in the middle of a public meeting and loudly proclaim:

"I believe that all people are equal!"

What did I just do? First, notice that it's not a statement about people being equal: it's a statement about me. That's actually quite important. It's a clue.

Second, notice that *what* I claim to believe is false: In most factual ways, all people are not equal. They are taller or shorter, fatter or thinner, richer or poorer, law-abiding or criminal, with different interests, personalities, and abilities.

Therefore, my statement is kind of a mess. It's not about what it pretends to be about, and what it pretends to be about is obviously untrue. It seems to do this:

- It asserts that I believe "All people are equal."

- It suggests that all people are equal.

- It signals that I am a virtuous person in ways with which people around me agree.

I'm communicating at least three things. Two of them are about me, and one of them signals that I share moral beliefs with the other people present. Unless I'm at a meeting of the Ku Klux Klan, everyone else will nod in agreement and think I'm a nice person. They will also think that they know what I believe. If they interact with me, they will base their actions on that assumption. Will they be right? It depends on what we think belief *is*.

Examples of belief give us clues

If you want to know what kangaroos are, it won't suffice just to make up a description at your desk. You've got to look at some real kangaroos. The same applies to beliefs. If you want to know what beliefs are, you've got to look at some beliefs, not just make up a description and insist that all beliefs must be like what you described.

Remember that one of our goals for a definition of belief is to cover all the things we would normally call belief, and only the things we would normally call belief. So let's look at more examples.

Example #1: Words that require action

Suppose that you're a newly-hired technician at a nuclear power plant. At your workstation, I point to the computer screen and hand you a piece of paper that says "Loss of coolant."

I say that if you ever see those words on the computer screen, you must shut down the reactor and evacuate the power plant.

A couple things are interesting here. First, notice that a fact (words on a screen) implies that you must do some actions (shutting down the reactor and evacuating the power plant). That takes a lot of logical steps for granted and leaves them unspoken:

1. Loss of coolant can cause a core meltdown.
2. A core meltdown will release large amounts of radioactive material into the vicinity.
3. Exposure to large amounts of radioactive material harms humans.
4. Shutting down the reactor can prevent a core meltdown.
5. Evacuating the plant reduces the risk of human exposure to large amounts of radioactive material.
6. If possible, prevent harm to humans.
7. Therefore, shut down the reactor and evacuate the plant.

Steps 1 through 5 are purely factual, but step 6 is different. It introduces a moral principle in the form of an imperative: if X, then do Y. Step 7 follows by simple logic.

Suppose you're a poorly trained technician and you don't know what "loss of coolant" means. You know the individual words, but not the meaning of the phrase so that you could give an equivalent phrase in English. Does that lack of understanding make any difference in your behavior if the phrase appears on your screen? No. You can reach the necessary conclusions and take the required action even if you can't explain what it means. You hold this belief:

> *"If 'loss of coolant' appears on my screen, it means I must shut down the reactor and evacuate the power plant."*

We often think that "what a phrase means" is an equivalent phrase, either in English or in some other language. You cannot give an equivalent phrase or explain the original phrase. However, you believe something without knowing, in that sense, what it means: You know how to behave if a certain thing happens. In summary:

- You can't give the linguistic meaning of your belief – *i.e.*, you can't state it in different words – because you don't know what "loss of coolant" means.

- You can't form a coherent mental picture of your belief for the same reason.

- You *can* act correctly on the basis of your belief. To the extent that your belief has meaning, its meaning is that it points to a particular sequence of behavior.

Therefore, in a practical sense, you *do* know what "loss of coolant" means: it means certain facts and actions. You can't give an equivalent phrase. You can't picture it in your mind. But you understand what to do. That's enough. You believe it, and you do it. Lives are saved.

Example #2: Gibberish that requires action

You're still a newly hired technician at a nuclear power plant. However, this time the plant is in Japan and you're an American who understands no Japanese. You took the job because the salary was a million yen per year, and that sounded like a lot of money (it's about $9,300).

I'm your Japanese supervisor and, considerate fellow that I am, I'm explaining your job in English. I point to your computer screen and hand you a piece of paper with this written on it:

冷却水の喪失.

I say that if you ever see 冷却水の喪失 on the computer screen, you must shut down the reactor and evacuate the power plant.

In the previous example, you understood the individual words but couldn't give an equivalent phrase in different words. Now, you have even less idea what the writing on the paper means. You not only don't know what the words mean, but you're not even sure where one word ends and the next word begins. All you know is that if you see that string of characters on your screen, you've got to shut down the reactor and evacuate the power plant. You hold this belief:

"If 冷却水の喪失 appears on my screen, I must shut down the reactor and evacuate the power plant."

As before, you believe something but you don't understand what it means in the sense that you cannot give an equivalent phrase. Your belief points to required actions in case there's a loss of coolant. If you see that string of characters, your belief tells you how to behave. So you know the meaning. It's not an equivalent sequence of words: it's a required sequence of actions.

Example #3: Religious doctrine that requires action

You're no longer a technician in a nuclear power plant. You got your first paycheck and it was barely enough for a week's worth of *bentos*, Japanese lunch boxes that you can buy at the local convenience store. You decided that religion might pay a little better. You considered becoming a Catholic priest, but there's that whole celibacy thing, so you decided to be a rabbi. Thanks to your non-religious but still stereotypically Jewish mother, you've got street cred for that.

At the yeshiva, your teacher is instructing you about basic Jewish beliefs. He says you must believe that:

"God gave the Torah to Moses at Sinai."

Can you believe it? Yes, you can, but there are some problems.

The first problem is one from our first example: you don't understand some of the words in the belief, just as you didn't understand "loss of coolant." Jewish and Christian thinkers agree that we can't understand God, so we have no ordinary conception of what the word "God" means. The same applies to other words when we apply them to God. What we logically understand of the belief is essentially *"Blank blank the Torah to Moses at Sinai."*

As for the rest -- the Torah, Moses, and Sinai -- it's all good. The Torah consists of five books, Moses was a man, and Sinai is a mountain. We've seen books, men, and mountains. As long as we don't insist on historical or archaeological evidence, we can believe that part. The Torah says it happened, and that's good enough for us.

And just as before, you do know what the belief means. You can't give an equivalent statement in different words because you'd need to understand all the words of the belief. However, you know what actions the belief requires. You always state the belief in appropriate situations. You never deny it. And you act consistently with it. So you believe it.

But in your own private thoughts, do you really believe what you're supposed to believe?

Do you really believe it, or are you just acting like you do? How would anyone else know? For that matter, how would *you* know?

That is the real problem. If believing something requires a specific thing to happen in your mind – the same thing that corresponds to the belief in your teacher's mind -- then how can you know if the thing in your mind is the correct thing?

You can't.

Your teacher told you to believe that "God gave the Torah to Moses at Sinai." You think your belief is correct if it's the same as what the teacher believes. You're right about that, but wrong about what it means.

You can observe what your teacher says and how he acts, but not what's in his mind. It is impossible for you to know what you're supposed to believe "mentally." The teacher can't communicate that to you at all. He can only tell you the words and show you the behavior. If you faithfully recite the words and consistently exhibit the behavior, then you believe. If your words and behavior match those of the teacher, then so does your belief.

Every person who believes "God gave the Torah to Moses at Sinai" might have a different mental experience of what it means, and none of us would ever know.

When nobody can know even in principle if their mental experience of belief is correct, then the word "correct" loses its meaning. *Whatever* your mental belief is, it's correct as long as you consistently say the right things and exhibit the right behavior. If your mental experience (A) is hearing "Stairway to Heaven," and the teacher's experience (B) is hearing the words of the belief, then each of you matches that experience (A or B) with your other experiences and behaviors associated with the belief. As long as you both do it consistently, it works fine. You can communicate.

Even if you examine your mental states and find that they are correct, you have no independent check on your judgment that they are correct – which in this case, means that they match your memory of what they were yesterday. And because your mental states are private, nobody else can help you. As the philosopher Ludwig Wittgenstein said (*Philosophical Investigations*, section 258):

> *"Whatever is going to seem right to me is right. And that only means that here, we can't talk about 'right'."*

Your mental state must exist, or else you're not conscious. As we normally think of belief, a corresponding mental state is a *necessary* condition for having a belief: otherwise, you can't believe anything. But the specific content of your mental state drops out. If you say and act, then you believe.

When we think about other people's beliefs, we often imagine our own internal experience and attribute it to them. We assume that for them, believing "God gave the Torah to Moses at Sinai" (or anything else) is associated with the same mental experience as we have when we think about the belief. However, two points should by now be clear:

- We cannot even in principle know the contents of other people's private mental belief experiences.

- And more significantly, it doesn't matter at all for the meaningfulness of beliefs.

As long as we remain aware of those facts, it is harmless -- and probably unavoidable without clumsy literary constructions -- to talk about beliefs as if they were mental experiences. But it's generally not true. Beliefs are public acts with public meaning, even though they must be connected with private experiences that serve to "anchor" them in our consciousness.

Notice one other thing. Even though we can't know the contents of other people's private experiences of belief, we *can* infer how the beliefs are related to each other.

If John says "This book is blue, therefore this book is colored," there's no way for us to know how he privately experiences either of those beliefs. However, based on his behavior, we can infer that he connects the beliefs and that the first belief leads to the second. What's private is the content of the experience. The structure of the experiences can be public. We also assume that other people are having some kinds of experiences that correspond to the structures shown by their verbal and non-verbal behavior.

Example #4: A law-school wannabe that requires action

Sadly, you flunked out of the yeshiva because your teachers said that you couldn't even speak coherently, let alone engage in theological discussion. For your own good, they sent you back to the first grade. Since you're 25, none of the other first-graders have tried to bully you. They just wonder what you're doing there.

Your teacher is talking about the names of different colors. It's a much simpler example than any we've discussed. No nuclear power, no reading Japanese, no theology. Just a palette of colors on the wall with their names written next to them.

Your teacher points to a blue-colored patch and says, "This is BLUUUUE." She enunciates the word very slowly and carefully because in her private mental states -- remember those? -- she thinks that first-graders are idiots. She wishes that she could have gone to law school instead. Unfortunately, she went out drinking the night before the LSAT exam, with predictable results. So here she is, teaching a bunch of rotten kids about the color BLUUUUE instead of earning a six-figure salary on Wall Street.

"All together now, children: BLUUUUE."

You and all the other first-graders say "BLUUUUE."

Your teacher points at the word next to the color patch: "BLUE." She says, "This is how the word looks if you write it," she says. "Write the word 'BLUE' in your workbooks." You and all the other first-graders write "BLUE."

It's just the color blue, but you might as well be talking about a beetle in a box. Do you know what the teacher sees when she looks at something blue? Do you know what any of the other kids see? No, you don't. You can't. But if they say that something is blue, you know what they mean: it's the same color as the patch on the wall, or similar enough to count as the same. As long as you all identify the same things as blue, say the correct words, and exhibit the correct behavior, you know what "blue" means to everyone in your group.

Belief isn't what we thought

Our examples highlighted surprising facts about belief. It's not connected as intimately with mental experiences as we expected, though there is a definite connection. It's much more tied to speech, writing, and behavior than we initially thought:

- Belief doesn't depend only on words.

- Belief does more than just make statements.

- Belief is a social phenomenon learned from and taught to other people in a social group by associating words with public behaviors.

- Language has only public meaning, not private meaning. We can describe mental states only in terms of people's behavior and its structure. That applies even to our own mental states, including beliefs.

- Still, if you're not conscious, you can't have beliefs. We assume that other people have some kinds of mental experiences corresponding to their beliefs.

So how should we define belief for our current purpose? It's starting to look like belief is behavior. Unfortunately, that suggestion bothers anyone with common sense:

"Sure, belief is connected to behavior, but seriously: Isn't belief still really mental? We behave in certain ways because we have mental

beliefs. If I believe something, it means I have a mental experience, no matter how you describe it or argue about it."

It's a persuasive argument. Private mental experiences are necessary for having beliefs. However, so is being alive. If you're not alive and conscious, you can't have beliefs. So where do we draw the line? What do we count as part of belief and what not?

Philosophy distinguishes between first-person explanations ("I believe") and second- or third-person explanations ("You believe," "he/she believes").

Our conviction that belief requires private mental states comes exclusively from our own first-person viewpoint. Any time we talk about our own beliefs, we think of our private experiences, whatever they are. We don't think about how we behave based on our beliefs. Other people see our behavior more clearly than we see it. As a result, we naturally think of belief in terms of how we experience it, not an objective third-person viewpoint that sees only our behavior.

Conversely, when we talk about other people's beliefs, all we really know is their behavior, but we unthinkingly assume that their private mental experience is just like ours. We have no way to know anything about that. If we talk about their beliefs, their private experience drops out. If we talk about our beliefs, we use the same public language, so our private experience drops out.

Belief is behavior

Let's go back to the criteria that we discussed in Chapter 1. A good definition:

- Should pick out all and only the things we would normally call belief.

- Should explain a lot of things.

- Should be useful in promoting happiness, morality, and social peace.

Therefore, I propose that for social, political, and moral analysis, we should define belief as behavior.

Does that satisfy the criteria for a correct definition?

It satisfies the first criterion. We learn to talk about belief by associating words with behavior, so our definition picks out all and only the things we would call belief. When we talk about other people's beliefs, all we can observe is their behavior. Even when we talk about our own beliefs, the only language we can use is public language that refers to public behavior. We have private mental experiences but we have no private language with which to talk about them.

As for the second and third criteria, the rest of this book argues that defining belief as behavior explains many human problems and can help us solve them. If that's so, then the definition has explanatory power and it is useful. Belief consists of:

- A set of verbal and non-verbal behaviors taking place over a period of time,

- which are given meaning by their relation to a network of other beliefs (including behaviors, etc.),

- defined conventionally by the believer's social and linguistic group.

A person believes X if he or she consistently behaves as if X were true, never denies X, and never acts inconsistently with X being true. The person might or might not verbally affirm X.

Let's pause for a moment to contemplate what that means about each individual belief.

In specific contexts, verbal and non-verbal behaviors express beliefs according to the rules and expectations of the believer's social and linguistic group. Each of the behaviors, such as saying "There's been a coolant loss" and taking actions to deal with the loss, express the belief.

We often forget that beliefs develop, and almost invariably occur, in the context of other beliefs and other people. If I believe that democracy is the best political system, then my belief cannot exist or be meaningful without a context of other beliefs, such as beliefs about other possible political systems. If you alter or remove the other beliefs, then you change the meaning of the first belief. Believers might:

- State their belief in words that match the belief they're stating. If I say, "It's later than 8 o'clock," I'm typically stating a belief that matches the words I use.

- Express their belief in words that don't match the belief they're stating. If I say, "It's later than you think," I'm typically stating a belief that doesn't match the words I use.

- Express their belief in non-verbal behavior. If before an 8pm party, I rush around the house straightening things up, I express non-verbally the belief that it is shortly before 8pm. Conversely, if I then put on a bathrobe and sit down in front of the television set, I contradict that belief without ever having to say a word.

Belief can be actions instead of words

Just as behavior can express belief, beliefs can imply or be associated with behavior. When those behaviors are central to a person's life, laden with emotion, or connected with important experiences, the link is even stronger. As a result, people feel as if rejecting the belief means rejecting the behavior and everything else associated with it.

If as a child you went to church or synagogue with your parents every week, prayed with family, friends, and loved ones, those experiences were not only pleasant but were also an important formative influence in your life. They've become part of who you are as a person. When anyone suggests that you reject the beliefs associated with all that behavior and life experience, it feels like you're being asked to reject your family, your loved ones, all those wonderful moments, and even important parts of yourself.

Is it any wonder that so many people can't do it and don't even *want* to do it?

Belief is a social phenomenon

Could a person have beliefs if he or she was raised by wolves and had never interacted with other human beings?

We might think that the answer is "yes," but think again. It's true that individual people have beliefs. However, it is not true that they could acquire or express those beliefs except as part of a community of intelligent beings who use language.

Consider our wolf-boy. Just like the wolves who raised him, he would learn to associate things with each other. The call of a bird means there's food nearby. A growl from the wolf pack leader means he'd better be careful. But he could not articulate any of those associations in speech or writing. That knowledge can only be developed in a human community.

From childhood through adulthood, we learn most of our beliefs from other people. As children, we learn arithmetic from our school teachers and morals from our parents. As adults, we learn from other people everything that we do not personally discover or verify, such as the principal export of Norway, the plot of a currently popular movie, or scientific results reported in a journal article we've read.

We test and refine our beliefs in conversation and debate with others. We modify our beliefs in response to new evidence reported by others, as well as to fit in with peer groups and social groups. Even generating new beliefs is a skill we learn from participation in a community.

Without testimony, support, and challenge from other people, any beliefs we had would be only inarticulate associations. The sophisticated intellectual infrastructure that we deploy even in the simplest daily tasks would be beyond us. Even the language in which express our beliefs is far beyond the ability of any human being to create on his or her own.

There's another side of that phenomenon. Not only do we learn our own beliefs in cooperation with other people, we *teach* beliefs to others by our verbal and non-verbal behavior. Just as what other people say and do affects us, what we say and do affects others, both for good and for ill. If our behavioral expressions of belief help the community and its people, they are in that respect good. Conversely, if our behaviors have a negative effect, they are in that respect bad.

Belief is not an individual phenomenon, but a social one that has some individual aspects. The private mental experiences we associate with our own beliefs are important to us, but they play no role in interactions with others or our membership in society. Only our verbal and non-verbal behaviors expressing beliefs are important in those areas.

The two-way effect of belief -- on us by others, and on others by us -- means that beliefs have moral significance beyond their mere truth and falsity.

Only behavior is socially relevant

Because mental experiences of belief are private to the person holding them, they can only be known to other people through the holder's verbal and non-verbal behavior. Only that behavior has any effect on other people or on the community. In addition, mental experiences of belief are often confused, vague, inconsistently held, and inconsistent with each other. Though they are a necessary condition for the existence of belief, they have no effect on its meaning.

For those reasons, communities cannot regulate mental experiences of belief. They can only regulate behavior. And since only that behavior has an impact on the communities and on other people, it is the only aspect of belief that is socially significant.

What the definition omits

Defining belief as behavior helps for analyzing the role of belief in human life and society. But it isn't any help in analyzing our first-person experience of the world. It doesn't exclude the reality of mental experience, but it doesn't say anything about it, either.

That's an omission, but it's harmless as long as we remember that stories (including definitions) have purposes. For example, when Aristotle defined humans as rational animals, his purpose was to classify humans as part of the animal kingdom. As a result, he omitted other human traits such as having two hands and two feet because they did not distinguish us from other animals. Even though his definition omitted those traits, it did not deny their existence.

Later in the book, our focus will shift to a more mentalistic view when we examine meaning, truth, and religious experience. Behavior will still be there, but in the background because it's less relevant to our purpose in those chapters.

We hold beliefs in three basic ways

If we look at real-life beliefs, we find that people hold them in three basic ways:

- Hold and apply

- Hold and do not apply

- Hold if X

Hold and apply

These are normal beliefs. In appropriate situations, we affirm them verbally or we base our non-verbal actions on them.

We weight such beliefs in terms of credibility, importance, and other factors. Although the scale is arbitrary, such beliefs might be weighted from 1 to 10. In case of conflicts between beliefs, we apply the beliefs with higher individual or combined weights. If we don't reject the losing beliefs outright, we place them in the "Hold and do not apply" category.

Hold and do not apply

These are beliefs that we put aside because they conflict with other beliefs to which we give more weight. We do not deny them, and if asked, we affirm them. But we do not apply them in inference or behavior.

For example, did you ever buy a lottery ticket? I buy one occasionally just to waste a dollar. For most, your chance of winning is less than 1 in 100 million. People who buy tickets often know they have almost no chance of winning. But they also believe they have a *slight* chance of winning. They hold both beliefs, but apply only the hopeful one.

Hold if X

These are beliefs that we hold only if a certain condition or conditions are true.

The most obvious case is when beliefs depend on matters of fact. Will I get wet if I go outside? I hold the belief ("If I go outside, I will get wet") if I look out the window and see that it is raining. If it is not raining, I do not hold the belief.

However, there are other cases of this type of belief-holding. In his book *Jewish Philosophy as a Guide to Life*, the late Harvard University philosopher Hilary Putnam told how he reconciled his religious and secular beliefs:

> "*As a practicing Jew, I am someone for whom the religious dimension of life has become increasingly important ...Those who know my writings from that period may wonder how I reconciled my religious streak and my general scientific materialist worldview. The answer is that I didn't reconcile them. I was a thoroughgoing atheist, and I was a believer. I simply kept these two parts of myself separate.*"

Putnam weighted his religious and materialist beliefs differently in different situations. When he was in religious situations, he assigned weight 10 to his religious beliefs and weight zero (do not hold) to his materialist beliefs. When he was in his office at Harvard, he assigned weight zero to his religious beliefs and some non-zero weight to his materialist beliefs.

Chapter 4:
Why Saadia and Maimonides Couldn't Believe -- But Did

"Belief is a notion that arises in the soul in regard to the actual character of anything that is apprehended."

-- Saadia Gaon

PREVIOUSLY, WE ARGUED THAT COMMON DEFINITIONS of belief are incorrect. They conflict both with how we behave in response to beliefs, but also with how we talk about beliefs when we're not trying to be philosophers.

In this and the next two chapters, we'll see how this conflict played out historically in the lives of several great thinkers. They all defined belief as mental and as only for making factual statements, but circumstances forced them to act against that definition.

Saadia Gaon (882-942 CE) and Moses Maimonides (1138-1204 CE) are textbook examples of that conflict. Both were Jewish intellectual leaders in societies dominated by Islam.

Direct challenges to their beliefs came from Islam and Christianity as well as from breakaway Jewish sects. Indirect challenges came from being second-class citizens in Islamic countries, as well as from political quarrels within the Jewish community.

How Medieval Islam challenged Judaism and Christianity

Islam has a bad reputation today among many Western people, mainly from terrorism and its treatment of women. But in the Middle Ages, Islamic civilization was – for its time -- tolerant and intellectually dynamic. Saadia and Maimonides lived in Islamic countries and wrote in Arabic.

Life as "dhimmi" in Islamic society

Even though they lived in Islamic societies, Saadia and Maimonides publicly defended their religious beliefs against arguments from Islamic writers. They could do so because whatever its shortcomings, Islam regarded Jews and Christians as kindred "people of the Book."

Most non-Muslims had to convert to Islam or be killed. However, Muslims saw the Jewish and Christian scriptures as part of their own religious tradition. Therefore, Jews and Christians had the status of "dhimmi," second-class citizens who enjoyed at least some legal protection. They could practice their religions without persecution as long as they paid a special tax.

Islamic scholars rediscovered Greek philosophy

In the 8th century CE, Baghdad became an important intellectual center as Islamic scholars translated ancient Greek works of philosophy, science, and mathematics into Arabic. They wanted to learn "falsafa" (philosophy) so they could argue more effectively for Islamic beliefs. They translated and studied the works of Aristotle and Plato, as well as Euclid (mathematics), Archimedes (mathematics and science), Galen (medicine), and Ptolemy (astronomy).

Based on what they learned from the Greeks – mainly from Aristotle -- Islamic sages wrote religious apologetics called "Kalam" (speech). They assumed that Divine revelation must be entirely compatible with reason and science. Jewish and Christian thinkers had to respond. Saadia and Maimonides gave part of that response. Just like Islamic writers, they accepted Aristotle's basic ideas and assumptions. So did Christian and Islamic thinkers. Each wanted to show that Aristotelian reasoning supported their own religion.

Even though Islam tolerated Judaism and Christianity, it was still the dominant religion of the societies. Conversion to Islam offered social, economic, and political advantages. Some Jews and Christians decided to convert for that reason, which alarmed both Saadia and Maimonides.

Rivalry between Palestine and Babylonia

Arguments with other religions weren't the only ball that Saadia and Maimonides had to juggle.

Palestine and Babylonia were rival centers of Jewish religious authority, and most communities followed one or the other. Saadia ended up on both sides of that dispute.

Saadia also had to deal with the Karaites, a breakaway Jewish sect that denied the validity of tradition and claimed only the Torah (the first five books of the Old Testament) had religious authority. Three centuries later, Maimonides confronted sects and various religious skeptics. And they both faced disputes that were partly about belief but mainly about political power.

Can you believe the unbelievable?

That was the context in which Saadia and Maimonides worked. The biggest intellectual problem they never solved is still with us today: Can you believe something that's *literally* unbelievable?

We're not talking about things that are merely *difficult* to believe, like a 45-year-old, overweight accountant winning an Olympic gold medal in gymnastics. That would be crazy -- and certainly worth seeing -- but it's not impossible. We can imagine that, so even by the mental-state theory of belief, we can believe it.

Instead, we're talking about things that are unimaginable, like something that has a color but occupies no space. Try to think of what that would be like. Try to think of a number that is both even and odd. You can't. And if you can't even imagine it, can you have beliefs about it?

Beliefs about God are like that. If you define God as transcendent and incomprehensible, then you can't even imagine Him. How can you have beliefs about what you can't even imagine?

That's a problem for any religion with a transcendent God and a naïve idea of belief. Alvin Plantinga, a contemporary Christian philosopher, summarizes it in his book *Knowledge and Christian Belief*:

> *"We human beings can't have any beliefs about God; God is beyond all of our concepts; our minds are too limited to have any grasp at all of him and his being."*

Plantinga rejects the problem mainly on the ground that it's a useless thing to believe, but he also offers kind of a neat logical argument against it:

> *"If we can't think about God, then (as Ramsey said) we can't think about him; and therefore can't make statements about him, including statements to the effect that we can't think about him. The statement that we can't think about God — the statement that God is such that we can't think about him — is obviously a statement about God; if we can't think about God, then we can't say about him that we can't think about him."*

Here's the instant replay, in case Plantinga lost you: He says that the statement "we can't think about God" is a statement about God. If we can make a statement about God, then we can think about Him. Therefore, the statement "we can't think about God" disproves itself.

A contemporary logician would reply that statements about what we can say or think are "in the meta-language" and aren't about God at all. But that's really bewildering stuff and it won't be on the test. So we'll skip it.

Notice that all of these arguments are *philosophical stories*. You can't test them experimentally. There's no historical or documentary evidence that would prove who's right in this debate. You just read the arguments and decide which story makes more sense to you.

The bottom line is that it was a problem for Saadia and Maimonides because they defined belief incorrectly. They never solved the problem, but they acted as if they had solved it. At some level they knew there was more to belief than their theories allowed.

Plantinga versus the Logicians

The meta-language debate really is interesting, but you can skip this little section if you want. Plantinga argues that if we can't understand God, we can't assign any meaning to the word "God" in the statement "We can't think about God." The statement turns into "We can't think about [blank]," which fails to tell us what we can't think about. Therefore, Plantinga argues, we have only two possible interpretations:

Interpretation #1: If the statement is meaningful, then "God" is meaningful. In that case, we are thinking about God when we make the statement. So the statement contradicts itself.

Interpretation #2: If the statement isn't meaningful because "God" isn't meaningful, then the verb "think about" has no object. So the statement isn't even a statement, and it tells us nothing.

Logicians would reply that "We can't think about God" isn't about God at all. Instead, it's a misleading way to say "We can't assign any meaning to the word 'God'." If that's right, then we're not talking about God. We're talking about a word, and we can think about the word. So there's no contradiction.

British atheist Antony Flew made that argument in his book *God and Philosophy*. Interestingly, he later changed his mind and started to believe in God, though in a way that didn't contradict his earlier argument. He didn't take God's existence as an article of faith, and he didn't think we could understand God. However, based on the evidence, he eventually decided it was probable that God existed in some sense, even it if was beyond our comprehension.

Would you believe Groucho Marx in Babylonia?

Groucho Marx, a famous 20th-century American comedian, poked fun at people who seemed gullible. After making some absurd statement about a situation, he often asked: "Who are you going to believe, me or your own eyes?"

Both Saadia and Maimonides would have understood that joke. By the standards of their time, they were world travelers. They spoke multiple languages. They had lived in different cultures, learned different customs, and seen different belief systems. Unlike most people even today, their background was "diverse." The contrast between different belief systems showed them examples of how beliefs worked – not just in logic, but in life. Their lived experience told them that belief had functions beyond making assertions and wasn't limited to private mental states.

But Aristotle, the ancient philosopher whose ideas they accepted, told them something else. They knew Aristotle only through Islamic translations and commentaries, but he clearly saw belief from a first-person (mental experience) viewpoint and thought it was only for asserting things about the world.

Neither Saadia nor Maimonides ever resolved the conflict between what Aristotle said and what they saw with their own eyes. In their theories about belief, they followed Aristotle. In their lives, they followed what experience had taught them was true. Let's explore how that conflict played out for them.

Saadia defends belief against all comers

Saadia is almost always called "Saadia Gaon," but that wasn't his name. Most people don't know his actual name, much as people think that the Mahatma Gandhi's name was Mahatma, which means "great soul" in Sanskrit. Gandhi's real first name was Mohandas.

Similarly, "Gaon" was Saadia's title as headmaster of a Babylonian Jewish academy. His full name was Saadia ben Joseph: "ben Joseph" means "son of Joseph."

Saadia was born in 882 CE in a small village of Egypt. His parents might have been Christians who converted to Judaism. Even if they weren't, he got plenty of exposure to Christianity. Since Egypt was dominated by Islam, he also got that. Finally, Egypt's Jewish community followed the teachings of Palestine rather than Babylonia. As a child, he grew up with the Palestinian side of the rivalry, then argued for the Babylonian side as an adult.

By the time he left Egypt at age 23, he had already written a Hebrew dictionary and polemics against the Karaite sect. Until 921, he traveled between Palestine, Aleppo, and Baghdad, and was often away from his family.

In 921, however, the Jewish officials of Palestine and Babylonia had a bitter dispute over which of them had the authority to define the Jewish calendar. Celebrating holy days was a religious obligation, so the side that defined the calendar controlled Jewish religious life. Saadia argued effectively on behalf of the Babylonian side, which won the dispute.

In 928, the leader (Exilarch) of the Babylonian Jewish community, David ben Zakkai, appointed Saadia as headmaster (Gaon) of the Babylonian Academy at Sura. He did so because Saadia was widely known from the calendar dispute and he was the best available scholar. Academy members had more parochial interests, and wanted Zakkai to appoint one of them instead.

Up to that time, the academy had focused mainly on study of the Babylonian Talmud. As a result, their rulings about Talmudic law were considered authoritative over those of rabbis in the academies of Palestine. However, that narrow focus also blocked them from wider knowledge, even of Jewish documents such as the Palestinian Talmud, which Saadia often used in his own writing. It seems strange, but academy members did not study the Bible, write commentaries on the books of the Bible, or write single-issue monographs, as Saadia did.

That narrow focus had put the Sura Academy in danger of closing. Even so, members feared that the cosmopolitan Saadia would import unwelcome new ideas. They warned Zakkai that he was too independent. On both points – fortunately -- it turned out that they were right.

Saadia's unwelcome new ideas broadened the focus of the academy and restored its reputation. That, at least, pleased Zakkai. Everything went smoothly until 930, when Saadia confirmed the academy members' warnings about his independence. As leader of the Jewish community, Zakkai issued a ruling in a real estate dispute. Despite his relationship with Zakkai, Saadia refused to endorse the ruling because he believed it was illegal.

Angered by Saadia's seeming disloyalty, Zakkai appointed a new Gaon. In retaliation, Saadia appointed a replacement for Zakkai as community leader. Zakkai eventually won the dispute and removed Saadia from his position, though the two men finally reconciled years later.

Saadia was thus well aware that belief, even when well-founded and sincerely held, could have serious practical and social consequences. At some level, that awareness undoubtedly affected his willingness to support or oppose certain beliefs.

How Saadia defined belief

His magnum opus, *The Book of Beliefs and Opinions* (known in another English translation as *The Book of Doctrines and Beliefs*), clearly supports the mental-state definition of belief. In the Prolegomena, he writes that belief is:

> *"a notion that arises in the soul in regard to the actual character of anything that is apprehended ... He deposits it in his soul for a future occasion or future occasions."*[6]

In other words, he thinks that belief is a kind of mental state. Its purpose is to help us direct our behavior successfully on a future occasion or future occasions.

His definition of truth sheds further light on the nature of this mental act:

> *"A true belief consists of believing a thing to be as it really is; namely, that much is much, and little is little, and black is black,*

---

[6] The two English translations use different wording but convey the same meaning. Quotes here are from Samuel Rosenblatt's 1947 translation, published under the title *The Book of Beliefs and Opinions*.

and white is white, and that what exists exists, and what is non-existent is non-existent."

Thus, Saadia thought a belief was an accurate representation, in the mind of the believer, of a fact outside the mind of the believer.

Saadia also wrote that because human minds are finite, they can only form representations of things that are themselves finite. To make the point clear, Saadia adds in Book II ("Concerning the Belief that the Creator of All Things is One") that:

"Science is capable of being grasped by man only because it is finite, for if it were thought to be infinite, it could not be grasped in its totality, and once that becomes impossible, it is no longer subject to the cognition of anyone."

If science can be grasped by human beings "only because it is finite," then it clearly follows that what is not finite cannot be grasped by human beings – according to Saadia.

How Saadia justified belief

The accuracy of the mental representation was determined in different ways depending on the type of belief involved. Saadia accepted four ways to validate beliefs:

- **By direct observation:** for example, that this apple is red.

- **By intuition of the intellect:** for example, that 1+1 = 2.

- **By logical inference:** for example, that people have souls because we see their effects.

- **By authentic tradition:** for example, that Moses confronted the Egyptian Pharaoh because it's what rabbis have taught for centuries. Note that this last test of truth amounts to reliance on the testimony of other people. Saadia's reference to "authentic" tradition makes his test circular: a belief is true because it relies on authentic tradition, and the tradition is authentic because it endorses true beliefs.

Saadia thought that perceptual beliefs were validated empirically, simply by inspecting the world around us. Other beliefs were validated by consulting rabbis or sacred writings. But as for logical and metaphysical beliefs -- including belief in God -- he advocated a different test: That the beliefs be clear and distinct. In the Prolegomena, he wrote:

> *"Now as for the intuitions of the intellect, anything that is conceived in our mind in complete freedom from accidents of any sort is to be regarded as true knowledge about which no doubt is to be entertained."*

Here, "accidents" refers to non-essential features of a thing. In the dominant view at the time, everything had a certain nature that made it what it was.

An apple had a certain "appleness" that made it an apple instead of a peach or a dog, and it shared this essential nature with all other apples. However, each apple also had "accidental" properties that its nature did not require. The apple that I hold in my hand might weigh eight ounces, but could just as easily have weighed six ounces or 10 ounces and still be an apple. An apple's weight, then, is an accidental rather than an essential feature.

For Saadia, to conceive something "in complete freedom from accidents" is to conceive it clearly and distinctly as it is by nature. If we conceive a belief clearly and distinctly, we know it is true.

It's worth observing that on this point, Saadia was far ahead of his time. Seven centuries later, the French polymath René Descartes (who indirectly got Spinoza in trouble) would make the same kind of "clear and distinct ideas" his test of truth:

> *"So I now seem to be able to lay it down as a general rule that whatever I perceive very clearly and distinctly is true."*

Saadia's epistemic agnosticism

But for Saadia, this "clear and distinct" test of truth causes a problem when it comes to belief in God: It leads straight to agnosticism, though it rules out atheism for the same reason as it rules out theism.

Later in *The Book of Beliefs and Opinions*, Saadia devotes a chapter to the nature of God. He writes that:

> *"The idea of the Creator, exalted and magnified be He, must of necessity be subtler than the subtlest and more recondite than the most recondite and more abstract than the most abstract and profounder than the most profound ..."*

So far, it's the same kind of florid praise that people routinely and without embarrassment apply to God. But then Saadia gets to the punch line:

> *"... so that it would be impossible to fathom its character at all ... what is infinite and endless cannot be embraced by the human mind."*

In other words, the human mind cannot form a representation of God. The human mind can only grasp what is finite, and God is not finite.

But on Saadia's view, a belief is a mental representation of a fact outside the mind of the believer. If we cannot mentally represent God, we cannot have beliefs about Him. We cannot believe that He is One. We cannot believe that he is good. We cannot believe that He gave the Torah to Moses at Sinai. We cannot even believe that He exists or doesn't exist.

As an observant and faithful Jew, of course, Saadia would have recoiled in horror from such suggestions. Most of *The Book of Beliefs and Opinions* is devoted to arguing for various beliefs about God.

Why the disconnect? Why did Saadia hold an explicit definition of belief, but then argue and act as if his own definition was false? Why argue for beliefs that on his view were impossible? Even if they came from "authentic tradition," they still referred to a Being whose nature could not "be embraced by the human mind."

The answer is that even though his definition of belief did not permit it, he knew from experience that beliefs were about more than just asserting things. They held society together, maintained personal relationships, and guided individual lives.

The evidence will become even clearer as we look at the other thinkers: Maimonides, Spinoza, and Mendelssohn. All of them, at least implicitly and sometimes explicitly, recognized that behavior was an essential component of belief. Mental affirmation might have been important, and spiritual commitment was definitely helpful, but only behavior was subject to morality and only behavior could affect society.

Maimonides insists on beliefs you can't believe

Like Saadia, Maimonides's famous name isn't his actual name. His name was Moshe ben Maimon, but he's usually called "Rambam" (short for for Rabbi Moshe ben Maimon) or simply "Maimonides."

He was born in 1138 CE in the relatively tolerant Islamic society of Andalusia (now southern Spain). A few years later, the region was taken over by the Almohads, a radical Islamic sect that allowed no dissent from its beliefs. Maimonides and his family had to run for their lives. As a young man, he moved around North Africa until he finally settled in Egypt in 1166.

When he arrived in Egypt, Maimonides had no status, no wealth, and no connections. Nevertheless, his hard work and brilliant mind soon made him a leader of the Egyptian Jewish community. He became a famous scientist and was the Egyptian Pharaoh's personal physician. He wrote the first systematic exposition of Jewish law in his *Mishneh Torah*, discussed the philosophical basis of Judaism in *The Guide of the Perplexed*, and wrote other treatises on logic, astronomy and medicine.

Of course, to do all that required more than just intellectual brilliance. He had to be a diplomat and a strategist. From childhood experience, he knew that beliefs could have deadly results and could tear society apart. From the contrast between tolerant Andalusia, various North African countries, and Egypt, he could see the ways in which belief either united or divided people.

Could he reconcile his lived experience with what Aristotle told him about belief?

Not very well, it turns out, but somewhat better than Saadia.

How Maimonides defined belief

In Chapter 50 of *The Guide of the Perplexed*, Maimonides clearly supports the mental-state view of belief:

"Belief is the affirmation that what has been represented is outside the mind just as it has been represented in the mind."

In other words, to have a belief is to represent in the mind a fact outside the mind: to affirm it in a mental act. If the representation corresponds to the fact, the belief is true; otherwise, the belief is false. That implies two crucial points:

- We can only have beliefs about things we understand or have experienced. If we cannot understand or have not experienced something, then we can't form a mental representation of it and can't have beliefs about it.

- A true belief must have an object outside the mind that is "just as it has been represented in the mind."

Beliefs required by Judaism

Apart from *The Guide of the Perplexed*, Maimonides is best known in Jewish circles for his list of 13 principles that he says are essential to the Jewish faith. In Chapter 10 of *Helek: Sanhedrin*, he wrote that Jews must believe:

- **First principle:** "In the existence of the Creator."

- **Second principle:** "That God is one, the cause of all oneness."

- **Third principle:** "That He is incorporeal."

- **Fourth principle:** "That the One (i.e., God) is absolutely eternal."

- **Fifth principle:** "[That only God] is rightfully worshipped, magnified, and obeyed."

- **Sixth principle:** That there are "certain people so gifted and perfected that they can receive pure intellectual form ... These men are the prophets; this is what prophecy is."

- **Seventh principle:** "[That Moses] was the chief of all other prophets before and after him, all of whom were his inferiors."

- **Eighth principle:** That "the whole Torah was given [to] us through Moses entirely from God ... it came to us through Moses who acted like a secretary taking dictation. ... The authoritative commentary on the Torah [by the rabbis] is also the Word of God."

- **Ninth principle:** "That this Torah was precisely transcribed from God and no one else."

- **Tenth principle:** "That God knows all that men do and never turns His eyes away from them."

- **Eleventh principle:** "That God rewards those who perform the commandments of the Torah and punishes those who transgress its admonitions."

- **Twelfth principle:** "That the Messiah will come."

- **Thirteenth principle:** "That the dead will be resurrected."

Impossible beliefs and other problems

However, according to Maimonides's definition of belief, some beliefs on his list are impossible to hold. As for the beliefs that aren't impossible, he either asserted them without believing them himself, or he reinterpreted them in ways that most people wouldn't recognize. The beliefs on his list fall into three groups:

- **Impossible beliefs:** Principles 1, 2, 3, 4, 5, 8, 9, 10, and 11.

  All those beliefs refer to God, of whom we cannot form a mental representation.

- **Reinterpreted beliefs:** Principles 1, 2, 6, 8, 9, 10, and 11

  Maimonides reinterpreted those beliefs to make them philosophically acceptable. However, he kept the traditional wording because he thought that most people were better off with simple beliefs even if incorrect. He agreed with the Islamic philosopher Averroes, who wrote in *On the Harmony of Religion and Philosophy* that for such beliefs, "the duty of the elite is to interpret them allegorically, while the duty of the masses is to take them in their apparent meaning."

- **Unproblematic beliefs:** Principles 7, 12, and 13.

  We can hold these beliefs without reinterpretation.

Maimonides thought that most people couldn't understand the impossible beliefs *at all*. Even the most gifted people could only understand them by reinterpreting them philosophically or stating them in negative terms: they couldn't know what God *is*, but they could know what He *isn't*.

Likewise, he thought that prophecy was completely different from how most people understood it. He knew perfectly well that the text of the Torah had changed over the centuries, contrary to the belief required by his eighth principle.

He thought that Divine reward and punishment operated by natural law. God didn't intervene in the world to reward the virtuous and punish the wicked. Instead, He set up natural law so that good actions usually succeed (rewards) and evil actions usually fail (punishments). Just as in the case of prophecy, his view was completely different from what most people believed.

Maimonides deliberately obscured his views on these issues because he knew that stating them clearly would upset the community and confuse most people. In *The Guide*, he wrote that:

"My purpose is that the truths be glimpsed and then again be concealed, so as not to oppose that divine purpose which one cannot possibly oppose and which has concealed from the vulgar among the people those truths especially requisite for His apprehension."

Let's look at each of these points.

God is incomprehensible

According to Maimonides, God is mostly incomprehensible even to the most intelligent and educated individuals. God is *entirely* incomprehensible to most people, whom he characterized in *The Guide* (Part II, Ch. 36) as "like domestic animals or like beasts of prey."

In the Introduction to *The Guide*, Maimonides writes that:

"You should not think that these great secrets are fully and completely known to anyone among us. They are not."

Among those secrets is the nature of God, about whom we can know nothing positive. In Book I, Ch. 56, he writes:

"Those who believe there are essential attributes that may be predicated of the Creator — namely, that He is existent, living, possessing power, knowing, and willing —to understand that these notions are not ascribed to Him and to us in the same sense."

In what sense, then, are they ascribed to God? Not in any sense we know about:

"His essential attributes, may He be exalted, in the existence of which they believe, must not be like the attributes of other beings ... Similarly the terms 'knowledge,' 'power,' 'will,' and 'life,' as applied to Him, may He be exalted, and to all those possessing knowledge, power, will, and life, are purely equivocal, so that their meaning when they are predicated of Him is in no way like their meaning in other applications."

By Maimonides's definition of belief as "the affirmation that what has been represented is outside the mind just as it has been represented in the mind," belief requires that we create a mental representation of our belief's object, which we can't do much in the case of God. For a belief to be true, its object must be "just as it is represented" in our minds, which he thinks we can't do at all in the case of God.

Those problems put him squarely into the same difficulties as Saadia and, in our time, Alvin Plantinga.

Maimonides managed to avoid the trap that later ensnared the great Christian theologian Saint Thomas Aquinas. Aquinas wrote (in his *Summa Theologica* under "The Names of God") that our knowledge of God's attributes was analogical: for example, our mind is to human nature as God's mind is to God's nature.

It might make a good SAT question to spot the error in that argument. We can use analogical reasoning to infer what a donkey's mind is like because we know what a donkey's nature is like: The human mind is to humans as the donkey mind is to donkeys. But we don't know God's nature, so the analogy is uninformative in His case.

Having avoided analogical fallacy, Maimonides fell into what psychiatrists call "word salad:"

> *"He exists, but not through an existence other than His essence; and similarly He lives, but not through life; He is powerful, but not through power; He knows, but not through knowledge."*

Centuries later, Spinoza (discussed in the next chapter) used similar language about God, but defined it differently. For the most part, Spinoza would have dismissed Maimonides's text here as nonsense. A more generous interpretation would say that it is mysticism. There's some basis for the latter view, because Maimonides said outright that the words don't mean anything with which we are familiar:

> *[The attributes of God] "cannot be considered through the instrumentality of the customary words, which are the greatest among the causes leading unto error. For the bounds of expression in all languages are very narrow indeed ..."*

One might as well say that *God is the Saturday ice cream cone of the amusement park*; it would be just as literally meaningful as "He lives but not through life."

But why say it, then? Why talk about God if we can't mentally understand what we are talking about? I would argue that Maimonides knew at a gut level that the words themselves were part of what made the belief important. The words and the behavior that goes with them are part of what holds the community together and gives people strength to survive. In addition, the words can -- unverifiably, but still can -- point to truths beyond our understanding. We'll look at that issue in Chapter 12.

Prophecy isn't what you think it is

Maimonides said at the outset of *The Guide* that he intended to conceal and obscure some of his ideas, and his discussion of prophecy keeps that promise. Like Aristotle, Maimonides saw the world as governed by natural law that left little room for Divine interventions, whether they were miracles like the parting of the Red Sea or less cinematic events like individual prophecy.

In his introduction to *Pirke Avot* (Ethics of the Fathers), he says that God's will applies to nature in general, not to specific things:

> *"The rabbis avoided referring to the Divine Will as determining a particular event at a particular time. When they said that man rises and sits down in accordance with the will of God, their meaning was that, when man was first created, his nature was so determined that rising up and sitting clown were to be optional to him; but they did not mean that God wills at any special moment that man should or should not get up, as He determines at any given time that a certain stone should or should not fall to the ground."*

In other words, God's will equals natural law.

For Maimonides, prophecy neither included nor required any supernatural component. It required study, reflection, and focus on the relevant issues. It also required imagination, which he called a faculty for "retaining things perceived by the senses, combining these things, and imitating them." It requires not only physical health, but intellectual preparation. In Part II, Chapter 36 of *The Guide*, he writes:

> *"That individual would obtain knowledge and wisdom ... [and] all his desires will be directed to acquiring the science of the secrets of what exists and knowledge of its causes."*

It's interesting to compare Maimonides's description of prophecy with a similar account from Bertrand Russell, the 20th-century British philosopher, two-time Nobel laureate, and religious skeptic. In describing how he analyzed philosophical problems, Russell wrote:

"After first contemplating a book on some subject, and after giving serious preliminary attention to it, I needed a period of subconscious incubation ... Having, by a time of very intense concentration, planted the problem in my subconsciousness, it would germinate underground until, suddenly, the solution emerged with blinding clarity, so that it only remained to write down what had appeared as if in a revelation." ("How I Write")

As a lifelong atheist, Russell would have been astonished to learn that he was a prophet, at least according to Maimonides's definition.

The point here is not that Maimonides was ahead of his time, even though -- just like Saadia -- he was. The point is that he said the same words about prophecy as other Jews, but *defined* those words in much different ways. He could honestly say that he believed in prophecy, but *what* he believed about it was wildly unusual and unorthodox. He found the ordinary meaning of the belief unacceptable, so he kept the words of the belief but redefined it as meaning something else. That strategy has been used countless times over the centuries as scientific beliefs, morals, and society have changed.

One question remains: In what sense can he have thought that he and other Jews believed in the same principle about prophecy?

He knew that they all used the same words and behaviors in public statements about prophecy. Their mental beliefs might have been completely different, but their words and behaviors were the same. To borrow a phrase he used in a different way, the public "external meaning" of the principle was the same, even if everyone had a different private interpretation. The latter had no effect on the community. It was the public meaning that promoted cooperation and social peace.

The Torah's text has changed

Modern archaeology, historical research, and textual analysis has convinced most academic Biblical scholars of three things:

- The text of the Torah was assembled by ancient editors (redactors) from various source documents, the most important of which are called J, P, D, and E. Most of the work was completed by the 6th century BCE. Scholars disagree about details, but agree about the broad outlines of the theory, called "the documentary hypothesis."

- Many stories in the Torah are similar to earlier stories from other cultures of the Ancient Near East, suggesting common human origins of the text. For example, the story of the flood in Genesis 6-8 corresponds point-by-point to the flood story in the Sumerian "Gilgamesh" epic, and even uses some phrasing from Gilgamesh that appears nowhere else in the Bible.

- In the 10th century CE, Jewish scholars called the Masoretes produced a standardized text of the Torah from different versions that had been in circulation.

Maimonides knew about the Masoretes' work to standardize the Torah's text. He probably also knew about the similarities between the Torah and other ancient writings. Even so, he argued that a belief in the Torah's Divine origin and unchanged text were essential for faithful Jews.

Why? For the same reason he was willing to say the same words about prophecy as other members of the community. No matter how people interpreted the beliefs as individuals, their shared verbal affirmation of the beliefs promoted cooperation and social peace.

Providence is natural law in action

Maimonides analyzed providence in much the same way as he analyzed prophecy. It's described in his faith principle 11:

> *"God rewards those who perform the commandments of the Torah and punishes those who transgress its admonitions. The greatest reward is the world to come; the worst punishment is extinction."*

Divine providence distributes the rewards and punishments, but it does so through the operation of natural law. If you understand natural law and live consistently with it, you'll be more likely to succeed and be rewarded. If you don't understand it, or try to ignore it, then you'll be more likely to fail and be punished. In Part III, Chapter 17 of *The Guide*, he writes:

"Providence is consequent upon the intellect and attached to it ... [each person] will be reached by providence to the extent to which he is reached by the intellect."

Maimonides saw providence as a kind of wisdom that we can acquire by studying natural law. It enables us to see life and the world clearly, and to plan our actions rationally. It doesn't exempt us from the hazards of chance or the infirmities of age, but it helps us live wisely, justly, and serenely. Maimonides almost sounds like the Stoic philosopher Marcus Aurelius: *Act rationally, accept what you can't control, and don't get upset about it.*

Once again, we see Maimonides saying the right words: "God rewards those who keep the commandments and punishes those who don't." He was also an observant Jew, so he acted according to those words. But his own interpretation of faith principle 11 was far from anything believed or even comprehended by the vast majority of people, then or now. Recall how he stated faith principle 11:

"That God rewards those who perform the commandments of the Torah and punishes those who transgress its admonitions."

Maimonides was no egalitarian. He thought that most people were at least ignorant (a realistic assumption in his era) and probably also unintelligent: "like domestic animals or beasts of prey." He expected them to interpret the belief anthropomorphically, as referring to "a man in the sky"[7] who would punish them if they disobeyed Him. But his own interpretation of the belief was far different: That understanding natural law enabled people to live more successfully, and ignoring it caused them hardship.

For him, the beliefs that mattered were those embodied in words and behavior -- even though that attitude was inconsistent with his own theory of belief.

---

[7] That's how God is described in the 2009 comedy movie, "The Invention of Lying." I disagree with the movie's assumptions, but it's thoughtful and entertaining.

Metaphor in the Torah

Maimonides followed the same strategy in dealing with problematic passages in the Torah. For example, in Chapter 1 of his *Mishneh Torah*, he writes in 1:8 that God does not have a physical body. Therefore, in 1:9, he argues that the Bible is engaging in metaphor when it refers to God's physical body:

> *"What is the meaning of the following expressions found in the Torah: "Beneath His Feet" (Ex. 24:10); "Written with the finger of God (ibid. 31:18); "The hand of God" (ibid. 9:3); "The eyes of God" (Gen. 38:7) "The ears of God" (Num. 11:1); and similar phrases?*
>
> *All these expressions are adapted to the mental capacity of the majority of mankind who have a clear perception of physical bodies only. The Torah speaks in the language of men. All these phrases arc metaphorical, like the sentence "If I whet my glittering sword" (Deut. 32:41). Has God then a sword and does He slay with a sword? The term is used allegorically and all these phrases are to be understood in a similar sense."*

Maimonides wants to keep the words of the Torah but change their meaning to something that is more philosophically defensible. Once again, we see his operating principle: it's not what we believe mentally that matters, but what we say and do: our behavior.

Beliefs can be necessary even if they're not true

Maimonides's actual practice showed the emphasis he placed on verbal and behavioral beliefs, even if his theory had no place for that kind of belief. A clue is that when he talked about beliefs, he usually referred to what people "say" rather than to what they believe mentally. Only what they say and how they behave affect the community. What they believe privately has no impact as long as they don't act on it or talk about it.

In Part III, Ch. 28 of *The Guide*, he distinguished between necessary beliefs and true beliefs. He still thought of necessary beliefs as mental beliefs, but they might not be true and they might not be justified by logic and evidence. Their justification was mainly practical:

> *"The Law also makes a call to adopt certain beliefs, belief in which is necessary for the sake of political welfare. Such, for instance, is*

*our belief that He, may He be exalted, is violently angry with those
who disobey Him and that it is therefore necessary to fear Him and
to dread Him and to take care not to disobey."*

Maimonides's attitude is an example of what I call "this is our
story and we're sticking to it." When radio comedian Jack Benny insisted against all evidence that he was 39 years old, his audience went
along with the joke. Interviewed on the radio in 1951, Benny said that
he had been born in 1912, making him 39 years old. He then admitted
that he had been drafted into the U.S. military in 1917. When the in-
terviewer asked how he could have been drafted when he was five
years old, he replied "I had a tough draft board, and shut up!" Everyone laughed.

For Maimonides, insisting on the truth of the Jewish tradition was
no laughing matter because the welfare and survival of his own people
were at stake. He wanted to give an account of Jewish beliefs that intelligent, educated people could accept in good faith, but that simpler
people could follow without crippling doubts. That's what he tried to
do. If moral health and social survival depended on a few logically dubious but "necessary" beliefs, he wasn't going to quibble about their
logic. In life, he'd seen both the good and the harm that beliefs could
do. He wanted to promote beliefs that supported the good, regardless
of the evidence or lack of it.

Chapter 5:
Why Spinoza Could Believe -- But Didn't

"A true idea must agree with that of which it is the idea."

-- Spinoza

IN THE PREVIOUS CHAPTER, we saw how both Saadia and Maimonides behaved inconsistently with their own definitions of belief. From their life experience, they knew that beliefs did other jobs besides just making assertions. However, they both wanted to say the right words, regardless of how they privately re-interpreted those words. They were both members in good standing of the community and wanted to keep it that way.

Baruch de Spinoza (1632-1677) didn't care about saying the right words. On the contrary, he often seemed to go out of his way to say the *wrong* words. His Biblical interpretations feigned sincerity but dripped with obvious sarcasm at what he considered harmful superstition. Some of his unorthodox beliefs are like those of Maimonides. But unlike Maimonides, he didn't try to conceal his beliefs.

Spinoza's religious motivation

Even the most scrupulous thinkers have non-intellectual motives that affect their beliefs, and Spinoza was no exception.

Born in Amsterdam to a middle-class Jewish family in 1632, he grew up in a tolerant Dutch society that unofficially appreciated its Jewish residents. He went to synagogue and at least outwardly observed Jewish law. His intellectual curiosity, however, led him outside the Jewish community to study the ideas of French polymath Rene Descartes and other philosophers. He became widely known as an expert on Descartes.

Then, for reasons that even now remain uncertain, the leaders of his synagogue condemned and excommunicated Spinoza from the Jewish community:

> "... having long known of the evil opinions and acts of Baruch de Spinoza, they have endeavored by various means and promises, to turn him from his evil ways. But having failed to make him mend his wicked ways, and, on the contrary, daily receiving more and more serious information about the abominable heresies which he practiced and taught and about his monstrous deeds ... they have decided ... that the said Espinoza should be excommunicated and expelled from the people of Israel. By decree of the angels and by the command of the holy men, we excommunicate, expel, curse, and damn Baruch de Espinoza, with the consent of God, Blessed be He ..."

That's pretty intense stuff. What could have prompted it, since Spinoza was at that time still observing the law and participating in the community?

It appears that Spinoza fell into a trap that later ensnared the German Jewish philosopher Moses Mendelssohn, though the results for Mendelssohn were only embarrassing instead of catastrophic.

In a private conversation, two students begged Spinoza to tell them his real beliefs. They swore to keep his remarks private, so he told them what he really thought: that he found nothing in the Bible about God being incorporeal (having no physical body) or about the human soul being immortal. The students then broke their promise and told the Jewish leadership what Spinoza had said. Apart from being condemned for believing what he considered the truth, he must have felt very bitter about the students' betrayal of his trust.

That incident pushed him away from the Jewish community. But he was also finding his way *toward* something that he highly valued.

Spinoza's rationalism was based in a kind of religious fervor. He sounds at times like a person who had a religious conversion experience and "got saved." However, he found salvation not in the worship of God, but in the worship of reason.

In his semi-autobiographical *Treatise on the Emendation of the Intellect*, he wrote of his disillusionment and redemption:

> "*After experience had taught me that all the things which regularly occur in ordinary life are empty and futile ... I resolved at last to try to find out if there was anything which would be the true good ... if there was something which, once found and acquired, would continuously give me the greatest joy for eternity ... I would be giving up certain evils for a certain good.*"

Can I get a "hallelujah"?

Spinoza's worship of reason, and the fact that he saw it as something that "would give him the greatest joy for eternity," accounts for some of the aggressiveness with which he attacked the Jewish tradition. He was a true believer, just as much as the most dogmatic of his critics – even though his faith was in reason and philosophy instead of traditional religion.

Spinoza's concept of belief

Spinoza never tells us explicitly how he defines belief. We have to construct a definition from his comments on other things. With Saadia and Maimonides, we could quote their definitions of belief and then compare them to their statements about God. We can't do that with Spinoza.

The short version is that for Spinoza, to believe something about X is to have an idea of X. But it was as clear to him as it had been to Maimonides that we could not form an idea of a God who was both transcendent and incomprehensible. If Spinoza was going to have beliefs about God, he thought that it had to be a God he could understand.

A little background information will help. Any philosophy about the world has to explain how:

- There are physical things with certain kinds of properties: place, weight, shape, color, spatial relationships, and so on.

- There are mental things with properties different from those of physical objects: feeling, intensity, reference, logical relationships, and so on.

- The two kinds of things interact somehow, or at least they seem to interact.

Spinoza's concept of God

Spinoza argued that thought (mental reality) and extension (physical reality) were the same thing, simply looked at in different ways. In his *Ethics*, Part II, Proposition 7, he wrote:

> *"Thinking substance [consciousness] and extended substance [matter] are one and the same substance, comprehended now under this attribute, now under that. So, too, a mode of Extension and the idea of that mode are one and the same thing, expressed in two ways."*

The 20th-century name for Spinoza's doctrine is "neutral monism." On Spinoza's account, the idea of a thing is just a different way of looking at the thing, while the thing itself is just a different way of looking at the idea. Therefore, ideas and their relationships exactly parallel things and their relationships. Ideas are part of the conscious order, while things are part of the extended (in space) physical order. The orders are the same thing, but viewed from different perspectives, as shown in the figure on the next page.

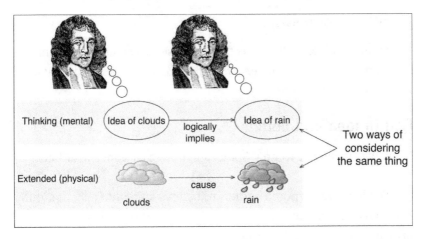

By the way, you might recall that as an example of something un-imaginable, the previous chapter listed "something that had color but took up no space." If you ever hear the same example in a philosophy class, the professor will say that the thing is "colored but not ex-tended." That comes from Spinoza's distinction between the con-scious order (ideas) and the extended order (space).

Through a complicated series of arguments in his *Ethics*, Part I, Spinoza decides that only one "substance" exists:

"By substance I mean that which is in itself and is conceived through itself; that is, that the conception of which does not require the conception of another thing from which it has to be formed."

The one substance exists necessarily, so it's impossible for it not to exist. It's infinite. And it causes itself. Everything else – stars, plan-ets, buildings, horses, you, me, bad music, etc. – is part of that one infinite, self-causing substance.

Think about that: It exists necessarily, is infinite, causes itself, and causes everything else. You don't need Google Maps to see where he's going with this:

"God, or substance consisting of infinite attributes, each of which expresses eternal and infinite essence, necessarily exists,"

On Spinoza's account, the only thing that qualifies as a substance is God. Everything else might or might not exist, is caused by some-thing else, and is finite in space and time.

*"Wait ... God is **what?!**"*

Spinoza thinks that God is the universe. If you are a convention-ally-minded rabbi in 17th-century Amsterdam, you just had what used to be called "a conniption fit."

God in idea and belief

Now, we finally get to how Spinoza applies that concept to belief in God.

For Spinoza, as noted earlier, to believe something about a thing is to have an idea of the thing. To have an idea of it is to know its principal attribute and its cause.

Its principal attribute is either thought (mental) or extension (physical). He believed that there were an infinite number of other attributes, but that we only knew about thought and extension. The ultimate cause of any finite thing is God, but it can also have more immediate and down-to-earth causes. In his usual turgid prose, Spinoza explains (*Ethics*, Part II, Proposition 9):

> *"The idea of an individual thing existing in actuality has God for its cause not in so far as he is infinite but in so far as he is considered as affected by another idea of a thing existing in actuality, of which God is the cause in so far as he is affected by a third idea, and so ad infinitum."*

In other words, if a horse exists, the ultimate cause is God. But the more immediate cause is that the horse was born to a mother horse, whose ultimate cause is also God. Complete and perfect knowledge of the horse would require complete and perfect knowledge of its ultimate cause.

For Spinoza, an idea is not just an image: it always asserts something. If you have an idea of a horse, then at the very least, it includes the implied assertion that "this is a horse."

To get a more complete idea of the horse, you might know part of its cause: that it was born to a female horse that's its mother. The more you learn about its cause (actually, the many things that jointly cause it) the better you understand the horse. The more you understand about the horse, the more "adequate" your belief is (*Ethics*, Part I, Axiom 4):

> *"The knowledge of an effect depends on, and involves, the knowledge of the cause."*

This means that having a belief is not an either/or situation. It's not a situation where you either have a belief or you don't. For Spinoza, there are *degrees* of belief and knowledge, based on the adequacy of your ideas. Only God, which is infinite, has perfect ideas and completely true knowledge. Of course, in Spinoza's view, we shouldn't say that God "has" ideas. God *includes* ideas, with each idea corresponding to a parallel extended fact in the natural universe.

And here's the most important point: Everything that exists is included in God, so the more you learn about the natural universe, the more adequately you can form an idea of God (*Ethics*, Part I, Proposition 15):

> *"Whatever is, is in God, and nothing can be or be conceived without God."*

And when you form an idea of God, even an inadequate idea, then you believe in God as Spinoza defines God.

That's a God Spinoza could believe in: what he called *deus sive natura*, the physical universe with its parallel system of ideas. We can understand it only very imperfectly, but we can understand it.

What Spinoza believed

So Spinoza *did* believe in God after all, but it was his own version of God as a rationally comprehensible being. What he *didn't* believe in was:

- **A transcendent and incomprehensible God:** "Whether therefore we say that all things happen according to the laws of nature, or are ordained by the edict and direction of God, we are saying the same thing."

- **A God that chose the Jewish people:** "On this issue then we can accept no difference between Jews and Gentiles; and therefore there is no election which is unique to the Jews ..."

- **A God who dictated the Torah to Moses:** "To interpret Scripture, we need to assemble a genuine history of it and deduce the thinking of the Bible's authors by valid inferences from this history."

Notice one final point: Spinoza did the same thing as Maimonides. For philosophical reasons, he could not accept the plain and simple interpretations of the beliefs. He redefined the beliefs in ways that made them rationally acceptable to him.

The big difference between Maimonides and Spinoza was that Maimonides still gave vigorous public support to the beliefs, concealing the fact that they meant something different to him. Spinoza didn't care about that. His people had already judged, maligned, and rejected him. He felt no need to conceal anything.

Chapter 6:
Why Mendelssohn
Changed the Subject

"Well done is better than well said."

-- Benjamin Franklin

IF SPINOZA WAS ONE OF THE FATHERS of the 17th-century enlightenment, Moses Mendelssohn (1729-1786) was one of its most influential children. He was a famous political philosopher as well as father of the 18th-century Jewish enlightenment (Haskalah) that reconciled Judaism with secular philosophy and non-Jewish society. As a bonus, he was the grandfather of Felix Mendelssohn (1809-1847), who -- in a life that was brief even by 19th-century standards -- composed some of the most beautiful classical music of that period.

The Socrates of Berlin

After he became famous, Mendelssohn was known as "the Socrates of Berlin" -- a nickname that put him on a pedestal with the ancient Greek philosopher who taught Plato. Growing up, however, he had never heard of Socrates, didn't live in Berlin, and didn't even speak German.

Born in the small town of Dessau, Mendelssohn started studying Torah and Talmud at the age of six. By 11, he had memorized the Torah and taught himself Hebrew grammar. That won him a place studying with Rabbi David Fränkel, an eminent scholar whom he followed to Berlin at age 14 in 1743.

Berlin was a turning point. There, he studied Jewish philosophers including Maimonides and Judah Halevi. He taught himself German, Latin, Greek, French, and English, thereby gaining access to non-Jewish literature and the wider non-Jewish world. In 1753, he formed a lifelong friendship with Gotthold Lessing (1729-1781), a Christian who shared his intellectual interests. Together, they studied Spinoza and jointly published a book about him.

In 1763, Mendelssohn's essay on reason in religion won first prize from the Berlin Academy, beating the second-place essay by Immanuel Kant (1724-1804), who was one of the most influential philosophers of all time. Mendelssohn's other work and his superb German writing style established him in non-Jewish society as a popular and respected thinker. At the same time, he remained religiously observant, making the Jewish tradition and the Jewish people the touchstones of his life.

He was both "the Socrates of Berlin" to the Christian intellectual world and a revered leader to the religious world of the Jews.

The Lavater affair

Sooner or later, those two identities had to come into conflict.

The first such conflict was "the Lavater Affair." Johann Lavater, a Swiss deacon, visited Mendelssohn in 1768 to discuss his ideas about reason and religion. Promising to keep the remarks confidential, he pressed Mendelssohn to reveal his opinion of Jesus. Eventually, Mendelssohn gave in to Lavater's entreaties and said that he respected Jesus as a moral teacher -- adding the reservation that his respect depended on Jesus not believing he was God.

Lavater, on the other hand, believed that Christianity was the only rational and true religion. He also believed that Mendelssohn was a brilliant thinker of high integrity. However, Lavater knew nothing about the intellectual foundations of Judaism. He could not understand why a smart man like Mendelssohn was not a Christian.

In 1769, he translated a book of Christian apologetics into German and dedicated it to Mendelssohn. The book argued that Jesus' miracles proved the truth of Christianity. In the dedication, he challenged Mendelssohn either to refute the book's arguments or convert to Christianity.

That put Mendelssohn in a terrible spot.

He agreed with Maimonides that many Bible passages were metaphorical. He shared Spinoza's skepticism about traditional beliefs.

But he was also a leader of the Jewish community. He knew that stating his doubts plainly and publicly would at best alienate most Jews, and might cause far worse results. Some Jews might lose their faith. It might damage the community and hurt the bonds of loyalty that had enabled Jews to survive disasters and challenges over the millennia. And he knew he might end up like Spinoza, excommunicated and cast out by his own people.

At the same time, his doubts about Jewish belief applied equally to Christianity. He had no desire to antagonize the Christian majority by arguing against their religion. Jews were tolerated and increasingly accepted, of which Mendelssohn himself was an example. He didn't want to ruin that. He thought that he had to respond, lest his silence be interpreted as agreement with Lavater's point. But he had to be very careful.

Mendelssohn replied to Lavater with an open letter he published in 1769. The letter shows Mendelssohn at his most tactful, answering Lavater's challenge by changing the subject. It was a maneuver that he would use later, and more ambitiously, in his book *Jerusalem*.

He opened by undermining Lavater's moral standing to make a public challenge, pointing out -- ever so politely -- that Lavater had both betrayed Mendelssohn's confidence:

"You cannot have possibly forgotten ... how much you and your friends had to press me before I dared to express my convictions on a subject that is so important to the heart. If I am not mistaken, assurances were offered in advance that no public mention should ever be made of the words that would emerge on this occasion. I

prefer to be mistaken, however, than to blame you for breaking this promise."

and that Lavater had misrepresented his position:

"And my great respect for the moral character of its founder [Jesus]? Had you not been silent about the condition that I explicitly added, I would have been able to concede it now."

Mendelssohn added that he hadn't just recently started thinking about religion, but had thought about it for many years. He had thoroughly investigated his own faith and satisfied himself of its truth. At this point, he deployed his two most characteristic tactics for avoiding arguments:

- **He changed the subject**, subtly misdirecting the readers to a peripheral issue so that he could avoid arguing against ideas that he thought it would be impolitic to dispute.
- **He used literary style** and flowery rhetoric to obscure the change of subject.

After explaining at some length (using verbosity to distract his readers) that Judaism does not seek to convert people from other religions, he got to the real bottom line:

"My religion, my philosophy, and my rank in civil life furnish me with the most important reasons for avoiding all religious disputes and for speaking in my public writings only of those truths that must be equally important to all religions."

Most interesting, however, was Mendelssohn's justification for his reticence.

As a Jew, he believed that key tenets of Christianity were incorrect. But he also believed that incorrect beliefs could have good consequences for moral behavior and social tolerance. In such cases, he argued, it is wrong to attack such beliefs unless people will accept alternatives that are both true and equally beneficial:

"Whoever cares more for the welfare of mankind than for his own renown will keep a rein on his opinions concerning prejudices of this sort ... in order not to overturn what he deems a suspicious ethical principle before his fellow men have accepted the true one that he wants to put in its place."

And even in the face of what he thinks is religious error:

> *"I am obliged to remain silent if these errors ... are accidentally connected to the promotion of the good."*

In other words, Mendelssohn believed that:

- Erroneous beliefs can have good consequences.

- If they do, then we should not argue against them unless we offer replacement beliefs that (a) are true, (b) are at least equally helpful, and (c) the believers will accept.

Mendelssohn's concept of belief

Mendelssohn does not give us an explicit definition of belief, but his other comments make it clear that he thinks of beliefs as mental acts, and that behavior -- though important -- is not a form of belief.

Menasseh ben Israel's 1656 book *Vindication of the Jews* had been published in England to argue that Jews should have full civil rights in British society. In 1782, Marcus Herz translated it from English into German. Mendelssohn wrote a preface for it. In that preface, he both alluded to his concept of belief and gave a preview of his main argument in his later and more famous work, *Jerusalem*.

In the preface, he distinguished between belief and behavior:

> *"Through contracts, we can obligate ourselves not to allow certain voluntary actions to depend on our own judgment or opinion, but rather to subject them to another's opinion and thus to renounce our own judgment to the extent that it carries over into our actions ... But our judgment itself is an inseparable, immovable, and therefore inalienable possession. Everything depends on this distinction."*

And:

> *"Renouncing opinion as it concerns action is one thing. Renouncing opinion itself is another. Action is immediately situated within our power of choice. Opinion is not."*

Mendelssohn's "search for light and right"

Distinguishing between belief and behavior was fine. However, his preface to *Vindication of the Jews* made another statement that got him into deep trouble even if it seemed harmless.

Mendelssohn had said that we control only our actions, not our opinions. But then he argued that while secular governments could banish people from the country, religious organizations had no such authority:

> *"It seems to me that every society possesses the right of expulsion except for an ecclesiastical society, for it is diametrically opposed to the ecclesiastical society's ultimate goal, which is collective edification and participation in the outpouring of the heart through which we show our thanks for God's beneficence."*

His statement denied that religious organizations had the authority to excommunicate members of the faith -- the punishment imposed so unfairly on Spinoza.

That statement caught the attention of journalist August Cranz (1737-1801), who anonymously wrote "The Search for Light and Right." Like Lavater, he challenged Mendelssohn to renounce Judaism – but for different reasons this time.

Cranz sympathized with Mendelssohn's earlier treatment by Lavater, who had betrayed his confidence:

> *"People were satisfied with your response [to Lavater] because they were dissatisfied with Lavater and felt that he had treated you unfairly by publicly embarrassing you. This time the case is different. You have now publicly provided a major reason for people to rightly expect and even demand fuller explanations from you."*

And what must Mendelssohn explain? How he can remain a Jew while denying a central belief of Judaism:

> *"In your remarkable preface, you ... rob the synagogue of its foremost power, by denying it the right of excommunicating from the congregation of the holy those who deviate from the faith of your fathers ... Perhaps you have now come closer to the Christian faith by throwing off the servitude of the iron bonds of the [Jewish] church and henceforth teaching the system of freedom of rational divine service."*

Like Lavater, Cranz saw enlightened Christianity as rational and Judaism as blind faith. But he also had a good point: Judaism had traditionally believed certain things, including the right of excommunication. Mendelssohn had publicly denied that belief. How could he possibly extricate himself this time and remain a Jew?

Mendelssohn took a bold and unexpected step. He responded to Cranz in Part II of his book *Jerusalem*, where Mendelssohn denied that Judaism required any beliefs at all:

> *"Judaism knows of no revealed religion in the sense in which Christians understand this term. The Israelites possess a divine legislation—laws, commandments, ordinances, rules of life, instruction in the will of God as to how they should conduct themselves in order to attain temporal and eternal felicity. Moses revealed to them propositions and prescriptions of this kind in a miraculous and supernatural manner, but no doctrinal opinions, no saving truths, no universal propositions of reason."*

As for doctrines and universal truths, those are revealed to Jews in the same way as they are revealed to everyone else: by experience and by the natural light of reason:

> *"These the Eternal reveals to us and to all other men, at all times, through nature and thing, but never through word and script."*

In other words, he says that Judaism doesn't care what you *believe*, as long as you *behave* in obedience to the commandments.

Mendelssohn's reply is, of course, nonsense. Obeying the commandments makes no sense unless one believes that they were ordained by God -- and indeed, that God communicated them to Moses, as Mendelssohn said. And since the commandments are mostly defined in rabbinic commentaries on the Torah -- the so-called "Oral Torah" -- it makes no sense to obey them unless one also believes that God communicated the Oral Torah to Moses, who in turn gave it to the rabbis who wrote the commentaries.

But the point is that Mendelssohn came back to what we have previously argued is a form of belief: verbal and non-verbal behavior. The behaviors he prescribes make no sense except as expressions or embodiments of traditional Jewish beliefs. Whether one mentally believes them or not, acting in accordance with those beliefs is what Mendelssohn says constitutes the Jewish religion.

Notice something astonishing about Mendelssohn's position: It entirely ignores the assertive function of beliefs, and focuses on the value from the behavioral and social functions of belief. He had a mental-act view of belief, so he couldn't explain it, but he certainly knew about the other functions.

Mendelssohn's key conflict

Mendelssohn's life and work were shaped by two conflicts, one intellectual and the other social:

- **Intellectually**, he knew and cherished the Jewish tradition as his cultural and religious heritage. But he also knew science and Enlightenment rationalism, including Spinoza and Leibniz, and he was convinced of their truth.

- **Socially**, he was loyal to his people and to his community. He wanted to protect their rights and promote their welfare. He was accepted and even celebrated by non-Jewish society. He wanted all Jews to enjoy the same acceptance as he did.

Mendelssohn resolved the conflict by focusing on verbal and nonverbal behaviors. It was those behaviors that united the Jewish community, inspired it, and strengthened it to survive and flourish through one challenge after another. Mental beliefs were private, had no social impact, and were -- he thought -- beyond our control. They existed but were not religiously important.

Chapter 7:
Belief and Biology

"Man is a credulous animal, and must believe something; in the absence of good grounds for belief, he will be satisfied with bad ones."

-- Bertrand Russell

BIOLOGY? WHAT DOES BELIEF have to do with biology?

Look in the mirror. What do you see? You are many things: interesting and important things. You might be a lawyer, a student, or one of three sisters. You might be an American, a Russian, or an Israeli. Or you might not be any of those things.

But there's one thing you definitely are: you're a living being. Biology applies to you. It doesn't make decisions for you, but it influences the decisions you make. It doesn't choose your beliefs, but it influences which beliefs seem natural or repulsive, which beliefs are helpful or harmful. It also lets you use beliefs to achieve your individual or social goals.

How? Why? That's the subject of this chapter. In the next chapter, we'll see how it applies to the social functions of belief.

If your biology biases you in favor of some beliefs and against others, then you might adopt untrue beliefs just because they appeal to you. Likewise, you might reject true beliefs simply because you instinctively don't like them. Understanding your biology helps you compensate for instinctive biases so you have a better chance of believing true things. Just as important, it helps you understand how religious beliefs and practices can support you in living a good life.

Biblical Biology 101

As soon as people started to think, they started to wonder.

Where does the sun go at night? How did we get here? Why are some plants and animals good to eat, but others make us feel sick?

For a couple thousand years, people in Europe and thereabouts thought that life originated as described in the Bible:

> *"God said, 'Let the waters bring forth swarms of living creatures, and birds that fly above the earth across the expanse of the sky ... And God created man in His image, in the image of God He created him; male and female He created them.'"*
> *-- Genesis 1:20 and 1:27*

Of course, the Bible wasn't the first to tell a story like that. Parts of the Genesis story are similar to the Babylonian *Enuma Elish*, as well as to the stories of Gilgamesh and Atrahasis. Far away from the ancient Israelites, the Greek writer Hesiod told creation stories in his *Theogony*. In Southern Africa, the Bushmen told legends of Cagn, who made the sun, moon, stars, plants, and animals. In India, the Hindus taught that a being named Parusha was sacrificed to create the world, with different parts of his body transforming into different parts of the world and into different groups of people. In China, Huang-lao brought order out of chaos.

Scholars of religion call all those legends "etiological tales," because they explain the causes (the etiology) of how the world and human society came to be as they are.

But biology, like history, is written by the victors. Judaism outlasted the older religions in the West, and Christianity adopted Judaism's account of creation. From ancient times to the 1800s, the Bible was Western civilization's premier biology textbook. God had created the world in six days -- or one, depending on which chapter of Genesis you believed. However long it took, that was when God created the earth, the plants, and the animals just as they are now. A horse is a horse is a horse. It's never a bird or a tree. It doesn't change into anything else.

Likewise, the earth itself was only about six thousand years old and hadn't changed since God created it. The Anglican Bishop James Ussher (1581-1656) calculated that God had created the universe on October 23 in 4,004 BCE. Not to be outdone, Dr. Charles Lightfoot at Cambridge University added that God had created the world promptly at 9:00am on that date.

Old Certainties Disappear

But as centuries passed, the old certainties seemed increasingly uncertain. The Copernican revolution had knocked the earth off its privileged perch at the center of the universe. Biologists noticed that many plants and animals looked like each other and had corresponding parts. For example, the internal anatomy of a human arm is like that of a dog's legs, a bird's wing, and a whale's fin.

Of course, the Deity might have used the same basic layout to make a lot of different creatures. It would have been efficient, and since He had already created the world by 9:00am on October 23, we know that He was big on efficiency.

But there was another obvious possibility. If Jim and Joe look a lot alike, we naturally wonder if they're related. What if different species of plants and animals were related somehow?

Even more puzzling was that embryos of animals had features found in the embryos of other animals. Human embryos, for example, have rudimentary gill arches like those in fish embryos. They also share features with embryos of amphibians and reptiles, as well as other mammals.

Geologists noticed that the earth seemed a lot older than 6,000 years. In sedimentary rock, layers upon layers had been deposited over the eons. The lower layers, which were older, had the fossilized skeletons of animals that no one had ever seen. The higher layers, which were newer, had fossils that looked more like living creatures. The closer the layer was to the present, the closer the fossils looked to the animals around us. By that time, a lot of people doubted the accuracy of the Genesis stories, but they weren't sure what the truth was. So they started thinking about how it all might have happened.

From creation to evolution

Most people today identify the theory of evolution with Charles Darwin (1809-1882). And that's essentially true, since he was the first to identify its basic mechanism and collect vast amounts of evidence that it had happened.

Scientists regard Darwin as something of a patron saint because he laid the groundwork for much of modern biology. Orthodox religious believers are split about the issue. Some still insist on a literal reading of the Book of Genesis, though that has its own problems because Genesis has two separate creation stories (1:1-2:3 and 2:4-2:24). Read literally, they contradict each other.

Orthodox believers who are scientists, such as Francis S. Collins (geneticist), Owen Gingerich (astronomer), and Gerald Schroeder (physicist) usually agree with their peers about evolution but add their own religious gloss on how it occurred. Essentially, they all argue for the theory of "intelligent design." On that view, life developed naturally under physical laws, but the physical laws *themselves* were "tuned" by a Divine intelligence to facilitate the development of life. Even though he didn't know about evolution, Maimonides had a very similar view of natural law.

Intelligent design is a philosophical story rather than a scientific story. It accepts the results of physical science, but then offers an explanation of why the results are the way they are. Note that intelligent design competes not against the scientific story of evolution, which it accepts, but against a rival philosophical story that says life developed through random, unguided physical processes. Both stories are about the *explanations* of scientific results instead of being about the results themselves, so they cannot be proven or disproven by looking at scientific results. Like most philosophical stories, they either "make sense" to you or they don't. Which story you prefer depends on your own psychology, assumptions, and experience.

What Darwin brought that was new

Darwin wasn't the first person to suggest that modern plants and animals developed by evolving from different species.

The best-known of his predecessors was Jean-Baptiste Lamarck (1744-1829) who thought evolution took place by inheritance of acquired characteristics. For example, giraffes evolved long necks because their ancestors kept stretching their necks to eat leaves high in trees. Over many generations, the stretching caused their necks to lengthen. Other advocates included Darwin's grandfather, Erasmus, who was a little vague about how evolution occurred.

Darwin, however, did bring something new to the discussion. He both assembled vast amounts of evidence that evolution had occurred, and he proposed a verifiable mechanism for how it had happened. It wasn't just armchair theorizing.

Even as a boy, he was an avid naturalist, studying all the animals and plants around the small English town where he lived. At his father's insistence, he tried studying medicine but couldn't stand the sight of blood. As a second choice, he enrolled in Cambridge University to study for the ministry. That made sense because most famous British naturalists were ministers. They preached a few sermons, heard confessions, and had the rest of their time free to peruse the various forms of plant and animal life in the countryside.

Darwin's big break came in 1831, when he signed on as a scientific observer for a British Navy ship that was mapping the coast of South America. For four years, he studied plants and wildlife of South America, but that was only a warmup for the main event. In the fifth and last year of the mission, the ship surveyed the Galapagos Islands just off the South American coast.

The Galapagos Islands had been created by undersea volcanic activity and had never been connected to the mainland. In spite of that, they were teeming with plants and animals. Some were the same species as Darwin had seen in South America. Others were similar to those on the mainland but were clearly different species. Some species were found only on individual islands and on none of the others.

Selection, natural and otherwise

Obviously, there was something odd going on. If God had created all plant and animal life at one time, why were there different types of plants and animals in the fossil record, with newer fossils being more similar to current species? And why would God create slight variations of the same species of plants and animals on different islands?

Darwin didn't know much about genetics, but he did know how farmers bred animals. In any population of animals, some have desirable traits and others don't. If you mate animals that have desirable traits, their offspring are likely to have the traits of their parents. Humans have used that technique for millennia to breed useful varieties of plants and animals.

The same kind of variation exists in nature. Some animals are bigger, stronger, more resistant to heat or cold, or harder for predators to see. When those traits increase an animal's chances of surviving to produce offspring, it has more offspring and they inherit the helpful traits.

At the same time, if an animal lacks helpful traits or has harmful traits, it is more likely to die off before producing offspring, or to produce fewer offspring. Its offspring are likely to have the same traits, so they, too, have fewer offspring.

Therefore, with each new generation, the animal population has a larger percentage with the helpful traits and a smaller percentage without them. Over many generations, that two-sided process alters the population so that animals and plants with helpful traits are most common, and the ones with unhelpful traits disappear.

That's natural selection, as opposed to the artificial selection used by animal breeders. Instead of breeders deliberately mating animals with desired traits and not mating others, nature kills off animals with undesirable traits because they can't compete with the more advantaged members of the species.

Notice that the emergence of new species is a special case of evolution by natural selection. Most evolution takes place within species, such as all the wildly different breeds of dogs -- some big, some small, with different features, personalities, and intelligence. New species only come into being when enough small changes accumulate that two groups descended from a common ancestor can no longer interbreed. That happens if the groups are geographically isolated from each other and exposed to different environments that make different traits helpful or unhelpful.

So according to Darwin, that's how evolution occurs: *them what's able, survive*; the others die off, either mostly or completely.

The problem of altruism

But there was a problem with Darwin's theory. Many animals -- not just humans -- exhibit altruistic behavior, where they risk or sacrifice their own welfare for the benefit of others. The others can be individuals such as family members or all the members of a group. For example:

- A duck that sees a wolf emits a warning cry to the other ducks in its flock, enabling them to take flight before the wolf can kill and eat them. But by making a noise, the duck attracts attention to itself, risking its own death for the sake of the flock.

- Bees protect their hives by stinging predators, but they die from losing their stingers.

- Vampire bats (yes, they really exist) regurgitate blood to feed other hungry bats.

- Dolphins help injured dolphins and carry them to safety.

- Whirligig beetles form large groups to skim across the surface of ponds. Each beetle has a greater risk of dying from a predator's attack, but a greater number of beetles survive.

- Men routinely fight and die to defend their families, their faiths, or their countries.

In all of those cases and many others, animals risk or sacrifice their own welfare for the good of others. As laudable as that sounds, it doesn't fit Darwin's theory of evolution.

If a tendency to altruistic behavior is genetic, then on Darwin's theory, it should quickly vanish. Altruistic animals tend to die earlier and more often than others, so they have fewer offspring. Nonaltruists live longer and have more offspring. In a few generations, animals inclined to altruism should die off, and the population should be dominated by "selfish" animals.

If only humans acted altruistically, we could say it was because of intelligence, conscience, or moral training. But since other animals do it, that explanation doesn't work. Lower animals don't think about their actions: they behave as they do because their genes program them to do it. A duck doesn't think about the welfare of the flock being more important than his own welfare. He just warns the flock, and the wolf eats him as a result. No more offspring for the do-gooder duck.

How is it that altruists are still around? And for another example from today's society, how is it that gays and lesbians are still around? They have fewer children than heterosexuals, if indeed they have any at all. If homosexuality is mostly biological, as scientists now believe, shouldn't evolution have made us all heterosexual by now?

On Darwin's theory, we should all be selfish heterosexuals. But we're not. Darwin's theory is at least incomplete. There is something about altruism, and other offspring-reducing traits such as homosexuality, that has survival value in the evolutionary struggle.

When it was finally discovered, the mystery's solution was surprisingly simple. Darwin couldn't see it because he was limited by the science of his time. He thought of evolution in terms of individual animals producing their own offspring. Some of his successors, trying to explain altruism, would go to the opposite extreme and focus on whole species. But the real answer was too small to see: It was a sequence of molecules called a "gene."

All of animals' visible traits -- speed, strength, intelligence, and so forth -- are largely determined by their genes. Environment ("nurture") has a definite influence that can help or hurt, but an animal's genes set the range within which its traits are most likely to vary. Beagles never give birth to pit bulls; families of short people rarely include professional basketball players. Here's a summary of the important points:

- Genes are sequences of molecules called nucleotides: Adenine, Thymine, Cytosine, and Guanine. A fifth nucleotide, Uracil, occurs only in the genes of viruses.

- The genes of all living things except viruses are in molecules of DNA (deoxyribonucleic acid) in their body cells. Viruses use RNA (ribonucleic acid) to encode their genes.

- Each living thing's DNA (or RNA, for viruses) is the blueprint for its physical body.

- A living thing's blueprint is called its genotype. The physical body created from the blueprint is called its phenotype.

Those genes do not control human behavior, but they influence it. They can predispose us to help others and to care about their welfare, to be indifferent to them, or to be hostile. In various contexts, they do all three.

But for the theory of evolution, our inclination to help others posed a particular problem. How could helping others -- especially at risk or expense to ourselves -- help us pass on our genes to the next generation? In other words, how can we reconcile the theory of evolution with the fact of altruism? Darwin lacked a good answer for that.

Four kinds of altruism

What most people don't realize, even today, is that altruism isn't just one kind of thing. It comes in four varieties, depending on how the altruist selects the beneficiaries. All of them are relevant to human behavior, though they vary in their impact on evolution.

Need selection

The need altruist selects beneficiaries based on perceived need. This is pure altruism: helping others with no expectation of selfish benefit. It's Mother Teresa territory.

You might think only human beings can be need altruists, but they're not the only ones. Other mammals, from chimps all the way down to rats, sometimes help others even when they get no benefit for themselves.

Therefore, need altruism isn't just a result of human moral training: It reflects something genetic. Altruism by lower animals suggests that the morals are based on the genetics, not the other way around.

The biological basis of need altruism is *empathy*, which enables animals -- mammals, mainly, and primates, particularly -- to feel the suffering or happiness of others. Thus even "pure altruism" has a selfish aspect: one animal might get no material gain from helping another, but it might get a good feeling from doing it. Need selection has only a small effect on evolution, but enough for Darwin to mention it in *The Descent of Man* (Part I, Chapter 4):

> *"The social instincts lead an animal to take pleasure in the society of its fellows, to feel a certain amount of [empathy] with them, and to provide various services for them."*

Game selection

Game selection makes a little more sense in evolutionary terms. The game altruist selects beneficiaries based on its own long-term self-interest: in other words, as a way of "winning a game." It's helping others based on the expectation of getting their help in return. The goal is not to benefit anyone else, but to benefit yourself: helping others is just a way to do it.

Just like need selection, game selection occurs in lower animals as well as in humans. Harvard biologist Robert Trivers argued in "The Evolution of Reciprocal Altruism" (*Quarterly Review of Biology*, March 1971) that evolution tended to punish "cheaters" who received help but later failed to return the favor to the altruist:

> *[Evolution] "will discriminate against the cheater if cheating has later adverse effect on his life that outweigh the benefit of not reciprocating."*

That's just the conclusion of Trivers's article, the full text of which is available on the web. Game selection has some effect on evolution, though not as much as kin selection.

Kin selection

Kin selection is the most important type of selection. It's the most common basis of altruistic behavior and it's one of the basic mechanisms of evolution. It's similar to need selection, but with a twist.

The altruistic animal helps others based on their need, but only if it perceives that they're its close genetic relatives.

Though better known today as a militant atheist, biologist Richard Dawkins became famous as one of the popularizers of kin selection theory. In his book *The Selfish Gene*, he argued that the basic unit of evolution was not the individual, population, or species, but the *gene*.

If we focus on genes, kin-selection altruism makes sense. We share more of our genes with our families and close relatives than we do with others. If we risk our lives to protect our relatives, we are protecting their -- and *our* --- genes' opportunity to continue in the next generation. Whether we have offspring ourselves or simply help our relatives do it, the result is the same.

That fits biologists' field studies which show that animals are most likely to commit altruistic acts to benefit their genetic relatives, that is, their kin. In the 1960s, biologist William Hamilton came up with a formula for determining when it is most likely to happen:

$c < r * b$

where c is the survival cost to the altruistic animal (in risk, food, etc.), r is the percent of genes shared because of a family relationship, and b is the benefit to the object of the animal's altruistic act.

Thus, kin selection explained how evolution worked together with altruism:

- It explained why animals committed altruistic acts.
- It explained scientists' observation that when animals in the wild commit altruistic acts, it's usually to benefit their relatives (children, siblings, etc.).

The converse of kin selection is *non-kin non-selection*, which inclines animals to fight with other members of their species who are genetic competitors.

Because they are members of the same species, the non-kin animals occupy the same biological niche and compete with animals' genetic kin for food, resources, and mates. Therefore, animals react with extra hostility and aggression to non-kin members of the same species, even more than they do to animals of other species that are physical threats.

For example, male hawk wasps will attack other male hawk wasps that invade their territories but will ignore birds and genetically unrelated animals. They attack the other male hawk wasps because they are genetic competitors who might mate with female hawk wasps in the territory, but their aggression against female hawk wasps is limited to attempted copulation.

The implications for humanity are obvious. All members of the human race occupy the same biological niche. As a result, they need the same kinds of things to survive and reproduce. When such resources are limited, people compete in order to get them. If they perceive others as their kin, they are more likely to cooperate peacefully for mutual benefit. If not, the results are often irrational and destructive. But as we will see in the final chapter of this book, there are ways to promote cooperation even without kinship.

Group selection

Sometimes, however, animals commit altruistic acts to benefit their group as a whole: a hive of bees, a flock of ducks, or -- among humans -- a group of people defined by ethnicity, nation, or religion. That doesn't quite fit the kin selection theory, but it's not too different, either.

First, if an animal is a member of a particular group, it probably shares a larger number of genes with other group members than it does with non-members. Second, animals use specific cues to determine who is and isn't related to them. Because it's loosely connected to relatedness, group membership is one of the cues. It's not an infallible cue, but it works well enough for evolution. That's especially true for lower animals. Unlike humans, who see cues in clothing, belief, and other factors, animals use only biological cues. Therefore, an animal that engages in altruism for its group has a better than even chance of benefiting its own genetic relatives, and thereby helping its own genes make it into the next generation.

How Animals Know Who's Who

All the types of selection promote altruism, but studying animal behavior in the wild, biologists have observed that it usually benefits animals' genetic relatives. Kin selection is by far the most powerful cause of altruistic acts. That raises two other problems:

- How do animals know which other animals are their genetic relatives?
- How do they know *how closely* the other animals are related to them?

These two questions go back to Hamilton's formula: The amount that an animal will "spend" for the benefit of another animal is less than the percentage of shared (by kin relationship) genes multiplied by the benefit to the other animal. If the two animals aren't related, the percentage of shared genes is zero, so the animal is unlikely to help the other at all. If the animals are related, then some relationships are genetically closer than others. A parent shares half its genes with its offspring, but less with cousins or more distant relatives.

It turns out that animals use four methods to identify their kin, as well as to determine how closely related they are. The methods aren't foolproof, but as people say in Washington, DC, they're "good enough for government work." Sometimes, animals act altruistically to benefit non-relatives, but usually, it's for their relatives. As P.J.B. Slater explains in *Behaviour and Evolution* ("Kinship and Altruism"), the methods are:

- **Context:** This includes the location of the other animal. Birds and rodents, for example, often care for any young in their nests even if they are not related. It's a fairly crude way to identify relatives, but it works more often than not. If an animal is in the right place at the right time, another animal might assume it's a relative.

- **Familiarity:** If unrelated animals are raised together, they treat each other with more care than they treat strangers, often even if the "strangers" are their genetic relatives.

- **Phenotype:** An animal's phenotype is its physical body, and biologists also include its behavior in this category. If animals look alike and act alike, they assume that they are related and are inclined to help each other altruistically.

- **Genotype:** An animal's genotype is the genetic blueprint encoded in its DNA. That is obviously not visible to other animals. However, sometimes genes create clues that other animals can perceive. For example, some genes affect the way animals smell, and that can indicate kin relationship.

Need selection, game selection, and group selection amount to imperfect "back doors" leading to kin selection. Need selection implies context and familiarity, since the beneficiary must be in the same location as the altruistic animal. Game selection and group selection also imply those factors. Those types of selection will sometimes lead animals to help unrelated beneficiaries but the same thing can happen with kin selection based on appearance and behavior.

The bottom line here is that animals are more inclined to help other animals if the other animals:

- Are in a certain location,
- Are already familiar,
- Look like them, or
- Act like them.

Below the level of consciousness, on a purely instinctive level, those four cues prepare an animal to help and cooperate with another animal who satisfies one or more of the cues.

You can probably guess how that's relevant to religious belief and behavior. Human beings might be created in the image of God, but their physical bodies share the same nature as other animals. On that level, they react in the same way as other animals.

Emotion as instant calculation

For most of Western history, we've regarded thought and emotion as opposing forces. To keep our thinking free of emotional influence was the ideal. The ancient Greek philosopher Plato said that strong emotion was like being chained to a raging madman, and he found few people in the ensuing millennia to disagree with his viewpoint.

However, we now know that Plato's view was wrong. Emotional reactions are not the enemy of reason, but instead, they are an integral part of it.

Emotions give us instantaneous calculations based on eons of evolution, faster and with more knowledge than we could do by "thinking" about situations. Sometimes, our emotional reactions are wrong, but just as often, they're right. If you think about emotion in the context of evolution by natural selection, that makes sense.

Emotion is more than just a mental "feeling:" it involves specific biological reactions that prepare us to act. In the face of a threat, it increases our heart rate, sends more blood and oxygen to our muscles, and prepares us to fight or run away. In other situations, it prepares us to cooperate with allies or get lovey-dovey with potential mates. If our evolutionary ancestors had reacted that way in the wrong contexts, they would have died without producing offspring. The ancestors who survived are the ones who reacted correctly. Their emotional reactions are coded into us.

In order for kin selection to work in evolution, animals must be able to identify their probable genetic relatives. As we saw in the previous section, they rely on cues such as appearance and behavior to help them make such identifications. Their emotional machinery, including its purely biological aspects, supports that. When they see another animal that they identify as a relative, their emotional biology prepares them to cooperate. When they see another animal that is not a relative and might be a threat, their emotional biology prepares them to fight or run away.

Humans have the same emotional and biological responses to fight, flee, or cooperate. As a result, they unconsciously look for signs that other humans fall into one of four groups:

- **Genetic relatives:** These humans share genes with us by common descent. We are emotionally inclined to cooperate with them.

- **Genetic competitors:** These are humans, and have the same basic needs as us, but they share few genes with us by common descent. As a result, they compete with us and our genetic kin for resources. In order to protect our genes, we are emotionally inclined to be hostile to them, to fight them, to keep them away from potential mates, and even to kill them if needed. This is the biological source of racism and other forms of hostility between human groups.

- **Physical threats:** These are other species that could harm us physically, such as wolves and snakes.

- **Non-competing non-threats:** These are other species that pose little risk to us.

Just like other animals, we automatically consider appearance, behavior, familiarity, and location when we decide whom to fight and with whom to cooperate. All that proceeds independently of any conscious thought they might have about the situation.

However, human beings are both biological and thinking creatures. When we react emotionally, it's a biological response based on our unconscious assessment of the person or situation. The response occurs instantly and without our conscious awareness of it. Those responses evolved in pre-human contexts, so they are often wildly inaccurate about some situations we face in modern society.

By itself, that wouldn't be a problem if our intelligence then subjected emotional reactions to rational scrutiny. But that's often not what happens. Instead, our minds take the reactions as a starting point, then they start fabricating "reasons" why the reactions are correct. As political scientist Howard Margolis observed in his book *Patterns, Thinking, and Cognition:*

> *"Given the judgments (themselves produced by the non-conscious cognitive machinery in the brain, sometimes correctly, sometimes not so), humans produce rationales they believe account for their judgments. But the rationales ... are only ex post rationalizations."*

Our minds go to work generating justifications for the conclusions our emotions have already reached. That's why smart people often hold stupid opinions. They don't get their opinions by thinking: they get them by reacting emotionally. They only start thinking when challenged to justify the opinions they've already chosen. Smart people are simply more adept at coming up with reasons for beliefs they adopted emotionally.

As a result, people's animal-level emotional reactions tend to bias all the thinking they do afterward. If they encounter another person and feel at a gut level that he is bad and a threat, their intelligence will go to work justifying the feeling. It will adduce reasons: *He follows an alien religion. He's of a different race. He's disloyal to our group.* And because their minds are primed to believe bad things about the person, they will discount any good reports and be inclined to believe terrible slanders based on no evidence:

> "The bottom line is that human minds, like animal minds, are constantly reacting intuitively to everything they perceive, and basing their responses on those reactions. Within the first second of seeing, hearing, or meeting another person, the elephant has already begun to lean toward or away, and that lean influences what you think and do next."[8]

Let's not be overly pessimistic. If rational moral judgment were impossible, then we would not have achieved even as much civilization as we have. It's not impossible, but it's difficult, and it's not the norm. We react first, and think second.

Remember how animals identify their kin: appearance, behavior, location, and context.

For us, those kin-identification factors operate at the subconscious level. They generate emotional reactions that prepare us to cooperate, help, fight, or flee:

> "What matters is not actual genetic relatedness, but the perception of relatedness ... the experience of having grown up together, having seen one's mother care for the other person, commensal meals, myths of common ancestry, essentialist intuitions of common flesh

---

[8] Haidt, J. (2012), p. 69.

and blood, the sharing of rituals and ordeals, physical resemblance, and metaphors ... Military leaders use every trick in the book to make their soldiers feel like genetic relatives and take on the biologically predictable risks."[9]

Unless we make a conscious and determined effort to override those reactions, our intelligence simply makes up justifications for why the reactions are correct. Most people do not make that effort most of the time, nor is it practical for anyone to do it *all* of the time.

As a result, signals that hook our "cooperate" reaction support social harmony. They tell us that people are our genetic relatives whom we should help and who are inclined to help us. Signals that hook our "fight or flee" reaction cause strife, hatred, violence, and social dissolution. They tell us that people are threats – predators or genetic competitors – whom we must either escape or destroy.

The neuroscience of practice

One more thing is relevant: how the brain responds to practice.

Did you ever learn to ride a bicycle? And how about learning to read? You don't need to think about the words you're seeing on this page. You just look at them and their meaning pops into your mind. When you were first learning to read, it was laborious. Now, it's automatic.

Likewise, what's your favorite song or melody? When you think of it, you don't have to think about what the next musical note should be. It just pops into your mind automatically.

That's because of long-term potentiation (LTP) in your brain. If you repeat an action over and over, your brain learns how to do it without requiring you to think about it anymore.

Animal brains have billions of cells called neurons. The neurons communicate with each other across little gaps called synapses.

When you practice an action, you make the same pattern of neurons activate repeatedly. And it does what you'd expect based on

---

[9] Pinker, S. (2011), loc. 7932.

common experience: It changes the structure of the synapses so that the practiced pattern of neurons activates more easily.

The next time you want to do that action, you barely need to think about it before the neurons are ready to activate and do it for you. That's what learning is.

And there's a bonus. You don't actually need to *do* the action to practice it. Just thinking about it tends to activate the same pattern of neurons as doing it.

The effect isn't as strong as actually doing it, but if you think of an action repeatedly, you get some of the same effect. That's why Olympic athletes, for example, engage in "mental practice" of visualizing their athletic events. If thinking about an action is associated with strong emotion or "sensory pageantry" such as bright color, music, or movements such as standing up or raising your hands, that strengthens your brain's learning of the neuron activation patterns.

In the Bible, Proverbs 23:7 was way ahead of its time:

"As a man thinketh, so is he."

Chapter 8:
What Beliefs Do

"The professor destroyed my core beliefs without replacing [them] with anything. He tore down my foundation and left me staring at the rubble."[10]

-- A Yeshiva University student

THE PREVIOUS CHAPTER COVERED THE BIOLOGY OF BELIEF, so you might think that we're done with biology. To start off this chapter, however, there's one more biological mystery to solve:

Why do you have such a big brain?

That's not meant to flatter you, though congratulations are in order since you've read this far in what is unavoidably a challenging book.

It's meant seriously. As a human being, you have a much bigger brain than a comparison with unrelated animal species would predict. Why?

Not only is your brain big, it's an energy hog. At three pounds, it accounts for about two percent of your body's weight but uses about 20 percent of your body's energy.

---

[10] *Moment* Magazine March/April 2014, "James Kugel: Professor of Disbelief."

Of course, some animals have bigger brains than you do. The brain of a sperm whale weighs about 18 pounds, but its average body weight is around 90,000 pounds. Relative to the size of your body, your brain is much bigger.

And your brain is also *better*. Most of a whale's brain is devoted to operating its massive body. But your brain has a neocortex that handles thinking, belief, and social relationships. A whale's brain doesn't have a neocortex at all. The brains of our primate relatives such as chimps have a neocortex, but it's smaller than ours relative to their total brain size.

Biologists have offered various explanations for human brain size. An early view was that as our evolutionary ancestors foraged for food, they needed big brains to remember where it was. On the other hand, bees have tiny brains but are better than humans at remembering where food is. And the truly distinctive feature of human brains is not their size, but the size of their neocortex, compared not only to the rest of the brain but compared to other primates.

Most biologists now accept the social brain hypothesis:[11] that we evolved larger brains with a larger neocortex in order to reason about social relationships in social groups larger than those formed by lower primates such as chimps. That ability means that we can think about who did what to whom, what it means, and how we should act as a result: in other words, it enables us to form reliable beliefs. A side benefit of social brains is that we can reason about non-social facts such as how nature works and how to make tools. As a result, we can deal with the world more effectively. We can form beliefs to guide us in many different ways in different situations.

Let's put that in a more general context. If we can form beliefs, what good does it do us? Why do we have beliefs?

I'm not talking about this belief or that belief. The question is more general: Why do we have *any beliefs at all*? Why is forming beliefs something that human beings do?

---

[11] "Large human brain evolved as a result of 'sizing each other up'," *Science Daily*, March 18, 2018.

Biological evolution favors traits and behaviors that help living things to survive and pass on their genes to the next generation. Does that principle also apply to beliefs?

Yes, it does. Recall that evolution favors traits and behaviors that:

- **Directly** help living things to pass on their genes by enabling individuals to get food, resist disease, use energy more efficiently, avoid predators, and so forth.

- **Indirectly** help living things to pass on their genes by enabling their group (including their genetic relatives) to survive in the same ways.

We have beliefs because they helped our ancestors pass on their genes to the next generation and ultimately to us. Having beliefs enabled them to live more successfully than other versions of our species that did not have beliefs, or didn't apply them in the ways our ancestors did. As a result, we inherited our ancestors' particular ways of having and applying beliefs.

And notice that for biological evolution, what matters are traits and behavior. Whatever beliefs are or are not "mentally," the reason we have them in the way we do is that they're embodied in our traits, biological responses, and actions. The main point of this chapter follows directly:

Beliefs do things for us.

That's "things," plural. Beliefs do a variety of things for us. Different beliefs do different things.

The fact that beliefs do different things suggests there are different kinds of beliefs. For example, consider three beliefs:

- The cat is under the bed.

- Joe lied to Sally and stole money from Bill.

- God rewards the good and punishes the wicked.

The first is an ordinary empirical belief. It can be verified or falsified by specific physical steps and specific observations. If you look under the bed and see the cat, your belief is verified. If you reach under the bed to retrieve the cat and get clawed, that's more verification. But if you look under the bed and do not see the cat, then reach under the bed and feel around but don't feel the cat, your belief is falsified.

Normally, that kind of belief also has specific empirical and physical payoffs: You find the cat. With some difficulty, you get it out from under the bed. With even more difficulty, you put it in the bathtub and give it a bath. Those are goals you value. The cat does not value them: hence your disagreement with the cat and your subsequent need for bandages.

The second belief is a more direct example of the social brain. It lists two social events: Joe lied and Joe stole. From those observations, we use our neocortex to deduce a further belief that we should neither believe Joe nor trust him with our possessions. If Joe then lied to us, we would not rely on his statement but would independently verify the facts: as a result, we would have a greater chance of acting successfully. If we had food or money, we would not leave them where Joe might steal them. As a result, the resources would benefit us instead of Joe. Once again, it enables us to act successfully, just it enabled our ancestors to survive and procreate.

Now, consider the third belief: "God rewards the good and punishes the wicked." It can be held in the face of almost any evidence. It is a sweeping general statement that covers a wide range of situations. Those situations differ in ways that the believer can invoke to maintain the belief, come what may. It gives people a framework to understand reality and to plan their actions.

"God rewards the good and punishes the wicked" is believed by many Jews and Christians despite millennia of evidence to the contrary. Maimonides considered it a "necessary belief," that is, a belief justified by its moral and social benefits even if its meaning or truth were dubious.

The Bible's Book of Job testifies to the difficulty of maintaining the belief, since terrible things often happen to good people and good things often happen to bad people. But there's always a way to save the belief. Job's friends speculate that he must have committed some sin, or else God wouldn't be punishing him. In the wake of the Holocaust, when millions of innocents were horribly murdered, modern writers such as Dennis Prager speculate that Divine reward and punishment must be after death, because it's obviously not happening on earth:

> *"To state this case as starkly as possible, if there is nothing after this life, then the Nazis and the children they threw alive into furnaces have identical fates. If I believed such a thing, I would either become an atheist or hate the God who had created such a cruel and absurd universe."*[12]

Prager's belief strategy is typical in a couple of ways:

- **He kept the words of the belief but changed its meaning.** "God rewards the good and punishes the wicked" looks like a factual statement about what happens in this life on earth, and that's how most people have always interpreted it. It's why in the Bible, Job's friends thought he must have done something wrong to deserve all the misfortune that God inflicted on him. But Prager thinks that meaning is obviously false, so he reinterprets the belief to make it true. He makes it true by making it invulnerable to any possible earthly evidence. No matter what happens in life on earth, Prager can continue to hold his belief.

- **His reinterpreted version of the belief *does something* for him.** Belief in a moral order under a just God enables Prager to avoid what he sees as the three common responses to moral nihilism: hedonism, utopianism, and despair.

Prager's attitude demonstrates what cognitive scientist Jason Slone calls "theological incorrectness." When they think carefully about their beliefs, religious people often give sophisticated explanations that match the tenets of their faiths. In casual reasoning, however, they use shortcuts such as simplistic, literal interpretations that actually conflict with their more sophisticated "official" beliefs.

---

[12] Prager, D. (1995), p. 236.

That kind of thinking is found in most religious traditions. American founding father Benjamin Franklin gave an almost identical argument in *The Pennsylvania Gazette* (1734):

> *"Many arguments to prove a future state have been drawn from the unequal lot of good and bad men ... to see virtue languish and repine, to see vice prosperous and triumphant: such a view, I confess, raises in us a violent presumption that there is another state of retribution, where the just and the unjust will be equally punished or rewarded by an impartial judge."*

General beliefs about complex situations tend to be like that, whether they're about morality, theology, or purely factual subjects. We understand the world by progressively reinterpreting such general statements to make them fit new evidence.

So what are some of the things that beliefs do for us?

Beliefs satisfy our psychological needs

We're not merely biological creatures. Thanks to our social brains, we're also thinking creatures. We think about our lives, what they mean, what we want, and how we fit in the universe. Such thinking makes us feel good, bad, fearful, or needy: that is, we have psychological needs. We crave security, belonging, family, love, certainty, structure, and self-expression. What differs are not the needs, but their intensity and importance for each individual.

The results of many beliefs are intangible, such as making us feel that we are more in control of our lives and our destinies. Beliefs in gods – whether or not they are factually true – have results that are mainly moral and psychological. Believing in God – or for those of a secular bent, believing in the natural order – helps us feel as if we can avoid many bad experiences and increase the likelihood of good experiences. Often, it's even true.

When the Bible's character of Job suffered misfortune, his friends believed that it had to be punishment for his sins. The belief made them feel safer because it implied that if they avoided sin, they could avoid the kind of misfortune that afflicted Job. Likewise, when modern people die young, we want to believe that we know why: because they smoked cigarettes, ate fried food, or did not exercise. We want to believe that if we avoid those "sins," we can avoid the punishment of premature death. We might even half-pretend that we can avoid death altogether. Belief gives us a result that, even though incorrect and intangible, comforts us and helps us get through life with more happiness and less anxiety.

It should be mentioned that simply because a belief satisfies a need, that doesn't mean it's false -- or true. It just means that it satisfies a need. The article "Therapeutic Superstition" by David Bentley Hart, *First Things*, November 2012, describes the case of a man who since childhood often saw angels. He lived an otherwise normal, productive life and was happy. After mentioning his visions during a routine physical exam, he was subjected to treatment for his visions, and medicine "cured" him. He no longer saw angels, and he was unhappy. Cured? It's debatable.

Some people need to be given "the answers" by an authority, whether the authority is a religious leader, a sacred document, or a famous scientist. It doesn't matter if they are completely convinced by the answers: what matters is that someone else has done the thinking for them. They don't have to worry about it. You don't drive on Shabbat. You fast on Yom Kippur. You don't mix meat and dairy. It's all settled, and you don't have to think about it.

By the same token, other people find the same situation to be stifling and intolerable, which is why they leave Orthodox Judaism, Evangelical Christianity, or Islam. They want to make up their own minds in ways that Orthodoxy's more structured faith and observance do not allow.

There is nothing shameful about wanting to let someone else decide the main issues of life for us. It's analogous to my own attitude about apple pie. I don't want a recipe. I don't want to make it myself. I want someone else to make it, give it to me, and let me eat it. In economics, it is called "division of labor." And it's fine.

Because people's psychological needs differ, there's no "one size fits all" belief system or way of life, any more than there's a "one size fits all" pair of shoes. The beliefs we adopt are one of the ways that we satisfy our own psychological needs.

Beliefs provide factual guidance

The most obvious function of belief is to tell us accurate things about the world. Having such accurate beliefs helps us succeed in life, both in our daily activities and in long-term plans. As a result, we are more likely to survive, prosper, and pass on our genes. Beliefs help us do things such as:

- Getting to the store.
- Treating a disease.
- Determining whom to trust or ask for help.
- Determining whom to help and how much.

The value of the belief is not in its factual accuracy per se, but in its ability to help us achieve our goals. If I want to buy some milk and I believe that the grocery is at a location on College Avenue, my belief is valuable to me if it helps me get the milk. The value of its factual accuracy depends on the result. If it helps me get to the grocery to buy some milk, it's valuable; if it doesn't, it's not valuable.

If I'm not interested in the result, then the belief might still be accurate but it has no value for me. The value comes from the result, not the accuracy. The accuracy is only a tool to get the result.

Sometimes the results are tangible and obvious, such as getting to the store or curing a disease. At other times, the results are intangible and less obvious.

It's also worth noting that beliefs can be helpful even if they are factually incorrect. For example, until the 20th century, doctors believed that the disease of malaria was caused by exposure to damp night air. People exposed to damp night air were more likely to get malaria than people who weren't exposed. The cause seemed obvious, but malaria is more specifically caused by mosquito bites that infect the sufferer with a microorganism called Plasmodium. Such bites are more likely to occur in damp night air, where mosquitoes are common.

Therefore, when people took their doctors' advice and stayed away from damp night air, they were less likely to get malaria. Their belief had value.

Beliefs provide "handles"

We use words and concepts as "handles" that allow us to think about complex ideas, or vast quantities of information, without getting bogged down in the details. That enables us quickly to assess situations and handle them successfully.

Consider the concept of a "dog." No actual dog corresponds exactly to the concept, so in a sense, the concept is inaccurate. But using the concept of a dog and its associated word allows us to think about issues related to dogs without getting bogged down in the details of individual dogs.

Similarly, concepts such as "electron" and "the quadratic formula" include details that might or might not be relevant to a problem about which we're thinking. If the details are relevant, we can use the concept and associated word to recall them. If the details are irrelevant, we can ignore them and simply use the concept without thinking about its full meaning.

Thus, a concept and its associated word are like a handle for the related information. When we hold the handle, we can use all the related information without having all of it in mind: we recall only the details that are relevant to solving our current problem.

Beliefs sometimes provide the same kind of efficient shortcut. "God gave the Torah to Moses at Sinai" appears to have a literal, empirical meaning (though in a later chapter, we will see that it doesn't); it has a metaphorical meaning about spirituality; and it also works as a handle for a vast number of associated beliefs in Judaism and Christianity.

When we assert that "God gave the Torah to Moses at Sinai," we seem to be making a literal statement, but we're not. We're using the belief as a handle to assert, and to express commitment to, a vast array of beliefs, practices, and attitudes to which the handle connects.

A contemporary example is that of political beliefs. Consider a belief such as "America is a nation of immigrants." If someone asserts that belief, we can deduce his or her probable beliefs about a wide range of other issues, as well as the political "tribe" to which he or she belongs. The belief itself says nothing about those things, but it serves as a handle to help us identify and interact with the person until we know more.

Of course, the proviso "until we know more" is crucial. Handles can be misleading if we ignore further information as it emerges. To use handles as the only way of understanding a person or group of people is to engage in harmful stereotyping.

Beliefs provide moral guidance

This function of belief is similar to factual guidance, but with a different goal. In this case, our goal is not to achieve specific factual situations -- though factual situations are involved -- but to act morally and to achieve factual situations that are *good*.

Thinkers have argued for millennia about what goodness is. What is it that makes some things good and other things bad? How is that related to our judgments that some actions are right or wrong? From an evolutionary perspective, what's right is what helps us survive and prosper to pass along our genes. That's not the only perspective, of course, but it's a reasonable one.

Regardless of our theories about what makes actions right or wrong, ordinary moral beliefs can help us guide our actions. "Stealing is wrong because it causes unhappiness." Whether or not a person can defend that belief logically, it's a useful guide for life. "I should be loyal to my friends and family" is likewise helpful even if a person never asks why loyalty is supposed to be good.

In morals just like in medicine (recall the example of malaria earlier in the chapter), beliefs don't need to be true in order to be helpful. During the Middle Ages, European Christians believed that prayers by the poor were particularly effective in helping them gain entry to

Heaven.[13] As a result, the rich often provided material help to poor people, as a way to gain their support in prayer. Their belief now seems risible, but it led to good results. Moral and religious beliefs, just like factual beliefs, can be helpful even if they are incorrect.

Let's take another look at the belief with which we started this chapter: "God rewards the good and punishes the wicked." We can't define "God," but we want to be rewarded and we certainly don't want to be punished. As very often happens, this belief looks like a factual assertion, but it has several functions. Most importantly, it's a moral command:

"Be good and don't be wicked."

This view recognizes that religious beliefs in particular are different from ordinary empirical beliefs and serve different functions in our lives:

> *"Wittgenstein, like Kierkegaard, would have regarded the idea of proving the truth of the Jewish or the Christian or the Muslim religion by historical evidence as a profound confusion of realms, a confusion of the inner transformation in one's life that he saw as the true function of religion, with the goals and activities of scientific explanation and prediction."[14]*

Beliefs encourage good behavior

As noted in the previous chapter, whenever we repeat an action, we strengthen the neural connections that implement it. Each time we repeat it, we "learn" it more thoroughly.

The first time we perform an action, we have to think about each step in the action – for example, driving a car. But after doing it a thousand times, we no longer have to think about each step. We just decide to do the action, and the practiced connections in our brains do the steps for us automatically. We just follow along with them.

Repeating beliefs works the same way. Each time we think of a belief, we strengthen the belief and its associated actions. If we

---

[13] See my article "Catholic Church" in *The Encyclopedia of World Poverty* (Sage Publications, 2006).

[14] Putnam, H. (2008), p. 13.

vocalize the belief, we strengthen it even more. If we vocalize the belief in unison with other believers, while surrounded with vivid "sensory pageantry" and emotionally-laden symbols (as in religious services or public events), we strengthen it further.

Most people hold the belief that they are honest, but the belief is more likely to work if they are reminded of their belief. In one study, people were supposed to get a certain amount of money but the cashier "accidentally" gave them too much. Only 20 percent corrected the mistake. But if the cashier specifically asked them whether or not the amount was correct, 60 percent corrected the mistake. They needed to be reminded of their own belief that they were honest.[15]

Beliefs indicate membership

As previously noted, emotions give us instantaneous calculations based on eons of evolution, faster and with more knowledge than we could do by "thinking" about situations. They evolved to help us distinguish between those who are friendly and those who might be a threat.

Because emotion occurs at a biological level, it uses the same criteria as lower animals use to distinguish between their genetic kin and non-kin.

Remember that among other things, animals use phenotype to identify their genetic relatives. The phenotype includes both appearance and behavior. In humans, it includes:

- **Physical appearance:** facial features, skin color, height, body shape, and so on.
- **Dress:** For example, a Star of David identifies the wearer as Jewish, while a cross identifies the wearer as Christian.
- **Language:** A speaker's language identifies him or her as a member of a particular national or linguistic group.
- **Beliefs:** Expressed through verbal or non-verbal behavior.

---

[15] Haidt, J. (2012), p. 96.

Animals also use location and context as a way of identifying their kin. In humans, those factors include:

- Presence at religious events
- Presence at community events

At the level of kin selection, our automatic reactions are a positive trait because they help us identify other people who share our genes, at least reliably enough for evolution to work. Those are the people we tend to help, trust, and with whom we tend to cooperate.

But humans are moral beings as well as animals. Preference for people we see as our kin has some morally negative effects. When we see people as non-kin, our biological response ranges from wariness to aggression because they are our evolutionary competitors.

At best, they might use resources that we and our kin need to survive and reproduce. At worst, they might attack *us* because we are *their* competitors. That's the root of racism. The Broadway musical "South Pacific" (1949) assures us that such beliefs aren't natural, but must be learned:

"You've got to be taught to be afraid

Of people whose eyes are oddly made,

And people whose skin is a diff'rent shade,

You've got to be carefully taught."

Contrary to the song's reassuring message, racism doesn't need "to be carefully taught." It's biologically hard-wired, with increased activity in the amygdala, part of the brain that regulates fear. The Implicit Association Test (IAT) showed that:

"... children as young as six years old have the same kind of race-based biases as adults. And, rather amazingly, an IAT developed for monkeys shows that they, too, exhibit implicit preferences for in-group members."[16]

Read that again: Not just adults. Not just human children. *Monkeys* have the same kind of response. *Monkeys* distinguish between in-group and out-group members. It's biological. When we react with

---

[16] Greene, J. (2013), p. 51.

wariness or hostility toward those who look different from us, act different, speak a different language, or profess different beliefs, we are expressing a deep biological impulse. We "need to be carefully taught" that such impulses are not necessarily reliable, and even then, we will still have the same impulses. We simply have learned to ignore them. Most people never do, and to assume the contrary is to invite social conflict. The impulses will bias our judgments, but we won't realize it because we've assumed we don't have them. We can't cope with a problem if we pretend it doesn't exist. Only by confronting it can we find a solution.

Shared beliefs foster social harmony because, expressed in speech and behavior, they hook into our biological kin-identification mechanisms. When other people look like us, dress like us, speak the same language, and profess the same beliefs, our biological impulses tell us that they are "kin" and not a threat; their impulses tell them the same thing about us. From the military to schools and workplaces, dress codes help people feel solidarity with each other. Languages and dialects do the same thing.

Shared beliefs also help at the level of game selection -- that is, choosing to cooperate with people who are likely to cooperate with us. When other people cooperate with us, it increases our chance of surviving, prospering, and producing offspring. Thus, shared beliefs operate via kin selection to make us help genetic relatives have offspring; and via game selection to help us have offspring ourselves. Naturally, each works in the other direction as well. Harvard biologist Edward O. Wilson observes that such group cohesion can make the difference between survival and extinction:

> *"The outcome of between-group competition is determined largely by the details of social behavior within each group in turn. These traits are the size and tightness of the group, and the quality of communication and division of labor among its members."*[17]

---

[17] Wilson, E.O. (2012), p 53.

Hostility toward perceived genetic competitors

Animals have a special hostility toward other members of their species who are non-kin and therefore genetic competitors. A lot of human behavior simply puts a thin intellectual varnish on top of these biological reactions to "explain" why they are the way they are.

Just as we perceive as kin those who look, talk, and act like us, and who profess the same beliefs, we perceive as competitors those who are similar to us but different in minor respects. Genetically unrelated animals of the same species are likely to share the same biological niche, requiring the same food, resources, and competing for the same mates. That causes hostility.

In our case, such differences activate our deep biological reaction to perceive them as genetic competitors, not as unrelated threats. That means, for example, that our most hysterical wrath is reserved for heretics, not members of completely different faiths. The greater the difference, the less we are biologically inclined to see other people as genetic competitors on that account.

A classic example appears in the Dead Sea Scrolls, which describe the beliefs and practices of the Essenes, an ancient Jewish religious sect at Qumran. According to the Community Rule (also known as the Manual of Discipline), members of the sect:

> "[Must] love all the sons of light, each according to his lot in God's design, and hate all the sons of darkness, each according to his guilt in God's vengeance."

The "sons of light" were members of the sect. The "sons of darkness" were other Jews who were not members of the sect. Other Jews who were not members of the sect were perceived as "the other" and singled out for special hostility. Just as hawk wasps don't care about birds, the Essenes didn't care much about Romans, Egyptians, Babylonians, or other non-Jews. But Jews who denied the sect's beliefs were unconsciously perceived as same-species members in the same biological niche who might compete for resources or mates. As a result, sect members were commanded to "hate" them.

Therefore, we use beliefs, expressed in behavior and appearance, to announce membership in our group, and to identify other members of our group. In the intra-group case at least, our animal impulses are on the side of the angels, and tend to reduce conflict. When we encounter members of other groups, well, not so much.

Beliefs express and encourage loyalty

Expressing loyalty is a variation on signaling membership. To hold the right beliefs, especially when they are implausible, shows that you committed to the group and therefore loyal. Many groups have such beliefs.

An example is "American exceptionalism," which people often take to mean that the United States is a uniquely wise and virtuous nation. To hail the United States as "the exceptional nation" or "the indispensable nation" is to declare one's loyalty to the country, its people, and its system of government.

Other examples are more personal. If asked to identify "the best wife in the world," a sensible man replies without hesitation that his own wife holds that honor. And she might indeed be a remarkable person. The absurdity comes from the notion that there is any reasonable basis to choose one woman as "the best wife" (or one man as "the best husband"). Likewise, some people might claim that their college, club, or city is uniquely important and interesting, and they will find no one among their friends and neighbors to disagree. But they aren't stating any facts. They're expressing loyalty to their group, which might – but need not, by itself – also imply hostility toward other groups.

Human beings are more than just animals: We are thinking beings. However, our thoughts, beliefs, and behaviors have been fine-tuned by millennia of evolution to help us survive, act successfully based on accurate factual analysis, and work together in social groups. Beliefs do a variety of things for us. But which of those things can justify our holding beliefs, and when?

It is to those questions that we turn in the next chapter.

Chapter 9:
What Justifies Beliefs

"It is wrong always, everywhere, and for anyone, to believe anything upon insufficient evidence."

-- W.K. Clifford

WHEN MOST PEOPLE THINK ABOUT what justifies beliefs, they come up with the same answer: A belief is justified if there is adequate logical support or empirical evidence for its truth.

But that's a special case of a more general principle. Two factors determine the kind of justification a belief requires: what kind of a belief it is, and what functions it performs.

When people have difficulty, it's often because they tried to apply one kind of belief to a different kind of problem, or tried to apply one standard of justification to a different kind of belief.

Almost everyone makes two crucial errors when thinking about belief. Those errors mislead them about how beliefs are justified.

First, people assume that beliefs are purely mental. We discussed this error in Chapter 2. Mental states are private to the person who has them. Nobody else can know what they are. If beliefs are mental and private, then they have no public functions, don't involve behavior, and don't affect other people. Ordinary moral considerations don't apply to them.

Second, people assume that beliefs only assert things about the world. Even people who know that beliefs have other functions tend to fall back to "assertions only" when they think about how beliefs are justified. If belief's only function is to assert things, then the only kind of justification is the kind appropriate for making assertions.

However, as we saw in the previous chapter, belief has many other functions. The standard of justification appropriate for making assertions doesn't apply to beliefs whose main purpose is non-factual, such as beliefs signifying loyalty or providing psychological support. It does apply to factual beliefs that also perform non-factual functions. However, in that case, other standards apply as well, so we're back to our balancing act.

Conventional wisdom about justification

The idea that beliefs can only be justified by logic and empirical evidence has a long pedigree, both as common sense and as part of the Western intellectual tradition. Saadia Gaon, who we discussed in an earlier chapter, said that belief could be justified by four kinds of evidence: observation, intuition that some things are self-evident, reasoning, and tradition. Other thinkers, both religious and secular, have given similar lists.

In his book *Jerusalem*, Moses Mendelssohn alluded to the view:

"[Beliefs,] by their very nature, permit no coercion or bribery. They belong in the realm of man's cognitive faculty and must be decided by the criterion of truth or untruth."

Because Mendelssohn held a naïve theory of truth, his criterion means that beliefs can be justified only by appeal to logic and empirical evidence. He ruled out any role of good or bad consequences in justifying belief ("no coercion or bribery") – even though he elsewhere specifically endorsed considering such consequences.

In passing, note that even when we justify beliefs by looking backward at logic and evidence, we verify or disprove the same beliefs by looking forward at their results. If we have good evidence that the grocery store is two miles north on Ditch Road, we justify the belief by looking backward at the evidence. But if we then drive two miles north on Ditch Road and find a forest, the result of acting on our belief invalidates the previous justification, so we reject both it and the belief.

For modern skeptics, the gold standard of logical purity is the preachment of mathematician W.K. Clifford (1845-1879) in his essay "The Ethics of Belief." And it really *was* a preachment: his text sizzles with fire-and-brimstone religious fervor. After giving examples of tragedy or injustice resulting from factual beliefs that were based on inadequate evidence, Clifford concluded that:

> *"It is wrong always, everywhere, and for anyone, to believe anything upon insufficient evidence."*

Then he channeled the intensity of 18th-century American preacher Jonathan Edwards's sermon, "Sinners in the Hands of an Angry God:"

> *"If someone believes without adequate evidence, 'the life of that man is one long sin against mankind."*

Or as Edwards (1703-1758) put it:

> *"The Wrath of God burns against them, their Damnation don't slumber, the Pit is prepared, the Fire is made ready, the Furnace is now hot, ready to receive them, the Flames do now rage and glow."*

Clifford thought that belief is sacred and must not be defiled by the logically wicked:

> [Belief] *"is desecrated when given to unproved and unquestioned statements, for the solace and private pleasure of the believer; to add a tinsel splendour to the plain straight road of our life and display a bright mirage beyond it; or even to drown the common sorrows of our kind by a self-deception ..."*

To be fair to Clifford, he makes real arguments when he's not hyperventilating or foaming at the mouth. He argues correctly that factual beliefs are justified by factual evidence. I agree on that point, but I would add that the amount of evidence we need, and the care with which we are obliged to collect and evaluate it, depend on the consequences of our being wrong.

One of Clifford's examples tells of a man who owned a sailing ship and wasn't sure if it was seaworthy. Instead of investigating the ship's condition and repairing it, he hoped it would be good for at least one more voyage. The ship sank, and people died. Certainly, in the case of such a factual belief, factual evidence is required to justify it. If the consequences of error are serious, as in the example, then I would argue it's not the sin of unwarranted belief at issue, but that of ignoring risks to life. In any case, more evidence and investigation are required.

Clifford simply doesn't address non-factual beliefs or non-factual functions of belief. The idea seems not to have occurred to him. He does write about religious belief, but he doesn't talk about justification of religious belief per se. He does little more than recite familiar denunciations of "barbaric" doctrines about vengeful gods, sacrifices, and so on. Therefore, his writings about religious belief are not relevant here.

Justification backward and forward

As previously noted, conventional views of belief justification have in common that they see belief (1) as mental, (2) only for asserting things, and (3) only backward-justified. Justification of beliefs comes before the beliefs, both logically and in time.

But we've argued that belief consists mainly of verbal and non-verbal behavior. In other words, to hold a belief is normally to do something. Belief is not a special kind of thing, off in a corner, governed only by its own rules. To believe something is to *do* something. And what we *do* is governed, among other things, by moral concerns.

If belief is mainly behavior, then let's ask: What justifies *any* human behavior?

For thousands of years, people have given two basic answers:

- The behavior is justified because it *fulfills a duty* that we intuitively know is required. This answer is called deontological.
- The behavior is justified because it *produces good results*. This answer is called utilitarian.

Both are good answers, but they apply in different situations. And for biological, psychological, or cultural reasons, some people prefer one over the other.

So what about *belief* that's mainly behavior? In that case, the answers are the same as for any other kind of behavior:

- **Deontological:** The belief is justified because of the kind of belief it is: supported by logic and empirical evidence. This is backward-looking, toward the evidence.

- **Utilitarian:** The belief is justified because it generally (not necessarily in every case) produces good results. This is forward-looking, toward the results.

The arbitrary distinction between deontology and utilitarianism

It's worth noting that the division between deontological and utilitarian justifications is arbitrary. Both are ultimately based on moral intuitions that people take as axiomatic and as not requiring proof:

- On deontological grounds, actions are considered right (or wrong) because the actions or the rules they follow intuitively seem right.

  Hardly anyone feels a need to argue that it's right to help the needy and wrong to lie. It just seems obvious – that is, our intuition tells us it's true without requiring any proof.

- Utilitarian results are considered good (or bad) because the results intuitively seem that way.

  Hardly anyone feels a need to argue that pleasure is good and pain is bad. It just seems obvious – that is, our intuition tells us it's true without requiring any proof.

In Chapter 4 of his book *Utilitarianism*, John Stuart Mill (1806-1873) did give a loose argument that happiness was good. He said that because all people desire their own happiness, two conclusions follow. First, he argued that because happiness is desired, it is desirable. But he confused the fact that we are *able* to desire happiness with the belief that we *ought* to desire it. "Desirable" meaning "*able* to be desired" is quite different from "desirable" as "*ought* to be desired." Second, he argues that since we all desire our own happiness, we also desire the general happiness of everyone. But this is sleight of hand (and a fallacy of composition) since everyone experiences only his or her own happiness and has no direct stake in the happiness of others.

No matter how many arguments are made for it, even the most sophisticated ethical theory is based at least partly on subjective moral intuitions of the people who believe in it.

Maimonides on backward and forward justification

No less a thinker than Maimonides knew there was more than one way to justify beliefs, though he could never explain it because of his flawed definition of belief. In Part III of *The Guide for the Perplexed*, he distinguished between beliefs that are true and beliefs that are necessary. True beliefs are backward-justified by logic and evidence. Necessary beliefs (even if also backward-justified) are forward-justified by their good results:

> *"In some cases a commandment communicates a correct belief, which is the one and only thing aimed at-as, for instance, the belief in the unity and eternity of the Deity and in His not being a body. In other cases the belief is necessary for the abolition of reciprocal wrongdoing or for the acquisition of a noble moral quality-as, for instance, stance, the belief that He, may He be exalted, has a violent anger against those who do injustice ..."*

Necessary beliefs might or might not be true. Some of them, such as the belief that God gets angry at the perpetrators of injustice, were to Maimonides either false or metaphorical. In any case, they fell roughly into the category of what the Greek philosopher Plato called "noble lies." They were "lies" because he thought they were false; "noble" because they had good social and moral results. Maimonides saw their truth as being almost irrelevant, since their justification (or lack thereof) was in their results.

Factually correct beliefs are based on logic and evidence, and might not have any utilitarian value. Maimonides seems to have thought that factual beliefs often had no such value. They were backward-justified by the logic and evidence from which they could be deduced.

It's complicated

Justification of human actions can be complex, and the same applies to justification of beliefs.

For example, a general moral principle says that we should tell the truth. That is justified both deontologically and on utilitarian grounds. People feel intuitively that telling the truth is better than lying. And as for results, if most people didn't tell the truth most of the time, then society and human relationships would be impossible. Nobody would ever believe what anyone else said. That would prevent people from cooperating for their mutual benefit.

Truth-telling is kind of a standard example to illustrate moral reasoning, but let's go a little bit off the map. In his book *The Righteous Mind*, psychologist Jonathan Haidt describes some stories he made up to test people's moral reasoning. Consider this story:

> *A woman is cleaning out her closet, and finds her old American flag. She doesn't want the flag anymore, so she cuts it up into pieces and uses the rags to clean her bathroom.*

Or this one:

> *Jennifer works in a hospital pathology lab. She's a vegetarian for moral reasons— she thinks it's wrong to kill animals. But one night she has to incinerate a fresh human cadaver, and she thinks it's a waste to throw away perfectly edible flesh. So she cuts off a piece of flesh and takes it home. Then she cooks it and eats it.*

Did the people in the stories do anything wrong? On utilitarian grounds, no. What they did was fine. No living person was harmed, and they got a benefit from their actions. They believed that what they did was fine. But for most of us, their actions just seem wrong somehow. They make us uncomfortable. We can't quite believe that they're morally acceptable.

Those examples show how actions can be justified one way (producing benefit) and unjustified another way (intuitively seeming wrong). Let's consider a different example that's fairly standard in studies of moral psychology. In the "trolley dilemma," the only way you can stop a runaway train from killing five people is by pushing one person off a bridge onto the track below.

On utilitarian grounds, the right action is as clear as it is unintuitive and disturbing: Sacrifice one life to save five lives. Cost: one life. Benefit: Five lives. Net benefit: Four lives. It's the kind of moral calculation we might expect from a computer, not from a human being.

On deontological grounds, it's a lot tougher. We feel intuitively that we should save five lives, but we also feel intuitively that we should *not* kill an innocent person. We're conflicted and confused. We don't know what to do.

The point of these stories is not to discourage flag-cutting, cannibalism, or trolley travel. Judge them on their merits. The point is that justification is complex. Our behavior can be justified in some ways while at the same time unjustified in other ways. The same thing applies to belief.

For example, suppose a man believes that exercising and eating a healthy diet will help prevent him from going bald. His belief is probably false, but it's not directly falsifiable. If he does those things, he can't know how much hair would fall out if he *didn't* do them. Some of his hair might still fall out, but he assumes that healthy habits reduce his hair loss even if they don't eliminate it. His doctor might obliquely encourage the belief but avoid saying that it is correct. If the man made a diligent study of the relevant scientific literature, he would find little support for his belief. So is his belief justified or not?

- Looking backward at the evidence, his belief is not justified.

- Looking forward at the results -- better health in general -- his belief is justified.

- Then the question becomes: On balance, overall, is his belief justified?

There's no simple, cookie-cutter answer. The answer depends on whom you ask, and on that person's intuitive values. Which is more important, evidence or results? It's complicated. And it depends. Moral judgment depends on both reason and emotion; that's why people with certain kinds of brain damage show poor judgment even if their logical intelligence is intact.

When we evaluate anything -- ice cream, political candidates, beliefs, or whatever -- we usually follow three steps:

- Perceiving what we think are the facts. (We're often careless about this step.)
- Deciding how we feel about what we think are the facts.
- Applying general moral rules to justify how we feel about what we think are the facts.

Moral judgments involve both complicated factual situations and possibly conflicting feelings about those situations. That's why people disagree with other people, and even on occasion with themselves.

Remember that an emotion is both a mental and a biological reaction to some situation. The biological side of our reaction heavily influences the mental side, and the biological side was programmed into us by natural selection. We have certain moral emotions because they had survival value for our ancestors. Other prehistoric people who had different, unhelpful moral emotions were eliminated by natural selection because their feelings either didn't help them survive to produce offspring or actively hurt their survival and reproduction chances.

Our basic moral intuitions are *prima facie* helpful because if they weren't, our ancestors who had them would not have succeeded in the evolutionary struggle.

Misapplying justification

To assess a belief's justification, it's necessary to use the appropriate standards of justification. Sometimes, more than one standard applies. Those cases are the most challenging. Let's look at a couple of examples in which we might apply the wrong standard.

Consider this example of a logical argument:

1. All men are mortal.

2. Socrates is a man.

3. Therefore, Socrates is mortal.

To any normal person, the validity of the argument is obvious. If all members of the group "men" are mortal, and Socrates is a member of the group "men," then Socrates is mortal. If you want to justify your belief that Socrates is mortal, then you have two ways to do it:

- Refer backward to the premises of the argument: All men are mortal, and Socrates is a man.

- Shoot Socrates and see if he dies. This method is not recommended. Ancient Athenians tried a variation on it and they got a lot of bad publicity.

What's *not* valid in this case is to refer to the moral results of the belief. It's a purely factual belief. Whether it's good or bad for Socrates to be mortal is irrelevant. That's not the appropriate standard of justification.

Consider another example. Believing that we can achieve our goals is almost a necessary condition for achieving them. If we don't believe that we can do it, then we won't even try, or at best we'll try half-heartedly. As American industrialist Henry Ford said, "Whether you think you can or you think you can't, you're right."

Before you have actually achieved your goal, can you prove that you'll be able to do it? No, and even less can you offer a logical proof like you would have to give for a geometric theorem. The justification of your belief is in its results. If it helps you achieve your goal, then your belief was justified. That's the appropriate standard of justification. To criticize such a belief as "unproven" is to miss the point of that kind of belief and what justifies it.

In his book *The American Republic*, 19th-century political theorist Orestes Brownson (1803-1876) offered a similar justification for political revolutions. According to Brownson, results were what mattered: if a revolution succeeded, then it was justified; if it failed, it was unjustified. But note that this is also a mixed case. A revolution might succeed and be justified in that way, but cause terrible suffering and install a regime that was far worse than the old one. And looking backward at moral principles, it would – as all revolutions do – result in the killing of innocent people, which is wrong. As in many cases, justification is complicated.

Is factual truth intrinsically good?

The principal objection to justifying beliefs by their results is that it slights the importance of factual truth. But does it?

Things can be good in two ways:

- **Instrumentally good:** These things aren't good in themselves, but they help you get good things. Money is a prime example. You can't eat it. You can't wear it. You can only exchange it for other things. That's its value. It's an instrument to get other things that you consider good. (Misers and coin collectors are a special case.)

- **Intrinsically good:** These things are good in themselves, and not just as a way to get other things. We value them for their own sake.

It's surprisingly hard to find examples of things that are intrinsically good. Pleasure is often suggested as a candidate, but there are problems even with that. John Stuart Mill puzzled over the question of whether it was "better to be Socrates dissatisfied or a pig satisfied." If pleasure is intrinsically good, and a stupid pig has more pleasure than wise Socrates, then the pig is better off and we should all want to be pigs. Mill ultimately decided in favor of Socrates by claiming that his pleasure was of a higher quality than the pig's. But let's leave those problems aside.

We need intrinsic goodness to avoid an infinite regress, in which everything is good because of something else but we never find out what they're all good *for*.

For practical tasks, such as designing airplanes or finding your way to the grocery store, factual truth is important. And notice that even in those domains, the value of the truth is not in the truth itself: it's in the ability of accurate, truthful information to produce the results that we value: A plane that won't disintegrate in mid-flight. Getting groceries. And so forth. In other words, truth is instrumentally good. It helps us act successfully and get things we value.

Our feeling that there's something intrinsically good about factual truth is a deontological feeling, programmed into us by natural selection. Accurate factual knowledge helped our evolutionary ancestors survive and reproduce, so we inherited a preference for accurate factual knowledge. However, modern human life is much more complex than primitive humans' life on the African savanna. As a result, the kinds of goodness we can pursue, and the ways we pursue it, are more varied. Our deontological feelings sometimes mislead us, and in the case of truth, they do.

That being so, our obligations to believe or disbelieve are not purely logical. They also involve considerations of social benefit, personal character, group loyalty, and self-definition. We may believe things for logical reasons only, moral reasons only, or for both.

In some cases, moral reasons outweigh purely logical ones -- especially when our logical duties are not settled by the available evidence and the moral reasons are of great consequence. We are sometimes morally justified in holding beliefs to which logic and evidence give little support. On the other hand, we can be logically justified in holding beliefs on the basis of overwhelming evidence even if their results are negative. It depends on the balance between good and bad.

Chapter 10:
Belief in the Braino
Machine

"There is no spoon."

-- "The Matrix"

WE'VE LOOKED AT WHAT BELIEFS ARE, what they do, and how they're justified. But that leaves some important questions unanswered:

What makes beliefs meaningful?

Consider "the book is on the table" vs. "it's a good book." Both are meaningful but in different ways. If we don't know how they're meaningful, it's easy for us to get confused about what they mean. For example, we might think that being good is like being on the table, and that it's related somehow to the position or physical properties of the book. Believe it or not, people sometimes get confused about things like that.

How can you know if beliefs are true?

This is more obviously important. If we don't know how to determine if beliefs are true, then we can't have confidence in any of our beliefs. And there's one more important question:

*What does it **mean** for beliefs to be true?*

In a way, this asks what our world is like. Is it really true, as Hamlet wondered, that "there is nothing either good or bad but thinking makes it so?" Or is there a reality beyond our beliefs that makes them true or false?

The answers are the subtext of the 1999 movie "The Matrix." The movie got them from millennia of smart people thinking about those questions. The next few chapters will answer them in more detail. In this chapter, we'll set the stage to make the answers easier to understand.

What if nothing you perceive is "real"?

The hero of "The Matrix" is Thomas Anderson, an employee at a software company who spends his nights online as a hacker named "Neo." He discovers that the world he sees around him isn't real. It's only an illusion created by wires attached to his brain. Even his own body, as he perceives it, is an illusion. His real body sits in a pod that extracts energy from it, in a dark chamber that uses billions of human bodies as living batteries.

In one of the movie's early scenes, Neo has to escape from agents of the Matrix. He climbs out his office window onto a ledge high above the city street. He believes that if he slips, he'll fall to the pavement and die.

But he's not really on a ledge. He's not high above the street. The pavement isn't even there, nor is his body. Even so, he has beliefs about all of those things. As long as the virtual world around him stays consistent with his previous experience -- as long as there's no "glitch in the Matrix" -- his beliefs seem true. But are they? Do they mean what they seem to mean? And is he justified in believing them?

"The Matrix" is an entertaining movie, not a philosophy seminar. It raises serious questions but doesn't try seriously to answer them. For millennia, some thinkers have tried to answer them.

Plato's cave prisoners see shadows

The earliest known ancestor of "The Matrix" comes from ancient Athens. In his book *The Republic*, the philosopher Plato (427-347 BCE) told "the allegory of the cave." For their entire lives, prisoners have been chained in a cave where they face away from the entrance and can't see each other or themselves. As people outside the cave walk past the entrance, they cast shadows on the wall faced by the prisoners. The shadows are the only reality that the prisoners have ever known. They can hear each other, so they discuss the activities of the shadows and theorize about them.

One of the prisoners escapes from the cave and makes his way to the outside. Though at first blinded by the sunlight, he eventually realizes the truth: What he's seen all of his life and took to be real were only the *shadows* of people in the real world. He makes his way back into the cave and tells the other prisoners what he discovered. He tells them haltingly and with great difficulty, because even though he's seen the world outside, he has no words to describe it.

The other prisoners don't understand what he's talking about. They don't have any frame of reference for it. All of their ideas come from thinking about shadows on the wall. The ideas of open space with ground, sky, trees, and sunlight make no sense to them because they can't be translated into shadow-speak. They think that the returned prisoner must be insane.

Plato wanted to know the nature of our world. Is the world real and substantial, or like a series of shadows on the wall of our cave?

Descartes thwarts his evil demon

Two millennia later, the French philosopher René Descartes (1596-1650) told a similar story but with a different question. He wanted to discover if he could know anything for certain.

And he had a pretty high standard for what counted as certain. What he perceived with his senses seemed pretty certain – but was it really? In his *Meditations on First Philosophy*, he considered:

> "... I am here, sitting by the fire, wearing a winter dressing-gown, holding this piece of paper in my hands, and so on. Again, how could it be denied that these hands or this whole body are mine?"

What if he was asleep and was only dreaming about sitting by the fire? The possibility meant that he couldn't even be certain about what he perceived at the moment.

The situation was even worse: What if (like Neo) he didn't have a body at all, and was only dreaming that he did? Sure, it was kind of a goofy idea, but it wasn't impossible. If it wasn't impossible, then it was possible that he was mistaken about having a body. The whole world might be an illusion. It was possible that a malicious demon:

> "...has employed all his energies in order to deceive me. I shall think that the sky, the air, the earth, colours, shapes, sounds and all external things are merely the delusions of dreams which he has devised to ensnare my judgement. I shall consider myself as not having hands or eyes, or flesh, or blood or senses, but as falsely believing that I have all these things."

Was there anything at all that he could know for certain?

Just one thing, he thought: His mind existed, because if he could doubt that his mind existed, then he had to have a mind with which to doubt it. Whatever else might be doubted, he existed as a thinking being. He could know that for sure.

"Cogito, ergo sum!"

he cried, and leapt to his feet, startling the other patrons of the tavern in which he'd spent the evening.

"Cogito, ergo sum" means "I think, therefore I am." If he was thinking, he had to exist.

Tragedy almost struck a few hours later when the tavern was about to close. The bartender asked, "Would you like another drink, Mr. Descartes?" Descartes pondered for a moment and then replied, "I think not."

Poof! He disappeared in a puff of logic. Luckily for us, he reappeared a moment later, laughing. It was one of his favorite party tricks. We know that for certain.

Reid's common sense strikes back

The story of Descartes would be incomplete if I failed to mention his most perceptive critic, the Scottish philosopher Thomas Reid (1710-1796).

Descartes' argument "I think, therefore I am" is usually considered a pretty good one, but Reid would have none of it.

Reid argued that certain assumptions were necessary for any thought at all. As a result, you couldn't prove them without circular reasoning because in order to prove them, you first had to assume that they were true. Such assumptions included your own existence, the existence of the world, and the laws of logic.

According to Reid, it was crazy to reject such assumptions even if they could never be proven. His book *An Inquiry into the Human Mind* is where we get his devastating critique of Descartes.

> *"A man that disbelieves his own existence is surely as unfit to be reasoned with as a man who believes he is made of glass. There may be disorders in the human frame that may produce such extravagances, but they will never be cured by reasoning."*

Reid himself couldn't quite believe that Descartes was serious:

> *"Descartes would make us believe that he got out of this delirium by his logical argument Cogito, ergo sum. But it is evident he was in his senses all the time, and never seriously doubted his existence. He takes it for granted in his argument, and proves nothing at all. I am thinking, says he, therefore I am: And is it not as good reasoning to say, I am sleeping, therefore I am? Or I am doing nothing, therefore I am?"*

As we've seen in earlier chapters, these arguments are *philosophical stories*. Neither Descartes' view nor Reid's can be proven conclusively. One story probably makes more sense to you than the other. Or you might think that since neither story makes a practical difference, it just doesn't matter. For practical purposes, you'd be right. It doesn't make any difference in how you live your life. But if you're curious about the world, the dilemma might bother you a little. It's bothered a lot of people, and it still does.

Putnam puts brains in a vat

Plato's allegory of the cave gets its best contemporary retelling by the late Harvard philosopher Hilary Putnam (1926-2016). Although "The Matrix" told a version of the story, its focus was on entertainment rather than on the philosophical problems it raised.

Putnam's version is usually called "the Braino machine story." All people's brains have been removed from their bodies and plugged into the Braino machine.

Plato wanted to know what our world was like. Descartes wanted to know if he could know anything for certain. Putnam wanted to know how beliefs had meaning and what it meant for them to be true. In Chapter 1 of *Reason, Truth, and History*, he explains:

> *"Suppose that the automatic machinery is programmed to give us all a collective hallucination, rather than separate unrelated hallucinations. Thus, when I seem to myself to be talking to you, you seem to yourself to be hearing my words. Of course, it is not the case that my words actually reach your ears – for you don't have (real) ears, nor do I have a real mouth and tongue."*

All of us in the Braino machine seem to perceive the same world, but it's a virtual-reality copy of the physical world instead of shadows on the wall of a cave. We can communicate with each other, but we can't actually see each other or ourselves: we just believe that we do because the Braino machine creates the illusion.

The only world we know is the world portrayed to us by the Braino machine. When we see a tree, we're not seeing a real tree; we're just getting the result of electrical impulses sent to our brains by the machine. And when we believe that the tree is tall – what, exactly, is our belief about? Is it about a tree, because that's what we seem to perceive? Or is it about an illusion?

A lot depends on how we got into the Braino machine and how long we've been there. Based on Putnam's points, we can say that:

- If we previously lived in "the real world," then we have seen real trees, people, and so forth.
- If we have always lived in the Braino machine, then we have *never* seen real trees, people, and so forth.

If we previously lived in the real world, then our ideas about it were derived from real things. Our words and our beliefs refer to real things even if we're currently in the Braino machine looking at a series of illusions. When we were children living in the real world, our parents pointed to a real tree and said, "That's called a tree." Now that we're in the Braino world, we think that when we see a "tree," we're seeing at the same kind of thing as we learned about when we were children. But it's not. In that case, our beliefs about things in the Braino world are simply mistaken.

If we have always lived in the Braino machine – like Neo at the start of "The Matrix" – then our ideas about the world were derived from illusions. When we were children living in the Braino world, we perceived our parents pointing to one of the Braino reality's virtual trees and saying, "That's called a tree." As adults in the Braino world, we think that when we see a "tree," we're seeing at the same kind of thing as we learned about when we were children. *And we are.* Our words and beliefs refer to the illusions. In that case, our beliefs about the world are (or can be) correct.

To put it in terms of the allegory of the cave, the cave prisoners' only experiences have been of shadows. They've formed their language and ideas based on the shadows they've seen. If they believe something about "a man," they can't mean a real man because they've never seen one. "A man," to them, means the shadow of a man, but they don't even know it's a shadow because they don't have the concept of a shadow. They think it's the real thing. So if they see a shadow of a man on the wall and believe, "that's a man," their belief is true. Their concept of "a man" is that of a shadow. Their belief refers to a shadow, and that's what it is.

As a result, neither the Matrix prisoners, the cave prisoners, nor the Braino machine prisoners can refer to the real world or anything in it. There might not even be a real world outside of the worlds created by the Braino machine. We only know that there is -- at least, we think we know -- because we're not prisoners in the Matrix, the cave, or the machine. We're outside of them.

And there's the problem, according to Putnam:

"... although the people in [the Braino] world can think and 'say' any words we can think and say, they cannot (I claim) refer to what we can refer to. In particular, they cannot think or say that they are brains in a vat (even by thinking 'we are brains in a vat')."

To believe that we are brains in a vat requires us to have some concept of a world outside the vat: otherwise, saying that we are "in the vat" has no meaning.

But if we are lifelong Braino prisoners, then even our idea of "outside" refers to illusory spatial relationships that we've perceived inside the Braino machine. Those perceptions were generated by the machine, not by the real world. If we try to think about what's outside the reality created by the machine, we still end up thinking about the reality *inside* the machine. Just like the prisoner who escaped from Plato's cave and returned, we have no language or concepts with which to think about anything outside the reality created by the Braino machine.

For us even to think that our perceptions are illusory and our beliefs mistaken is impossible. When we seem to see a tree, the tree we see is the same kind of thing we've always seen when we saw a tree. Our beliefs about the tree are about the same things they've always been about. We aren't wrong.

What we see *is not an illusion:* It's exactly what we think it is. What we believe is true, in the sense relevant for someone who has always lived in the world of the Braino machine.

And we have no way to know if we're in the Braino machine or not.

That's our predicament. By definition, the Braino machine creates an illusion of reality so flawless that it contains no evidence of anything outside it. Since we can't know if we are in the Braino machine or not, all the conclusions about our beliefs that would apply in the Braino machine also apply to us:

- Our ideas are derived from our experienced reality, not from anything outside our experience.

- Our words and beliefs refer to the reality we've experienced, not to anything beyond it.

To verify that a belief is true, we look at related experiences and beliefs based on those experiences. We check to see if the belief is consistent with them.

For a belief to be true means that it accurately describes the experiences to which it refers. Those experiences are shaped by our thoughts and circumstances.

Meaning and truth cast their shadows

The next four chapters look at meaning, evidence, and truth in more detail. But what can we learn from Plato's cave, Descartes's demon, and Putnam's machine?

From Plato and Descartes, we learn that what reality is and how we perceive reality are not always the same thing. Our goal is to make our perception of reality more accurate, but our concepts and circumstances can make it more difficult.

From Putnam, we learn that we can't even *talk* about perceived realities that transcend our experience because we have no language or concepts with which to do it. To test a belief for truth, we look at more experiences. For a belief to be true means that it's consistent with those experiences.

Let's look again at the quote from "The Matrix" that begins this chapter: "There is no spoon."

It turns out that there really *is* a spoon after all. It's just not the kind of spoon we expected.

Chapter 11:
How Beliefs Have
Meaning

"You keep using that word. I do not think it means what you think it means."

-- Inigo Montoya, "The Princess Bride"

THIS CHAPTER IS ABOUT HOW BELIEFS HAVE MEANING. And we'll get to that. But as a way into the topic, let's start with a related question that's more familiar:

What is the meaning of life?

It's a good place to start because it reassures us that we're on the right track. If our analysis applies to something as offbeat as the meaning of life, it probably applies to more conventional examples of meaning, such as "dog" or "the book is on the table."

The meaning of life is one of those questions that people have argued about for centuries without ever coming close to agreement. In his novel *The Hitchhiker's Guide to the Galaxy*, science fiction writer Douglas Adams (1952-2001) showed why the argument has been difficult to resolve. Seriously.

In the novel, a team of scientists built a powerful computer called "Deep Thought" to answer the ultimate question of life, the universe, and everything -- in other words, to tell them the meaning of life. But in Chapter 28, when Deep Thought gave them the answer, they didn't understand it:

> *"'I think the problem, to be quite honest with you, is that you've never actually known what the question is' [explained Deep Thought].*
>
> *'But it was the Great Question! The Ultimate Question of Life, the Universe, and Everything!' howled Loonquawl.*
>
> *'Yes,' said Deep Thought with the air of one who suffers fools gladly, 'but what actually is it?'*
>
> *A slow, stupefied silence crept over the men as they stared at the computer and then at each other.*
>
> *'Well, you know, it's just Everything ... Everything ...'' offered Phouchg weakly.*
>
> *'Exactly,' said Deep Thought. 'So once you know what the question actually is, you'll know what the answer means.'"*

I won't tell you Deep Thought's answer: read Douglas Adams's book! However, if we know what the question is, then it can show us how beliefs are meaningful.

Meaning starts with connection

The question played itself out in the life of John Stuart Mill (1806-1873), a philosopher and economist who is most famous for his book *On Liberty*. He found meaning in life, then he lost it. Eventually – through the love of a good woman, just like in a romance novel – he found it again.

Mill was an activist as well as a thinker. From his early youth, he wrote and campaigned for individual freedom, against arbitrary restraints on people's ability to live as they wished.

His father was a political reformer with radical ideas about education, and he tested those ideas on his son. From infancy, Mill was subjected to intensive schooling. His father even hired tutors to speak Ancient Greek in the nursery, so Mill learned it as a native language just like he did English.[18] By his teens, he was writing articles about political philosophy. His unusual education made his great mind even greater, and psychologists estimate his IQ was over 200.

But all that knowledge and understanding came at a price. Mill had become (in his words) "a reasoning machine" dedicated to political reform as the purpose of his life. At age 20 in 1826, he asked himself a question, and the answer devastated him:

> *"'Suppose that all your objects in life were realized; that all the changes in institutions and opinions which you are looking forward to, could be completely effected at this very instant: would this be a great joy and happiness to you?'" ' And an irrepressible self-consciousness distinctly answered, 'No!'*
>
> *At this my heart sank within me: the whole foundation on which my life was constructed fell down. All my happiness was to have been found in the continual pursuit of this end. The end had ceased to charm, and how could there ever again be any interest in the means? I seemed to have nothing left to live for."*

Then what's really the question?

For Mill, the meaning of life was to work for the achievement of his social and political ideals. His life was meaningful because he connected it to things he valued:

- His goals of a free society, the rule of law, and enlightened social institutions.

- His activities to help achieve those goals in the future.

- His pride in past accomplishments to achieve those goals.

Notice two key clauses: "he connected" and "he valued." Both of those clauses indicate that a conscious mind has done something. Another person might see no connection between his or her life and the rule of law, but Mill did see it for his own life. And what we value depends on us: our background, experiences, and psychology.

---

[18] Until the late 20th century, educated people in Western civilization were expected to have at least some familarity with Ancient Greek language and literature.

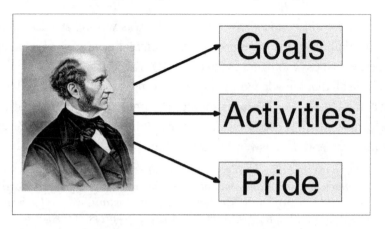

The reason nobody can answer "What is the meaning of life?" is that it has no single answer. It's like asking "What is the height of the people in New York?" There are many answers.

The question is really this:

What does person X value enough to feel that it makes his or her life worth living?

As expected, it implies consciousness (the person is aware of something), connection (the person connects it to his or her life), and valuation (the person values it).

So the first lesson of Mill's example is that meaning depends on consciousness. If nobody is aware of them, things have no meaning. They get meaning only when a person bestows it on them by connecting them to other things.

Since you're reading this book, you and most of your acquaintances probably value some of the same things as Mill. They're meaningful because you connect them with ideas and experiences you know. But if you ask most people what they think about the rule of law, they'll either have no idea of what it is or they'll think it's about being tough on criminals. It's not a meaningful idea to them because they have no knowledge or experience with which to connect it.

The second lesson of Mill's example is more subtle: meaning is a matter of degree. The more connections we make to something, the more meaningful it becomes to us. The fewer we make, the less meaningful it becomes to us. Consider what would happen to the meaning of Mill's life if he had only goals and pride, but wasn't actually doing anything to accomplish his goals. Then all of his talk about freedom would be just hot air, and his pride would be less justified:

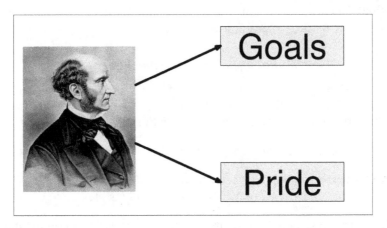

I call that "the take-away test." If something has meaning, but the meaning changes when you take away a certain thing, then what you took away was part of the meaning. If something has more connections for us, it tends to be more meaningful to us. If it has fewer connections, it tends to be less meaningful.

Mill's drama had a happy ending. He recovered from his depression in 1830, when he fell in love with Harriet Taylor (1807-1858). That restored his zest for life. They had only a platonic friendship until her husband died in 1849, whereupon they married. In the dedication of *On Liberty*, published after her death, he said that she was:

> *"the inspirer, and in part the author, of all that is best in my writings— the friend and wife whose exalted sense of truth and right was my strongest incitement, and whose approbation was my chief reward ... Were I but capable of interpreting to the world one-half the great thoughts and noble feelings which are buried in her grave, I should be the medium of a greater benefit to it than is ever likely to arise from anything that I can write, unprompted and unassisted by her all but unrivalled wisdom."*

And notice what happened. Initially, Mill felt that his life had meaning -- had value -- because he connected it to goals, activities, and pride that he valued. When he ceased to value them, his life's value connection was broken. His life regained value when he connected it to something new that he valued, his relationship with Harriet Taylor. His life got value partly by connection to something else that had value. When we talk about truth in Chapter 13, we'll see a similar process at work for various kinds of true beliefs.

The meaning of life and the meaning of truth

Connections that make our lives meaningful are similar to those that make beliefs factually true. The former make our lives meaningful by connecting them to things we value, like this:

If x, y, and z are true, then I feel good about myself and my life.

In Mill's case, x (goals), y (activities), and z (pride in accomplishments) made him feel good about himself and his life.

The latter make beliefs factually true in various ways by connecting them to things that produce results we value, like this:

If a, b, and c are true, then I can get to the store by driving north on Ditch Road.

How much meaning a thing has depends on the number of connections it has. But what kind of meaning it has depends on the kinds of connections.

The meaning of life affects how we feel about our lives, so we connect our lives to things about which we have feelings -- in other words, to things we value. The meaning of factual truth has to do with how to predict the results of our actions, so we connect it to things we can perceive, do, or experience in the world. Chapter 13 discusses truth in more detail.

Defining meaning

We're now in a position to define meaning in general. When we talk about the meaning of life, we're talking about the connections that individual people make between their lives and some things that they deeply value. And meaning in general is similar. If something has meaning, we connect it with other things. Let's review some of the facts we've identified:

- A thing has meaning if we connect it to other meaningful things.

- A thing becomes more meaningful by having more connections in a larger network that covers more of reality and is more internally consistent, and less meaningful otherwise.

Based on those facts, we can define the meaning of a thing for a person (a mind) as its set of connections to other things with which the person associates it. Moreover, anything can have meaning if a person can perceive, imagine, talk about, act on, or understand it.

Different kinds of meaning connections

We connect meaningful things to each other in a variety of ways. Some of the most common types of connections are:

- **Mere associations:** You might remember the restaurant where you had your first date. Thinking of the restaurant reminds you of the pleasant (or anxious) feelings you had.

- **Logical implications:** These can be either direct or indirect. Different thinkers use different terminology, but they always distinguish between what we know "by intuition of the intellect" (direct implication) and what we know "by inference" (indirect implication).

- **Direct implications:** For example, if a thing is colored, it occupies space; or if a whole number is even, it cannot be odd. You don't need to think about it.

- **Indirect implications:** You can see by indirect implication that if all humans are mortal and Socrates is human, then he must also be mortal. You apply rules that guide you through steps from one to the other. Each step is a direct implication.

Different kinds of meaning

The kinds of meaning something has depend on the kinds of things to which we connect it, such as:

- **Linguistic meaning:** We connect it to equivalent expressions in one or more languages.

- **Ostensive meaning:** We connect it to perceivable things to which we can point.

- **Emotional meaning:** We connect it to things about which we have feelings. For Mill, the things were his goals, activities, pride, and later, his love for Harriet Taylor. For people of various religions, the things are the texts, symbols, and rituals of their faiths.

- **Factual meaning:** We connect it to things we could achieve or discover by following specific procedures. (The fancy name for this is "empirical" meaning.) For example, I have no particular feelings about "the store is on Ditch Road," but I can arrive at the store if I follow the appropriate steps. A doctor might have no feelings about the fact that antibiotics cure some diseases, but administering the antibiotics can produce that result.

- **Moral meaning:** We connect it to rules that tell us how we should behave in order to be good people. For example, moral rules tell us not to lie, steal, or cause needless pain to other conscious beings (both people and lower animals).

What things mean, as opposed to the kinds of meaning they have, depends on the set of connections they have.

Does our definition do what it should?

As with belief, we want a definition that matches our intuitive sense of what we mean by "meaning." The reason is not that we're preoccupied with words, but because we want our definition to be about what we think it's about. Our definition should meet essentially the same criteria as we discussed for belief:

- **Requirement #1:** Pick out all the cases we'd ordinarily call "meaning." If we would say that "X means Y," then the definition should apply to that case. It should cover all the things we consider meaningful: words, phrases, statements, questions, experiences, relationships, physical phenomena, and so forth.

- **Requirement #2:** Pick out only the cases we'd ordinarily call "meaning." If we would not say that "X means Y," then the definition should not apply to that case.

Does our definition of meaning satisfy those requirements? We can't be totally certain, since it's always possible that someone will come up with a counter-example: either a meaningful thing to which our definition doesn't apply, or a meaningless thing to which it does apply. But let's look at a few examples to increase our confidence in the definition:

- "John" means John. We connect the word to a person we either see or remember.

- John means trouble. We connect the word to trouble because John is a bill collector.

- "Kaffee" means coffee. We connect the word to a life-giving brown elixir that we quaff on arising in the morning.

- "Disinterested" means "impartial" or "unbiased." We connect the word to other words that have the same or similar meanings.

- "Ich brauche Kaffee" means "I need coffee." We connect the statement to an equivalent statement in different words.

- Dark clouds mean that rain is coming. We connect the experience of seeing dark clouds to our memory of dark clouds being followed by rain.

- If John is 40 years old and Sarah is 35, it means that John is older than Sarah. We connect the premises to the conclusion by rules that seem self-evident.

The Morning Star versus the Evening Star

Defining meaning as a thing's set of connections solves a classic problem about meaning: the problem of "the Morning Star" and "the Evening Star."

Both phrases refer to the planet Venus, which appears in the Eastern sky in the morning and in the Western sky in the evening. They use different words and you can know the meaning of one without knowing the meaning of the other. They refer to the same thing, but they have different meanings. How is that possible?

The German philosopher Gottlob Frege (1848-1925) solved the problem by distinguishing between linguistic expressions' denotation and their "sense:"

- An expression's *denotation* is the thing to which it refers, such as the planet Venus.

- An expression's *sense* is an equivalent word, phrase, or sentence. For example, the sense of "your house" is "the house in which you live."

Frege's distinction got halfway to the solution of the problem. He realized that expressions could derive meaning both from connections to what they denoted and from connections to other words or phrases that said the same thing as they did.

We get all the way to the solution when we define meaning as a thing's set of connections to other meaningful things, including objects, feelings, memories, and linguistic expressions. A phrase like "the Morning Star" has a different meaning from "the Evening Star" because it has a different set of connections:

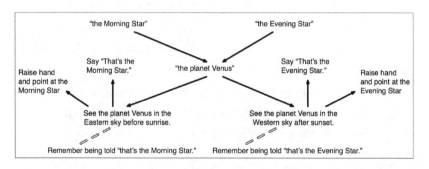

Look at what contributes to the meanings of the two phrases. We have:

- A verbal description
- Perceptual experiences of seeing
- Memories
- Non-verbal behavior
- Speech

If you take away any of those things, it decreases the meaning of the phrases "the Morning Star" and "the Evening Star." If you add things, it increases their meaning. We'll examine that issue in more depth a bit later.

And we've solved our astronomical problem. The descriptions "the Morning Star" and "the Evening Star" denote the same object, but they have different meanings because they are in different places in the network of expressions, experiences, and behaviors. In addition to the denotation that they share, each points to a different set of other things and is pointed to by a different set of other things: that is, each has a set of connections different from the other.

Meaning of general words and concepts

General words and concepts enable us to think efficiently and accurately. Consider an example. Here's a list of numbers:

08253704915761928346

Did you read it? Now cover the list and write it on a piece of paper. Very few people can do it. But let me give you the same numbers again:

00112233445566778899

You can do it this time. Why? Two reasons.

First, you were able to group the numbers, which reduced from 20 to 10 the number of items you had to remember. General words and concepts let you group related cases, just as you did with the list of numbers. It makes your thinking easier and more efficient.

Second, you saw the pattern (0 to 9, with each number repeated). That reduced the number of items to remember from 10 to three: the starting number, the ending number, and the pattern.

You could do that because you're intelligent. Together with opposable thumbs and coffee, it's what distinguishes humans from the rest of the animal kingdom.

Consider another example: "Dogs bark and cats meow." Apart from stylistic variations, there's only one way to say it. It's easy. It's efficient. It takes five seconds and not much brainpower.

But suppose for a moment that a few Chihuahuas find that statement insulting. They don't like being lumped together with German Shepherds, Bulldogs, and Collies.

A few Siamese cats are also in high dudgeon about it. They don't like being lumped together with British Shorthairs, Persians, and American Bobtails.

Therefore, to avoid offending Chihuahua dogs and Siamese cats, you must henceforth identify the dog and cat breeds any time you talk about dogs and cats.

There are 340 breeds of dog and 73 breeds of cat. Suppose that you now want to say (or think) "Dogs bark and cats meow."

You can't say that anymore. It's hurtful and politically incorrect. It means you hate Chihuahuas and Siamese cats.

Instead, you must enumerate all the combinations of breeds:

- "Labrador Retrievers bark and British Shorthairs meow."
- "Siberian Huskies bark and Bengal cats meow."
- "Beagles bark and Turkish Angora cats meow."
- ... and so on.

You end up with 340 x 73 = 24,820 statements you'll have to make in order to say "Dogs bark and cats meow." In order to make Chihuahuas and Siamese cats feel better about themselves, we have made it almost impossible to speak or think effectively about dogs and cats.

In summary:

- General words and concepts make our thinking more efficient and accurate.

- Humanity has the general words and concepts it does because they have proven practical for millennia in all kinds of societies.

- General words and concepts that weren't practical have disappeared because nobody wanted to use them, or because societies that used them died out.

- To prevent people from thinking clearly about a subject, require them to use general words and concepts that are unintuitive, numerous, impractical, and more complicated than necessary. Redefine the words frequently, so that no one can be sure what anyone else is trying to say. Or simply leave the words undefined.

Meaning for groups of people

What about groups of people? That's pretty important. In order to communicate and live in peace with one another, they must have some meanings in common, even if their meanings don't match exactly. This might be a little confusing, so we'll first look at the general ideas and then look at a simple example.

Suppose that we have a group of four people to whom the word "fribbit" is meaningful. The word's meaning to each of them individually consists of these connections:

- Frank: (A, B, C)
- Riff: (A, B, C)
- Brad: (A, C)
- Janet: (A, C, D)

The meaning of a thing for a group is the intersection of the thing's meanings for all the members of the group. In other words, it's the set of meaning connections that every one of the group members has for "fribbit:"

Frank	A	B	C	
Riff	A	B	C	
Brad	A		C	
Janet	A		C	D
Intersection	A		C	

The intersection of the meanings of all the members of the group is (A, C). That's the group meaning, so all members of the group can communicate about the A and C aspects of fribbits.

That's rather abstract, so let's translate it into an example. Suppose that everyone in the group uses "fribbit" to refer to what we'd call "rabbits." They all know that rabbits are (A) furry and (C) good pets. Frank and Riff know that rabbits are also (B) cute. However, Janet is the only biologist in the group, so only she knows that (D) rabbits aren't the same species as hares, and that they differ from hares about as much as sheep differ from goats.

If Janet starts talking about the D aspect of fribbits (rabbits aren't hares), then nobody else in the group will understand her: she's the only one for whom that connection is part of the meaning of "fribbit." Frank and Riff can communicate about the A, B, and C aspects of fribbits. However, the rest of the group will think they're talking only about A and C, because those are the only meaning connections they share with Frank and Riff. They will completely miss any references to the cuteness (B aspects) of fribbits.

Conflicting meanings cause miscommunication

A more dangerous breakdown occurs when meaning connections seem the same but are really different. Suppose that people have these meaning connections for "fribbit:"

Frank	A	B		C	D
Riff	A	B		C	
Brad	A		b	C	
Janet	A		b	C	
Intersection	A			C	

Frank and Riff connect it to a very positive idea (B, rabbits are cute), while Brad and Janet connect it to a very negative idea (b, Peter Rabbit caused great suffering to the innocent farmer Mr. McGregor). When Frank and Riff say nice things about fribbits because of B, Brad and Janet think they're endorsing b and that they want farmers to suffer. As a result, Brad and Janet believe that Frank and Riff maliciously enjoy causing harm to other people.

For a more realistic example, a Muslim woman might consider wearing a burqa to mean a commitment to peace and purity, while a non-Muslim might consider it an endorsement of terrorism. A Virginian might see the Confederate flag as meaning heroism and independence, while a New Yorker sees it as meaning racism and slavery.

These examples show that things can be meaningful relative to one system, but either:

- Have *no* meaning relative to a different network in which they have no pointing connections to other things in the network; or

- Have a *different* meaning relative to a different network in which they have different pointing connections to other things in the network. This kind of disconnect can cause wars. People use the same words but give different meanings to them. They think they're communicating, but they're not; instead, they lead the other side to beliefs that are doomed to disappointment, and that might be interpreted as betrayal.

How "unbelievable" beliefs have meaning

Beliefs about God and the transcendent are more difficult to explain.

In Chapter 4, we looked at how the philosophers Saadia Gaon and Maimonides struggled with belief. They both thought that:

- A belief is a mental representation of a real-world fact.

- Our minds can only comprehend what is finite. We cannot conceive of the infinite.

If Saadia and Maimonides had been atheists, those assumptions wouldn't have caused them a problem. But they both believed in God. They believed, as Saadia wrote in *The Book of Beliefs and Opinions*, that God is infinite,

> *"so that it would be impossible to fathom [the idea of God] at all ... what is infinite and endless cannot be embraced by the human mind."*

That leads directly to their problem, and to ours if we accept their definition of belief:

1. To believe something is to represent it mentally.
2. We can only represent mentally what is finite.
3. God is not finite.
4. Therefore, we cannot represent God mentally.
5. Therefore, we cannot hold beliefs about God.

Modest belief gives better results

According to Maimonides, Saadia, and thinkers of other religions (though they use different words), the transcendent is beyond our perception or understanding. We cannot understand God, and we cannot understand what our normal words mean when we apply them to God.

Relative to our normal experience, to say that "God is good" is equivalent to saying "Blank blank blank." We are in the peculiar position of making a statement without understanding what it means, at least in terms we know from observing our world.

This problem occurs with all religions that affirm the existence of transcendent realities, though those most familiar to us in the West are Judaism, Christianity, and (increasingly) Islam. It goes back to a question we discussed in Chapter 4:

Can we think about or talk about things we can't even imagine?

Yes, we can.

Saadia, Maimonides, and other thinkers require for belief that we represent facts mentally. However, in this chapter, we gave a more modest definition of belief:

The meaning of a thing for a person is its set of connections to other things with which the person associates it.

Based on that definition, we can hold beliefs about things we can't imagine. The beliefs can be meaningful in two ways:

- They can be meaningful by their pointing connections *to each other*.

- They can be meaningful by our associating them with imaginable things that have pointing connections to other imaginable things.

This resembles Spinoza's answer to how we can know about God. He identified God with the universe (*Deus sive natura*), so the more we knew about the universe, the more we knew about God. It was a matter of degree, not an all-or-nothing dilemma as with Saadia and Maimonides.

Similarly, on this book's definition of belief, the meaningfulness of our beliefs about God is a matter of degree. It depends on the number and strength of connections to other meaningful things in our belief networks.

Meaning within a belief network

Let's look at some beliefs about the transcendent, according to Maimonides:

- God exists.
- God is one.
- God is the creator of everything.
- The first being created everything.

The meaning network might look like this:

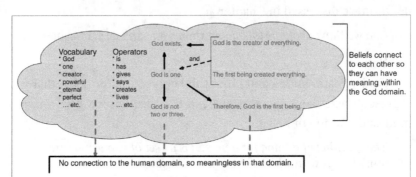

"God is one" points to "God exists" and "God is not two or three." God is the creator of everything, and the first being created everything; since God is one, therefore God is also the first being. And that God created everything points to "God is powerful."

If we believe Maimonides, we can't know what any of those statements means *outside* of the transcendent meaning network. We can't know what they mean for our ordinary world because they don't connect to our ordinary world at all. Even the words we use to describe transcendent reality mean something different from what they mean when we talk about ordinary reality.

However, we can know that our expressions for transcendent realities have pointing relations *within* the network. On that basis, they have some meaning even to us. Of course, it's a network "as seen by us," so we can't even know for sure what the pointing connections denote. But we can take our best shot, and make as much sense out of it as we can.

The problem of meaning with mixed domains

Now we come to the trickiest problem in our survey of meaning. We know what ordinary-world statements mean because they connect to each other and to our experience. In a more limited way, we know what transcendent-world statements mean because they connect to each other -- even though their pointing connections are all we can know about their meaning. The two domains do not connect to each other in any obvious way. Thus, within each domain, expressions from the other domain are disconnected and meaningless.

Notice something else about statement-beliefs that apply to only one domain: Their different parts connect to each other. For example, consider a statement about the ordinary world:

John bought a car.

We know what all those terms mean, and moreover, we know what they mean relative to each other. John is a human. "Bought" is an activity that humans sometimes do. "A car" is a physical object that, given enough money, we can buy. And consider a statement about God:

God is omnipotent.

In terms of our ordinary world, we don't know what "God" means. We don't know what "is" means: "God exists, but not through an existence other than His essence," says Maimonides. We don't know what "omnipotent" means, since the idea leads directly to contradictions in our ordinary reasoning. Can God tie a knot that He cannot untie?

However, we do know that in the transcendent domain, all those terms are defined relative to each other and to other statements in that domain. They are meaningful relative to each other, they form a grammatically-correct statement, and the statement has pointing relations to other statements in the domain.

But what about statements that draw from both domains? From the examples we've just looked at, we can see a problem immediately: The words from the transcendent domain are not defined relative to the words from the ordinary domain, and vice versa. The parts of the statement don't connect to each other.

Consider the canonical belief from the Bible's Book of Exodus:

God gave the Torah to Moses at Sinai.

Let's agree at the outset that the statement means something. It is a statement in human language, and billions of people over two millennia have guided their lives partly by a belief in that statement. A theory that says the statement is meaningless is disproven immediately by the facts of human life and human history.

On the other hand, how can such a statement possibly be meaningful? It combines terms from both the transcendent and the ordinary domains. Terms in each domain are unconnected to terms from the other, so the statement as a whole doesn't hang together.

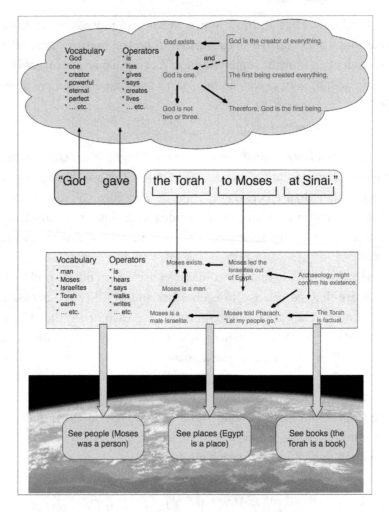

How mixed-domain beliefs are meaningful

Remember that the meaning of a thing for a person is its set of pointing connections to other things with which the person associates it.

166

Those associations can be either direct (thinking of John causes an image of John to appear in our imagination) or indirect (thinking of statements A and B leads to a conclusion C by direct steps, using rules we can explain).

Taken literally, mixed-domain statements are logically incoherent. In that sense, therefore, they don't mean anything. But human history, common sense, and our own experience show they do have meaning somehow. Moreover, their meaning isn't confined to woozy metaphors that might not say anything in particular. In their effects on our lives and behavior, they often have meaning that is specific and beneficial. But how? In three main ways:

- **By simple faith:** Unreflective people interpret the statements literally, as referring to anthropomorphic beings and earth-like realities.

- **By anthropomorphic substitution:** In practical situations, even reflective people substitute simple, anthropomorphic ideas of God for the more sophisticated ideas they use in other contexts.

- **By value connection:** Just as John Stuart Mill found value in his life by connecting it to things he valued, other people can find value and inspiration by connecting their lives to a transcendent "Something" that they value. People of simple faith see the Something as an anthropomorphic Deity. More reflective people see the Something as an indefinable source of comfort and courage.

Whether simple or reflective, substitution of anthropomorphic imagery enables believers to transform logically meaningless statements into meaningful and helpful beliefs. This is what cognitive scientist Jason Slone observed in his book *Theological Incorrectness:*

> "While religious believers produce theologically correct ideas in situations that allow them the time and space to reflect systematically on their beliefs, the same people can stray from those theological beliefs under situational pressures that require them to solve conceptual problems rapidly ..."

Suppose that a man finds a lost wallet containing several hundred dollars in cash. He wants to decide on the morally correct course of action.

He imagines God as a white-robed father figure in the sky, Who gave the Torah to Moses at Sinai and Who prescribed a demanding moral code. What would the father figure want him to do? Naturally — that is, supernaturally — God would want him to do the honest thing and return the wallet.

The man is not trying to do theology: he's trying to solve a practical problem. For him to "go full Maimonides" and start philosophizing about God's nature would mean he never gets around to returning the wallet. Instead, he imagines a quick, highly inaccurate, indubitably primitive image of God to tell him what to do. He gets the answer he needs.

If you cornered the man in a theology class, he might give you a sophisticated philosophical explanation; but that's a different context with a different purpose. In that situation, it's just as unhelpful for him to use a primitive father-figure image as it would be for him to use a theological explanation of God in trying to decide about a lost wallet.

In each case, the thinking he does is appropriate for the problem he is trying to solve, and his thinking is efficient in solving it.

Chapter 12:
How the Ineffable
Leads to Religion

"The world becomes apprehensible as world, as cosmos, in the measure to which it reveals itself as a sacred world."

-- Mircea Eliade

IN THE PREVIOUS CHAPTER, we saw how anthropomorphic substitution connects the unknowable and transcendent reality of God (or whatever you call it) to our ordinary beliefs about the world.

We are now in a position to understand in more depth how the same process leads to religion: to rituals, rules, institutions, and our choices in personal conduct.

Our religious beliefs generally depend on realities whose content we cannot describe or verify.

The fact that we can't describe or verify such realities means we can't know, in any normal way, that they even exist. Different people interpret them in conflicting ways. If we disagree with others about them, neither we nor they can prove that an interpretation is correct. Far too often in human history, such arguments end up with the frustrated participants trying to kill each other.

There are at least three explanations for our varied intuitions about ineffable realities:

- We sense only our own emotions, impulses, and fantasies, but people interpret them differently based on their individual beliefs, personalities, and cultural contexts.

- We sense ineffable realities, but people interpret them differently based on their individual beliefs, personalities, and cultural contexts.

- We sense both ineffable realities and our own emotions, impulses, and fantasies, but we cannot distinguish between them so we combine them into an interpretation based partly on reality and partly on our own fantasies.

Even most theists would concede that we sometimes mistake our emotions, impulses, and fantasies for more than what they are. The real question is whether or not we ever sense ineffable realities that exist beyond our own feelings. By definition, such realities can't be stated in any way that we could test scientifically. Therefore, reasonable people can believe in them or not. This book assumes that we do sometimes sense such realities, even if they are often colored by our feelings and fantasies.

Our unavoidable leap of faith

The challenge is to make the "leap of faith" from ineffable reality to beliefs that say something about ourselves and our world.

Here's why it's a leap of faith. Consider a simple process of reasoning:

1. John owns a car.
2. Therefore, John owns something.

So far, so good. Whether it's a good car or a piece of junk isn't at issue. Every step asserts a belief that is logically true or false. If the first step is true, then the second step must be true.

But suppose that the first step referred to something transcendent and ineffable. It wouldn't assert anything that was logically true or false:

1. Blah.
2. Therefore, John owns something.

As a logical argument, that just doesn't work. We can't rely on logic to get us from the first step to the second. The first step gives us nothing to work with. We could assume that if the first step is true, then the second step must be true. But that doesn't help us: the first step isn't true in any way we can understand. If we're going to reach the conclusion, we must make a leap of faith.

Your own perceptual leap of faith

The "blah, therefore X" argument might seem like a silly example, but here's a surprise: You're *living in it* right now, as you read this book.

Light waves hit the book page, which reflects them to your eyes. The reflected waves go through the lenses of your eyes and hit your retinas at the back of your eyes. In your retinas, cells for vision (rods and cones) activate and fire in the same pattern as the reflected light that hits them. Your optic nerves transmit the pattern to the visual cortex at the back of your brain, which interprets it in ways that we do not fully understand. From that process, you get sensations of light and darkness corresponding to the text on the page.

The sensations by themselves can't be true or false. They don't assert anything: they simply *are*. From those sensations – somehow – you get words and beliefs that mean something.

You've had such experiences often enough to remember them. Consider a simpler example.

Maybe you were just waking up, or the room was dimly lit. Your eyes registered a color, but it took a couple seconds for your mind to see it as the color. Your eyes gave you a sensation that was neither true nor false. On the basis of the sensation (and other sensations), your mind made a perceptual judgment that was true or false. From "blah," you deduced "that is blue."

Of course, you didn't make that inference consciously. You're an adult. From infancy, you've been taught to associate that particular sensation with the sound "blue." As soon as you have the sensation, your mind goes through a process that produces "blue." It's not yet a process of reasoning, and it's almost entirely unconscious:

1. Sensation pattern (eyes): blah.
2. Recognition (association): Your brain pops up a memory of the sound "blue."

> Even now, we have only a partial explanation of how this happens. If we are repeatedly exposed to two sensory patterns together, our brains form pathways between the memory of one and the memory of the other. After that, when we're exposed to one of the patterns, our brains send a message via the pathway to retrieve the memory of the other. If you want to know more about the process, look up "long-term potentiation." Scientists used to believe that specific memories were stored in specific brain locations, called engrams. However, more recent research suggests that even specific memories are distributed throughout the brain instead of being stored at only one location apiece.

3. Perceptual association (almost true or false): That [sensation] :: [memory of sound].
4. Explicit belief (true or false): "That is blue."

The last step – from things that aren't true or false to things that are – is a little more complicated than the example shows. However, what we've got is enough to make the point.

Every time you look at anything and recognize it *as* something, you make the leap from blah to blue. Even if you don't put it into words and say, "That is X," your recognition of it as something can be mistaken. If it can be mistaken, then it's true or false. It's a belief.

Therefore, you start with things that aren't true or false, and you deduce things that are true or false. As a matter of logic, that's not allowed. But as a matter of how the world works, it's very much allowed. It works for us very well. It enables us to survive and prosper.

What makes associations true or false

Like a bare sensation, an association by itself isn't true or false: it simply is. It has the potential to become true or false, but not all by itself. We need another factor. A simple change provides the missing factor. Suppose that in the dimly-lit room, you only saw the color for a second. You saw it, but you weren't sure what it was:

1. Sensation (eyes): fuzzy image (blah).

   You didn't see it clearly, so the image was indistinct. You saw it well enough for your brain to make some guesses.

2. Hypotheses (association): "blue"? "black"?

   Your brain pops up memories of two sounds that might match the indistinct image. The sounds ("linguistic pegs") provide entry into your system of language.

3. Sensation pattern (look again): "blue."

   You look again. This time, you pay careful attention to anything that might distinguish a sensation of blue from a sensation of black. You recognize it as blue.

4. Perceptual belief (true or false): "That-blue."

   The final step is true or false because it *excludes* other possibilities. It's the existence of other possibilities that make associations true or false.

Notice that your recognition of the image as blue is true based on the evidence you have in hand. Further evidence, however, could prove you wrong. If your spouse walks into the room and flips on the light, you might see that what looked blue or black was actually a light brown stain on the ceiling from a roof leak.

For people with normal vision, the sensations of black, blue, and light brown are different: we don't need logic for that. It's intuitive. Therefore, our association "that-black" conflicts with the association "that-blue," and both of them conflict with "that-light-brown." As a result, when we translate our sensations first into perceptual judgments and then into explicitly-stated beliefs, identifying an image as one color conflicts with identifying it as some other color. From (4) and a few other beliefs, we can logically conclude that:

- That is colored.

- That occupies space.

- That is not black.

If either the image isn't colored or it doesn't occupy space, then it can't be blue. If the image is black, then it can't be blue. As a result of other associations with which it could conflict, the association that-blue can be mistaken. It can be mistaken because if we accept that-blue, then we must accept that-colored, that-occupies-space, and that-not-black. By its connections, it has become true or false.

Recall from Chapter 11 that a thing's meaning is its set of connections to other things. We now start to see that its truth or falsity also resides in those connections. Those connections not only give meaning to things like associations, but also make them true or false, and provide the ways we can decide if they are true or false.

In order for something to be a true or false belief, it must at least implicitly have a subject, predicate, and sometimes an object. When an association has a connection, the original thing is the subject, the connection the predicate, and the thing at the other end of the connection is the object. Multiply that connection and you've got a meaningful belief that can be true (consistent with its objects) or false (inconsistent with its objects).

How we leap into religion

How does the leap "from blah to blue" occur in religion? How do we get from an unknowable transcendent reality to rules and rituals, prayers and priests, synagogues and churches?

From our analysis in the previous chapter, the figure shows the structure of the process:

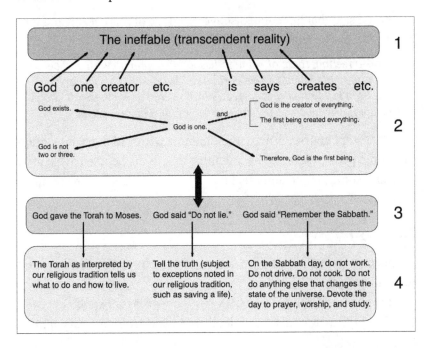

The transcendent (1)

Our experience starts with an ineffable layer that has qualities we can't describe.

Different people vary in their ability to sense the transcendent layer. Some people can't sense it at all. Others sense it very strongly. The former think the latter are superstitious. The latter think the former are spiritually barren.

Sigmund Freud, the founder of psychoanalysis, referred to the difference between those two groups of people in his book *Civilization and Its Discontents*. He recounted his correspondence with an "esteemed friend" for whom he obviously had some respect:

"I sent him a little piece of mine that treats religion as an illusion, and in his reply he said that he wholly agreed with my view of religion, but regretted that I had failed to appreciate the real source of religiosity. This was a feeling of which he himself was never free, which he had found confirmed by many others and which he assumed was shared by millions, a feeling that he was inclined to call a sense of 'eternity', a feeling of something limitless, unbounded – as it were 'oceanic'."

Freud said that he "could discover no trace of this oceanic feeling" in himself, but he summarized the situation as follows:

"It is a feeling, then, of being indissolubly bound up with and belonging to the whole of the world outside oneself ... ... The only question is whether it is correctly interpreted and whether it should be acknowledged as the fons et origo of all religious needs."

That is, of course, exactly the dilemma with which we now grapple. Some people have the feeling intensely, some people have a little of it, and some people don't feel it at all. The question is how to interpret those facts.

Theology (2)

Prophets associate words with the way they experience the layer and its qualities.

Prophets and religious leaders put the words into statements and relationships that are based on logic and ideas from ordinary human life.

The statements and relationships have meaning *relative to each other*. They can be understood within their own network, but not outside of it.

Bridging beliefs (3)

Prophets and religious leaders combine words and beliefs from Level 2 and from the normal world to create bridging beliefs between Level 2 and the normal world.

Prophets state bridging beliefs in terms of their own era's concepts, cosmology, traditions, customs, and mores.

The personalities of prophets and religious leaders also influence what they state as bridging beliefs.

As historian Mircea Eliade observed in his classic book *The Sacred and the Profane*, "Since the religious life of humanity is realized in history, its expressions are inevitably conditioned by the variety of historical moments and cultural styles."

Moral beliefs (4)

Religious leaders codify moral beliefs, rituals, required behaviors, and sacred dogmas backed by the authority of bridging beliefs.

They enhance the bridging beliefs by telling various stories about their origins.

Why look for transcendence?

Why do people look for transcendence in the first place? There are many reasons, but one of them is that they can't find the answers they need in their ordinary experience of the world.

Their quest for answers starts with the seen, such as night, day, stars, moon, sun, youth, maturity, age, and death. Sometimes, the earth shakes for no apparent reason. Sometimes, terrible storms or epidemics occur. They know what happens, but not why.

To satisfy their need for a "why," they infer the existence of unseen forces that can explain it. They explain the unseen in terms that are familiar to them and their group, such as their history, dominant psychologies, attitudes, and customs:

- **Seen:** Thunder, earthquakes, war, life, health, illness, death.

- **Anxiety:** Why do bad things happen? How can we prevent them? How can we make good things happen instead?

- **Need:** Anxiety prompts a need for answers to restore feelings of security and control.

- **Answers:** Posit unseen forces (gods, God, etc.) to explain observed events.

- **Down to earth:** Bridging statements describe unseen forces in anthropomorphic terms, prescribing rituals to make the forces do good things and not bad things to the faithful.

Note that the worldview need not be religious in the traditional sense. Mental illness, for example, was long ago explained as demon possession; then in a later era as moral failure; still later as a result of unhappy childhood; and today, often, as an imbalance of brain chemistry. Each era uses concepts that are widely accepted at the time.

How Judaism made the leap

Judaism provides one example of the leap from the ineffable to the mundane. Jews look to the Torah (the first five books of the Old Testament) as their ultimate source of authority on religious questions. The Torah makes a variety of statements about the transcendent, often combining primitive anthropomorphic imagery with sophisticated philosophical ideas. Exodus 19:3-4 shows the influence of earlier Israelite beliefs that God was a mountain god similar to other supposed deities of the Ancient Near East:

> *"The Lord called to [Moses] from the mountain, saying, 'Thus shall you say to the house of Jacob and declare to the children of Israel: 'You have seen what I did to the Egyptians, how I bore you on eagles' wings and brought you to Me.'"*

Elsewhere, however, the Torah hints at God's transcendence and ineffability. For example, Exodus 19:18-21:

> *"Now Mount Sinai was all in smoke ... The Lord said to Moses, 'Go down, warn the people not to break through to the Lord to gaze, lest many of them perish.'"*

Exodus 33:17-20 adds that even Moses, the greatest of the prophets, could not see the unseeable:

> *"And the Lord said to Moses, 'I will also do this thing that you have asked; for you have truly gained My favor and I have singled you out by name.' [Moses] said, 'Oh, let me behold Your Presence!' And He answered, 'I will make all My goodness pass before you, and I will proclaim before you the name Lord, and the grace that I grant and*

the compassion that I show. But,' He said, 'you cannot see My face, for man may not see Me and live.'"

In spite of its depth, the Torah provides few direct answers for practical questions of life. Over the centuries, ancient rabbis debated about what Torah passages required or forbade people to do. The official record of these debates is the Talmud, which constitutes "the Oral Torah."

But how authoritative was the Oral Torah? Mainstream Jews believed that the written Torah was authoritative because God gave it to Moses at Sinai. But if the Oral Torah was just some rabbis' interpretations of the written Torah, then why should other Jews accept their interpretations as, pardon the expression, "Gospel"?

The rabbis had an answer. At Sinai, God didn't just dictate the written Torah to Moses. He also dictated all the debates and interpretations that ancient rabbis would give in centuries to come. According to Maimonides in his *Introduction to the Mishnah*:

"Every commandment that the Holy One, Blessed be He, gave to Moses our Teacher, may he rest in peace, was given with its clarification. First, He told him the commandment, and then He expounded on its explanation and content, including all that which is included in the Torah."

Maimonides goes on to explain that after God had taught the Torah and Talmud to Moses, Moses then taught them to Aaron. After he taught them to Aaron, he taught them to Aaron's sons Elazar and Itamar. Then he taught them to the 70 elders of the Israelites. Then he taught them to "the masses of people:"

"The result is that Aaron heard that precept from Moses four times, his sons three times, the elders twice, and the remainder of the populace once."

After that, Aaron, Elazar, Itamar, and the elders taught the Torah and Talmud once again to the populace. Following the events at Sinai, they continued teaching them to groups of Israelites.

Thus, Judaism asserts that both the written Torah and the Oral Torah came from God. Because they both came from God, they have the same Divine authority and are binding on all Jews.

Even granting that the events at Sinai were supernatural, such an assertion strains the credulity of any unbiased observer. To recite the entire Torah would take a considerable amount of time. To recite both the Torah and Talmud repeatedly to various groups of people would take much more time. And of course, the Talmud records discussions that would not occur until centuries in the future.

However, belief in the Divine origin of the Oral Torah serves the twin goals of providing moral authority and uniting the Jewish people. It's not applied to other things, and it serves a useful social goal. It gets very little support from historical and archaeological evidence, but it gets very strong support from its moral results. Reasonable people may hold it as a justified belief.

How Christianity made the leap

Christianity has trod a similar path from the transcendent to the mundane.

When I was in high school, my roommate was Catholic. The priest who did services at the school was an endearingly cantankerous old fellow who smoked awful cigars. Whenever my roommate missed Mass, the priest showed up in the dorm that evening to scold him. I'm sure that my memory has enhanced the situation to make it more interesting, but I recall him blowing cigar smoke in my roommate's face and asking why the hell he had been absent.

At any rate, two things puzzled me about Catholicism. The first thing was that my roommate was constantly going to confession, a Catholic ritual in which someone confesses his or her sins to the priest, does some tasks as penance, and receives absolution. I couldn't imagine what my roommate had to confess, since I could rarely think of anything I would have needed to confess, and I didn't think I was a better person than my roommate.

The second puzzlement was more germane to our current topic. I occasionally engaged the priest in conversation about theology since it was a subject of mutual interest. And it seemed that whenever I asked a really interesting question, his answer was always "It's a mystery." In other words, we had come up against the ineffable and transcendent. From such mysteries, the Catholic church had to establish explicit beliefs, rituals, institutions, and rules of conduct. And in order to do that, it had first to establish its authority to do so.

Appropriately enough, it looked to the Bible -- to the Christian New Testament, of course -- for its source of authority. Matthew 16:18 reports that Jesus said to his disciple Peter:

> *"Thou art Peter, and upon this rock [petros = rock, so he makes a pun] I will build my church, and the gates of hell shall not prevail against it."*

The Catholic Church, based in Rome, maintains that Peter traveled to Rome and established the church there. By what Catholics call "apostolic succession," authority passed from Peter to the first Bishop of Rome, who passed it to his successors. Thus does the Catholic Church maintain its own authority as having a Divine origin.

Of course, the story about Peter has some of the same plausibility issues as the story about the Oral Torah. Peter wasn't exactly a poster boy for courage or for loyalty to Jesus. John 18:15-27 reports that after Jesus was arrested by the Romans, Peter three times denied knowing him. In addition to that, secular historians think it improbable that Peter ever visited Rome.

However, belief in the Divine authority of the church via apostolic succession has served Catholics reasonably well over the centuries. It's not applied to other things, and it serves a useful social goal. Reasonable people may hold it as a justified belief.

Note that Catholics' reasonable belief in the Divine authority of the Catholic church does not preclude other beliefs from being reasonable even if they conflict with it. Jews, Protestants, and Muslims all deny the Divine authority of the Catholic church even if they agree with many of its teachings. All of the beliefs rest on their moral and social results; logic and evidence are just so much window dressing. If their beliefs help people of faith to lead happy, moral, productive lives that do not include hating and killing each other, then their beliefs are justified.

Chapter 13:
How Description
Shapes Truth

"To thine own self be true,
And it must follow, as the night the day,
Thou canst not then be false to any man."

-- Hamlet, Act I, Scene 3

ARE YOU BEING TRUE TO YOURSELF?

We started Chapter 11 with a question about the meaning of life because it was a good way to start thinking about meaning. We discovered that the meaning of life was different for everyone. It depended on what people valued enough to feel that it made their lives worthwhile. Moreover, things can be meaningful in different ways.

Likewise, the question about being true to yourself is a good way to start thinking about truth. What does it mean to be true to yourself? How can you know if you're being true to yourself? How do those questions connect (or do they) to more conventional cases where things can be true or false and you can know it, such as:

- That is blue.

  (Recall the previous chapter's example of waking up in a dimly-lit room, seeing something, and deciding that what you see is blue.)

- The area of a circle is approximately equal to that of a square with sides whose length is 8/9ths the diameter of the circle.

- Abraham Lincoln was 16th President of the United States.

- Dogs are mammals.

- It's wrong to lie.

From those examples, as well as from the example of being true to yourself, you might start to wonder about a couple of things:

- Are there different ways for things to be true (or false)?

- Are there different ways to know that they're true (or false)?

For now, just keep those questions in the back of your mind and we'll get on with the chapter. At the end, we'll return to the question of being true to yourself. You'll be surprised how well it fits.

Just as most people never give any thought to the nature of belief, they never give any thought to the nature of truth. They believe vaguely that a true statement somehow matches a fact in the world, but that's about as much thought as they've given to the matter. Even great thinkers like Maimonides and Bertrand Russell tend to adopt similar though more developed views of truth.

In this chapter, we'll examine three aspects of truth:

- How foundational descriptions shape the truth: How a belief network's basic concepts and assumptions determine which of its beliefs are true.

- How we test for truth: How we can decide if beliefs are true. Philosophy books often call this the "criterion" of truth.

- How we define truth: What it means for beliefs to be true. Philosophy books often call this the "nature" of truth.

The three aspects are intimately related, since they all involve connections of beliefs within a network of other beliefs (which, to recall, include verbal and non-verbal behaviors, memories, feelings, and so forth). However, they ask different questions that we can answer separately.

Since it's impossible to determine if we are or aren't in some version of the "Braino machine," our answers must apply to either situation. But there's also good news: the Braino possibility makes it a lot easier to understand the second aspect (the test of truth) and the third aspect (the definition of truth).

How foundational descriptions shape truth

In the chapter about justifying belief, we looked at the difference between two types of good things:

- *Instrumentally* good things are good only because they help us get other good things.

- *Intrinsically* good things are good in themselves, not just because they help us get other good things.

We need at least one thing to be intrinsically good because otherwise, we'd be trapped in an infinite regress, where everything was good because of something else and we never got to the end of the line.

We're in a similar situation when it comes to knowing about things in the world. To justify or explain a belief is to tell a story about why you think it's true. But every story you tell must have endpoints, both at the beginning (with "Once upon a time ...") and at the end (when you stop talking or write "The End"). If it didn't end, then you'd have to go on talking forever, which would be bad because you've got tickets to the opera this evening. You'd be trapped in another infinite regress.

Foundationalism and self-evident beliefs

To avoid the infinite regress, philosophers (at least since Aristotle, and probably even earlier) came up with the idea of *foundationalism*. It argues that all our explanations depend ultimately on foundational beliefs requiring no justification beyond themselves. They are the bedrock on which we build our house of knowledge. In school, you might have learned the famous words of the U.S. Declaration of Independence (1776):

> *"We hold these truths to be self-evident, that all men are created equal, that they are endowed by their Creator with certain unalienable Rights, that among these are life, liberty, and the pursuit of happiness. -- That to secure these rights, governments are instituted among men, deriving their just powers from the consent of the governed ..."*

Foundational beliefs are said to be "self-evident." If you understand them, then you know they are true. You don't need to know anything else. Of course, people disagree about what is self-evident, so philosophers joke that "self-evident" means "evident to oneself."

Many supposedly self-evident beliefs, such as the ones in the Declaration of Independence, depend on many other assumptions and beliefs. As a result, they're arguably not self-evident at all. What the Declaration of Independence means by "self-evident" is:

> *"Obviously and indisputably true based on assumptions of Western European, particularly British, post-Enlightenment Era thought."*

But that's quite a mouthful, so the Declaration settled for calling the beliefs "self-evident" instead. Are any beliefs actually self-evident? If self-evident just means they're evident if you understand them, then yes, there are some, such as the statements that:

- The whole of a thing is more than a part of the thing.

- Black and blue are different.

- $1 > 0$

But -- and it's a crucial "but" -- remember that to understand something means you can tell a story about it, connecting it to other things. None of those supposedly self-evident beliefs can stand on its own, any more than "all men are created equal." If you can't tell a story about it, then you don't understand it or know what it means.

If you know *only one thing*, then you really don't know anything at all, because you can't tell a story about the one thing.

And understanding beliefs is only half the battle. Whether or not they're "evident" -- that is, whether or not you're justified in believing them -- depends on the story you tell. That applies both to supposedly self-evident beliefs and to perceptual beliefs from which foundation-alist philosophers want to construct our reality.

Such basic beliefs, combined with how you describe them and the story you tell about them, are a foundational description of a situation. It lays out the basic concepts and assumptions that you will use to talk about the situation, and shapes what you will see as meaningful, true, or false. It differs from "foundationalism" as discussed by philoso-phers because foundational descriptions include a lot of things beyond supposedly self-evident beliefs.

The same applies in writing fictional stories: you start with a foun-dational description. You give some background details, describing the stage on which the action will take place. Often, you give some information about the main characters:

Time: "Once upon a time, ..."

The opening phrase implies that the events occur far in the past.

Place: "in a peaceful kingdom by the sea, ..."

You give some details of the setting. You omit other details because they're either implied by your description or are common enough that readers will assume they exist, such as a castle and a beach.

Protagonist: "a wise and courageous king ruled over a free and happy people."

Then you introduce the purpose of the story. Usually, it's either a con-flict or an antagonist:

Antagonist: "But one day, a terrifying monster emerged from the sea. Its baleful gaze drove people insane, and its fiery breath incin-erated whatever it touched. Legends said its name was "Schreck-lichkeit." (Its name had originally been "Smiley," but the monster changed it for business reasons.)

Without that foundational description, the rest of your fictional story wouldn't make any sense. The same is true of non-fictional sto-ries, whether they are factual, procedural, or moral.

Notice that even in a fictional story, your foundational description determines the meaning and truth of events that occur later in the story. If you described the king as "reckless and violent," it would change the implications of any battle with the monster. If you said that the monster was a handsome prince under an evil spell, that would change it again.

Foundationalism's insight and errors

As described by various philosophers, foundationalism gets one big thing right and two smaller things wrong.

What it gets *right* is that knowledge has to start someplace. Philosophers usually locate the beginning in our sensations, like C.I. Lewis in his book *Analysis of Knowledge and Valuation:*

> *"Our empirical knowledge rises as a structure of enormous complexity, most parts of which are stabilized in measure by their mutual support, but all rest, at bottom, on direct findings of sense."*

However, philosophers tie themselves into knots trying to figure out how they can get from sensations that *aren't* true or false to beliefs that *are*. The problem results from their naïve (though often ponderously elaborated) theories of truth and meaning. We looked at the issue briefly in the previous chapter under the heading, "How associations become true or false."

Confusion about that issue leads to the things they get wrong.

First, they think that foundational beliefs are completely *certain*, so that the beliefs can't become more or less certain than they already are. Additional evidence is irrelevant to them.

Some foundationalists avoid this mistake by claiming only that the beliefs are justified, not certain. But that remedy suffers from circular reasoning.[19] It also rejects the essential idea of foundationalism and moves toward the view in this book: that beliefs get their meaning, justification, and truth from a network of other beliefs that they also support (called "coherentism"). It's an entirely different model of

---

[19] If you are interested in this issue, see Appendix A, "Why Modest Foundationalism Is Circular Reasoning." That material is not needed to understand the main arguments of this book.

knowledge. Foundationalism justifies all beliefs from the bottom up, by reliance on the foundational beliefs. Coherentism justifies all beliefs -- including "foundational" ones -- by connections in a network of beliefs, whether bottom-up, top-down, or sideways.

Second, they think that foundational beliefs are *immutable*, so their meaning can't change or expand as more connections are added to them.

But we've seen already that if we add more connections to a belief, we add to its meaning; and if we subtract connections (as in the take-away test), we diminish its meaning. Even foundational beliefs are not immutable.

If foundational beliefs aren't immutable, then they can't be certain. For example, "A=A" is as certain as beliefs get. If you can change its meaning, you can add connections to it, such as "+Bill has a headache." Then the belief's meaning is "A=A and Bill has a headache," which is not certain because Bill might not have a headache.

Thus, foundationalism and coherentism *agree* that knowledge has to start from beliefs that we accept without proof. They *disagree* about what happens after that. Foundationalism treats the initial beliefs as untouchable and unchangeable.

By contrast, coherentism treats them as a "starter set" of beliefs whose meaning, justification, and truth evolve with the growth of their belief networks.

What is a foundational description?

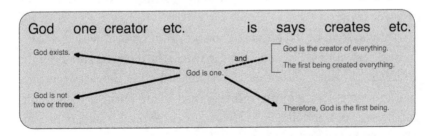

We've talked previously about the role of descriptions and how they are related to purposes, but we haven't yet specified what we mean by a description:

A description is a finite set of connected concepts and beliefs about the basic features of a particular thing, area, event type, or aspect of reality that is of interest.

You can describe the same thing or situation in different ways depending on your purpose, your viewpoint, and the concepts you already have available. Afterward, how you described it affects how you understand the things in it. That applies especially to new things. You interpret them in terms of what you already believe.

For example, depending on your purpose, you can describe a cell phone as a product of labor, as a thing for which consumers will pay, or as a complex electronic device. Each description focuses on a different aspect: the first on production, the second on sales, and the third on engineering. But they're all correct descriptions. And note:

- If you see a new handheld device to talk wirelessly to other people, you'll probably consider it a cell phone because that's in your existing stock of descriptions.

- Depending on whether you're a factory worker, a salesperson, or an engineer, you'll connect your idea of the cell phone to different experiences and beliefs.

Another example is a boat. The boat is just one thing -- unless you are recycling it for lumber. Then, it's a hundred or so pieces of wood, in various sizes and shapes. Your goal determines whether it's one thing or many.

Any system of beliefs about the world must deal with the same basic observations. The sun seems to rise in the morning and set in the evening. The stars and other astronomical bodies move in repeated patterns every day, month, and year. People are born, grow to adulthood, grow old, and die. Life is to some degree predictable, but seems also to include an element of chance, or luck if you prefer.

Once you've decided on your basic description, some beliefs:

- Will make sense, or not.

- Will be verifiable, or not.
- Will be true, or not.

Relatively foundational descriptions

Descriptions can be foundational at different levels. Describing the universe as a physical system is foundational at a very basic level. It covers everything that exists, but only in terms of physical properties and relationships. It tells you about a lot of things, but says nothing specific about any of them. If your goal is simply to understand the laws governing all physical objects, then it works fine. But if your purpose is more specific, you need simply to assume the physical description and push it into the background. Then, you start your story at a different level that's better suited to your goal:

- Somewhat higher, based on that description, we can describe the human body as a biological system that follows the same laws as other systems in the physical universe.

- Even higher than that, we can describe "Bill's body" as the biological system that we see standing in front of our desk.

- Still higher, we can refer to Bill, the person who (in some manner) inhabits Bill's body and nags us about forgetting to put cover sheets on our printed reports at the office.

- At higher levels, we think only of the description level immediately below them. When we talk about Bill, we don't see him in terms of a truly foundational description of the universe. We see him only in terms of a relatively (relative to Bill) foundational description of human beings.

Fictional stories work similarly. The story about the kingdom omitted descriptions of the castle and the beach because those are standard images that occur in many stories, just as the laws of physics apply in all stories about physical objects. If the fictional story spent its first five pages describing the castle and the beach, it would have both wasted the readers' time and obscured the more important aspects of the story.

The same applies to non-fictional stories. If you had to explain physics, biology, anatomy, and neuroscience before you could explain why Bill has a headache, then by the time you finished explaining, the headache would be long gone. Instead, you just say it's because Bill didn't get enough sleep last night. You simply assume all the lower-level descriptions that underlie your statement. Foundational descriptions focus on what is relevant for the story's purpose.

The reason that it's important to know the idea of relatively foundational descriptions is that they affect how we perceive situations and what we believe about them. Describing humans as mere animals with delusions of grandeur leads to beliefs far different from those we get if we describe them as children of God with a moral sense.

Similarly, if we look at immigration through the lens of 1939 in Europe, we'll arrive at beliefs far different from those we get if we view it through the lens of the latest terrorist attacks in Europe and North America.

Let's consider a couple examples of foundational descriptions.

A scientific example

Astronomy provides an example of how purpose affects basic description, and description determines what is true or false. Consider a true proposition that's known to every school child:

> The earth revolves around the sun, and the sun does not revolve around the earth.

What most people do *not* know is that for predicting observations of astronomical bodies, the choice between the Copernican (sun-centered) and Ptolemaic (earth-centered) view of the solar system is arbitrary. Astronomers say that the earth revolves around the sun not because it is true in some absolute sense -- it isn't -- but because it makes astronomical calculations simpler.

The Ptolemaic and Copernican descriptions of the solar system had related but different goals. Both wanted to explain and predict movements of stars, planets, and other heavenly bodies. However, the Ptolemaic model was complicated, clumsy, and unaesthetic.

Copernicus believed that the sky was an area of heavenly perfection, but complicated and clumsy were imperfect. So he wanted a basic description that made planetary movement simpler, astronomical calculations easier, and all of it more aesthetically pleasing.

If one adopts the Ptolemaic view of the solar system, one starts with the proposition that the sun revolves around the earth, as do the other planets and the stars.

But therein lies a problem when you look up at the sky to observe the movements of the planets and stars. The planets appear to move backwards a little bit (retrograde motion), then forward in their orbits, then backward a little bit, and so on.

In the Copernican model, we explain planetary retrograde motion by saying that the earth is also moving relative to the other planets: that's a basic assumption of the Copernican description. Copernicus thought that all the planets, including earth, had circular orbits because heavenly motion had to be perfect and circles were perfect geometric figures. Today, we modify his picture of the solar system to show that the orbits are elliptical.

In the Ptolemaic model, however, the earth isn't moving. Ptolemaic astronomers had to find some other explanation for planetary retrograde motion. The explanation had to fit all the same observed facts as the Copernican model, but with the earth at the center of the universe. To solve this problem, Ptolemaic astronomers said that as planets and stars orbited the earth, each one of them made smaller circles along its orbit, called "epicycles" (epi = on, cycle = orbit).

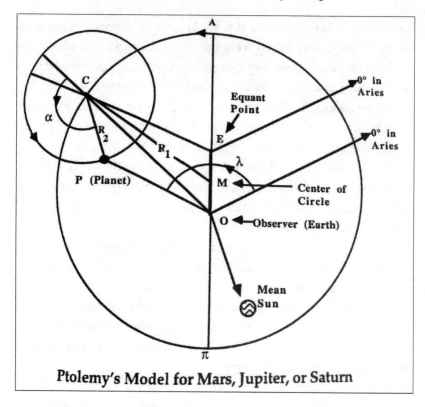

Ptolemy's Model for Mars, Jupiter, or Saturn

The Ptolemaic model fit observed facts just as well as the later Copernican model did, and it enabled astronomers to predict the movements of heavenly bodies. However, it was more complicated and difficult than the Copernican model. Simplicity might not equal absolute truth, but it has its advantages. So now we all "know" that Copernicus was right, Ptolemy was wrong, and that the earth revolves around the sun.

Under the Ptolemaic description, for example, planets move in epicycles as they orbit the earth. Under the Copernican description, they don't. Which is right?

The answer is that *relative to their basic description* of the situation, they are both right. Relative to the other description, they are both wrong.

An ordinary-life example

Let's look at something more down to earth. Imagine a man sitting on a bench just south of a railway track that goes east and west.

A train passes him, traveling west at 50 kilometers per hour. Having keen eyesight, he looks through one of the train windows and sees another man sitting at a table with a coffee cup in front of him. The man on the bench believes that the coffee cup is moving west at 50 kilometers per hour.

The man on the train is also looking at the coffee cup. He believes that the cup is not moving except for a slight vibration owing to the movement of the train.

So we are presented with two beliefs:

- The cup is moving west at 50 kilometers per hour.
- The cup is not moving.

Common sense tells us that the beliefs don't really conflict. Each man views the coffee cup from a situation whose basic description differs from the other. The basic description implies which belief is correct.

Suppose someone asked you if the cup was "really" moving, and if so, with what direction and speed. You could not answer without knowing the basic description. Without that, the question *has* no answer. And depending on the description, different answers are true or false.

Only the most basic facts are given to us. Their interpretation -- for example, if the cup is moving, how fast, in which direction, even its size and color -- depend on the foundational description. Without an explicit or assumed foundational description, statements about the cup are neither true nor false. They make no sense. The man in the train car applies a description with beliefs that:

- The train car is the standard to determine if something is moving or not.
- The coffee cup is not moving relative to the train car.
- Therefore, the coffee cup is not moving.

But the man on the bench applies a different description, including beliefs that:

- The ground is the standard determine if something is moving or not.
- The coffee cup is moving relative to the ground.
- Therefore, the coffee cup is moving.

Those considerations apply in other areas:

- In physics, relativity (for astrophysics), quantum mechanics (for sub-atomic phenomena) and classical mechanics (for engineering). Each works well in some contexts and not in others.

- In economics, the labor theory of value (a thing's price depends on how much labor is needed to produce it) and the subjective theory of value (a thing's price depends on how much consumers value it and will pay for it). Each works well in some contexts and not in others.

- In psychology, Freudian psychoanalysis, Gestalt, cognitive-behavioral therapy, and neuroscientific theories. Each works well in some contexts and not in others.

That doesn't mean there is no truth to be had. But it does mean we shouldn't assume some beliefs are false when they are just based on different foundational concepts and descriptions. Conversely, we shouldn't assume that some beliefs are universally true regardless of how we describe the world.

It also doesn't mean that all descriptions are equally useful for particular purposes. In economics, you can treat economic value either as subjective or based on labor. Each leads to a viewpoint that is more helpful in analyzing some situations than others. However, you can usually make an argument for any unwieldy description of reality, depending on how many logical acrobatics you'll do to keep it.

The main theories of truth

Descriptions shape truth. But how do we know what is true? And what is truth?

Truth is such integral part of our intellectual world that it's hard to answer the questions without sounding trivial or being totally obscure. The ancient Greek philosopher Aristotle put it this way:

"To say of what is that it is not, or of what is not that it is, is false; while to say of what is that it is, or of what is not that it is not, is true."

Both secular and religious philosophers, from Thomas Reid (Christian) to Maimonides (Jewish), Thomas Aquinas (Christian), and Avicenna (Islamic) have found inspiration in Aristotle's ideas. In the 20th century, the secular philosopher Alfred Tarski gave a similar formulation:

"A sentence is true if it designates an existing state of affairs."

To realize how slippery the idea is, notice that none of those formulations gives a definition of truth. They all tell us *when* something is true, but not what it *means* for something to be true. What is involved, *exactly,* in a sentence "designating" a state of affairs?

Back in Chapter 1, we listed criteria for a correct definition of belief, such as that it should cover all and only cases we'd normally call belief. Notice that what Aristotle and the others give us is the same kind of thing. They give us criteria to determine if beliefs are true, but they don't tell us what truth *is*. They don't give us a definition.

As with belief, a reasonable approach is to look at some examples. And we will. But to provide some context, let's briefly look at the three main theories of truth.

Each has its own definition of truth and test of truth. Philosophers argue about which is correct, but the theories are much more alike than different. They all define truth as a relation between a belief and something else. They test beliefs by looking for the "something else." When you get past the details, their essential difference is in what they say the *something else* is:

- **Correspondence:** Truth is a relation between a belief and a non-mental fact in the world, such that the fact matches the statement. The nature of the "matching" is left vague. The statement is either true or false. There is no third option.

- **Coherence:** Truth is a relation between a belief and a network of other beliefs, such that the belief gives support to and gets support from other beliefs in the network. Depending on the size of the system and strength of support, a belief is more true or less true. Truth (like meaning) is a matter of degree, so there are in effect an infinite number of options.

- **Pragmatic:** Truth is a relation between an action-guiding belief and the result that the action is meant to produce. If the action succeeds, then the belief is true. If the action fails, then the belief is false. Since "success" can be a matter of degree, truth can also be a matter of degree. Some pragmatists accept that and some don't.

Using your Braino to figure it out

In a moment, we'll look in more detail at how these theories handle the test and definition of truth. At the outset, however, note that the Braino possibility simplifies the whole problem.

Recall that the Braino machine creates an "illusion" of reality so perfect that we have no way to know if we are in the Braino machine or not. When we look at a tree, are we really looking at a real tree, or are we only having an experience created by the Braino machine feeding electrical impulses into our brains? In the latter case, not only is the non-mental, physical tree not there, but in addition, our eyes are not there, nor our bodies, nor the rest of the non-mental, physical world we seem to perceive. There's only our perception of the tree and ourselves, possibly with our perceptions of other people confirming our belief.

However, our experiences are exactly the same whether or not we are in the Braino machine. As a result, we test truth in the same way whether or not we're in the machine. We might have spent our lives in the machine. If so, our concepts and beliefs refer only to the experiences that the machine generated for us, not to anything that exists outside of it. Whether or not we have always been in the machine, our experiences would have been the same.

For example, suppose we look at something and believe "that is a tree." If we're in the machine, the tree is a network of experiences created by the machine combined with our judgments about those experiences. We formed our concept of "tree" based on previous experiences of the same kind. Therefore, if we say "that is a tree," it refers to the same experiences we would have in the Braino machine or outside of it. Because the world looks the same to us whether or not we're in the Braino machine, the same definition of truth must work in either situation. Truth also means the same thing whether or not we are in the Braino machine.

Truth is always a relation between a belief and *something else*. Whichever theory we choose, that "something else" must be consistent with the Braino machine. Therefore:

- If we adopt the correspondence theory, then the something else is *nothing*, because we can have beliefs only about our experiences in the machine. We do not know about any non-mental facts.

- If we adopt the coherence theory, then the something else is a network of other beliefs. This is consistent with the Braino machine.

- If we adopt the pragmatic theory, then the something else results from an action guided by our belief. This is also consistent with the Braino machine, since belief, action, and results are all experiences we can have in the machine.

How we test for truth

To be sure, correspondence with fact is the most natural and intuitive theory of truth: that's why it's so popular.

Even coherentists, in their ordinary life, think and act as if correspondence were both the test and the definition of truth. Nobody looks at a rose and thinks, "I now see a red patch with a particular shape, I smell a pleasing aroma, I feel pain in my finger after moving it to touch a shape that looks like a thorn. Therefore, that's a rose." Instead, they look, they see a rose, and boom! It's done. That's a rose.

If you asked them how they tested the truth of their belief, they'd simply point at it and say, "Look. See? It's a rose." The rose is "something out there."

It's less clear in the case of historical beliefs: "Abraham Lincoln delivered the Gettysburg Address at the Soldiers' National Cemetery on November 19, 1863." Abraham Lincoln is long dead. The Soldiers' National Cemetery is quiet. The crowds are gone. The subject of our belief doesn't exist at present. On one hand, there's a belief; on the other hand, there's -- nothing?

No, not nothing, but nothing that corresponds to the belief. What exists is a vast collection of evidence: Eyewitness accounts. Newspaper clippings. Historical books. Comments about the speech written by Lincoln's contemporaries. We believe in the existence and accuracy of all that evidence. If we rejected the belief about Lincoln, we would be forced to reject those other beliefs as well. Therefore, what verifies the belief about Lincoln is not correspondence with facts that no longer exist. The belief is verified by connection to other beliefs about facts that do exist. That is to say, the belief is verified by its coherence with the rest of our beliefs:

> *"What really tests the judgment is the extent of our accepted world that is implicated with it and would be carried down with it if it fell. And that is the test of coherence."[20]*

So are beliefs about history verified by coherence, but beliefs about cats by correspondence? Let's take another look at the beliefs from the beginning of the chapter:

- That is blue.
- The area of a circle is approximately equal to that of a square with sides whose length is 8/9ths the diameter of the circle.
- Abraham Lincoln was 16th President of the United States.
- Dogs are mammals.
- It's wrong to lie.

---

[20] Blanshard, B. (1939), Volume II, p. 227.

Consider the first belief. You just woke up. You open your eyes. In the dim light, you see an object. You decide the object is blue. You then conclude that your belief is correct.

What is it that verifies your belief? Is it a non-mental, physical fact that the object is blue? The answer is "no," for three reasons:

- If the object is blue and you do not see it, the fact is the same but your belief is still unverified.

- If the object is blue, but you fail to recognize it as blue, then your belief is still unverified.

- If the object is not blue, but you mistakenly perceive it as blue, then your belief is still unverified and your perception was mistaken.

You test the other beliefs similarly, although the details differ:

- For the area of a circle, you do a calculation:

  ✓ The formula for the area is πr^2, where π is about 3.1416 and r^2 is the circle's radius multiplied by itself.

  ✓ The radius is half the diameter, so r^2 is $\left(\frac{D}{2}\right)^2$, or $\left(\frac{1}{4}\right)D^2$.

  ✓ So if a circle had a diameter of 9, its area would be 3.1416 times one-fourth of 81, which equals about 63.62.

  ✓ If you construct a square whose sides have length 8 (that is, 8/9ths the diameter of the circle), its area is 8 times 8 = 64, very close to the modern value. That's how ancient Egyptians calculated the area of circles. Their value for π comes out to about 3.16. Amaze your friends at parties. You're welcome.

- For the belief about Abraham Lincoln, you consult books and historical records.

- For the belief about dogs, you check the definition of "mammal" to see if dogs fit the definition.

- For the belief that it's wrong to lie, you consult wise people, books of moral instruction, your own experiences, and your conscience.

Despite the differences in detail, in each case you are collecting more beliefs against which to compare your original belief. If the additional beliefs support the original belief, then it is verified. If they contradict it, then it is falsified. If the beliefs fit coherently into our network of other beliefs, we pronounce them true; if not, false.

People often believe that science is more reliable than religion because it's based on hard facts, not theories and assumptions. However, scientific beliefs are even more removed from anything resembling hard facts than are ordinary beliefs. The luminiferous aether, space bent by gravity, time altered by velocity, electrons as mathematical probability functions, or quarks that no one, even in principle, can perceive: all are the subjects of physical science. They are not facts given in our experience. They are creatures of theory, of the belief systems in which they play a part.

What is truth? Let's stay for an answer.

In case you think the section heading sounds odd, it's a riff on a quote that most people think appears in the Bible but which actually doesn't:

> "'What is truth?' said jesting Pilate, and would not stay for an answer."

That's from Francis Bacon's (1561-1626) "On Truth" in his book *Essays or Counsels Civil and Moral*. Bacon, in turn, was riffing on the New Testament's Gospel of John 18:38:

> "Pilate saith unto him, What is truth? And when he had said this, he went out again unto the Jews, and saith unto them, I find in him no fault at all."[21]

This section answers Pilate's question: perhaps not as well as Jesus might have answered it,[22] but at least the section's answer is in English instead of in Aramaic (the language of Jesus).

---

[21] Whether or not you're a believer, knowing the Bible is essential for understanding most of Western civilization.

[22] Neither the Tanakh (the Old Testament) nor the New Testament shows much interest in purely philosophical questions. Both focus more on practical, moral, and theological issues. Pilate's question was probably "What is *the* truth?", i.e., what are the facts? Jesus would probably have given an answer about God, not truth *per se*.

We've already got enough scratches from fighting with the cat, so let's consider a less injurious example: a pencil on a desk. That seems like a clear example of correspondence. You believe that "A pencil is on the desk." There's a pencil on the desk. The fact corresponds to your belief. Case closed.

Well, maybe not. Let's look at it.

After you flunked out of the first grade in Chapter 3, you managed to get your job back at the nuclear power plant. Yes, they've lowered their hiring standards a lot. As long as you haven't shot anyone or starred in a reality TV show, you can be a nuclear power technician.

Your supervisor needs to write down a phone number. He asks if you have a pencil. "Yes," you reply. "There's a pencil on the desk."

What does it mean for that to be true? Obviously, that there's a pencil on the desk. But what does that mean -- for a pencil to be on the desk?

Suppose that you looked at the desk and saw no pencil. You ran your hands over the desk surface and felt no pencil. You called over a few co-workers who repeated the same procedure. Nobody saw or felt a pencil on the desk. Could there still be a pencil on the desk?

"Excuse me," interrupts your supervisor. "Are you going to give me the damn pencil or just keep jabbering about truth?"

"Oh, sorry," you say. "Here you are ... wait a minute ..." You look for the pencil on the desk, but you forgot that we made it go away in the previous paragraph. You pull a pen out of your pocket and hand it to him. For the moment, your job is safe.

Your supervisor writes the number, returns your pen, and walks away. Now that he's out of earshot, we can take a minute to finish our discussion about truth.

You believed there was a pencil on the desk. You and other people tested your belief by performing actions that led to additional beliefs: "I don't see any pencil on the desk," "I don't feel any pencil on the desk," "Don't you ever clean your desktop?" Those beliefs tested your original belief by coherence. It failed the tests.

Can truth be correspondence with fact?

We test truth by coherence. But can truth itself be correspondence with fact?

The possibility that we're in the Braino machine suggests that it can't be. In that reality, we cannot discover any non-mental facts to correspond to our beliefs. And since we can't know if we are in the Braino machine or not, the same analysis must apply in both cases.

But there's an even stronger argument. Suppose that we test truth by coherence with beliefs, but truth is correspondence with non-mental facts. Let's see how it works with the pencil on the desk.

Suppose that "There is a pencil on the desk" is true (by correspondence), but fails every test of truth (by coherence). That means:

- You look at the desk but don't see the pencil.

- You feel every inch of the desktop but don't feel the pencil.

- You try to pick the pencil up from the desk and write with it, but you can't.

- You bring in scientific equipment to detect an invisible pencil, but it doesn't.

- You perform every other test you can think of but never detect the pencil.

- Other people do their tests, but nobody detects the pencil.

- Nobody remembers ever seeing the pencil on the desk.

In spite of all that, there's really a pencil on the desk. The belief "There is a pencil on the desk" is true because it corresponds to a non-mental fact.

What kind of pencil is it? It's a pencil that you can't see, can't feel, can't write with, can't detect with scientific equipment, and can't remember ever having seen.

In other words, whatever it is, *it's not a pencil*. If "There is a pencil on the desk" is true because it corresponds with fact, the fact with which it corresponds does not include a pencil. Therefore, the belief "There is a pencil on the desk" is false.

If coherence is the test of truth, then taking correspondence as the nature of truth leads straight to a contradiction. Either coherence is not the test of truth, or correspondence is not the nature of truth. We already established that coherence is the test of truth. Therefore, correspondence is not the nature of truth.

And because coherence is the test of truth, we have good reason to believe it is also the nature of truth. As Brand Blanshard observed:

> *"If the criterion A could be present while the B it was supposed to indicate was absent, and the criterion be absent when the thing indicated was present, the connection would be intolerably loose. A surgeon who operated or a jury that convicted on evidence of this kind would in most [people's] opinion be acting irresponsibly."*[23]

And note something interesting: Because our definition of belief includes behaviors, feelings, and other kinds of experiences, this definition of truth includes the pragmatic definition. Beliefs can include the results of our actions, so the pragmatic theory is bundled into it.

Blanshard's proof that truth's test and nature must be the same

Like "Plantinga versus the logicians," this section has information that's not needed for the main argument but is interesting to philosophy nerds. You can skip it if you want.

Brand Blanshard's book *The Nature of Thought* was a landmark in 20th-century philosophy. It took him 15 years to write, much of that time spent at a desk in the reading room of the British Museum. In the second volume of his book, he argued that coherence was both the test and the nature of truth.

Some philosophers conceded that we test truth by coherence, but still insisted that the *nature* of truth was correspondence. I've slightly simplified his reply:

1. Suppose the test of truth is coherence with systems of belief, but truth itself is correspondence with non-mental facts.

---

[23] Schilpp, P.A. (1980), p. 595.

2. Then we must be able to test the belief "Truth is correspondence with non-mental facts" by coherence with systems of belief.
3. But we can't test that belief by coherence, since it requires us to know about non-mental facts.
4. Therefore, if truth is correspondence, the test of truth can't be coherence.

Either we must accept coherence as both the test and the nature of truth, or we have to explain how we can know about the non-mental facts that correspondence requires.

Be true to yourself

Let's return to the question with which we started the chapter: Are you being true to yourself?

Being true to yourself means living in ways that connect to your most important moral values and your most heartfelt desires. Your life supports them, and they in turn support it.

You know that you are true to yourself by comparing how you live with your most important moral values and heartfelt desires.

Though more consequential, it's similar to believing "there is a pencil on the desk."

For a pencil to be on the desk means that your belief in the pencil connects with other beliefs that are relevant -- i.e., "most important." It connects to the belief that you see a pencil on the desk, you feel it, you can pick it up, and so forth. It supports them and they support it. Other beliefs are there, too, but they're less relevant: the desk is grey and has a scratch on the side.

You know that there is a pencil on the desk is by comparing your belief in the pencil with the other relevant beliefs you acquire by action and observation.

So be true to yourself, and it follows as night follows day, you cannot then be false to anyone. It's a good way to live.

Chapter 14:
Does It Make Any
Difference What We
Believe?

"'We were just discussing a most interesting subject,' said the earnest matron. 'Dr. Pritchett was telling us that nothing is anything.'

'He should, undoubtedly, know more than anyone else about that,' Francisco answered ...

'Just what did Hugh Akston teach?' asked the earnest matron.

Francisco answered, 'He taught that everything is something.'"

-- *Ayn Rand,* Atlas Shrugged

The previous chapter might suggest a good question: If all the truth we can know is relative to one or another network of beliefs, then isn't any "truth" just as good as any other? Does it make any difference what we believe?

Yes, it makes a lot of difference. The law of gravity is only true relative to some systems of belief, but if you step off the top of a tall building, those are the relevant systems and they will make you absolutely dead. Any philosophy that says otherwise is just plain nuts. The key is to remember:

- Each network of beliefs is connected to one or more *purposes*. A system about the physical universe has beliefs to help us succeed in physical reality. A system about our spiritual place in the universe has beliefs to help us succeed in living happily and morally. And many belief systems also serve the purpose of uniting people for mutual benefit in social groups. We rely on beliefs in each system to guide us for achieving our purposes in the corresponding area of life.

- A belief is true to the extent that it gives and gets support from other elements in a network of beliefs. The other elements can include observations, statements, behaviors, feelings, memories, rituals, and other such things.

- A belief with *more* supporting links is more true than a belief with fewer supporting links. If a belief is supported by a larger and more comprehensive system, it's more true than one that's supported by a smaller system because more of observable reality stands or falls (off a building) with the former belief.

Purposes are crucial. In the abstract, all of our belief systems are created equal, but practically they have different value for different purposes. And "practically" refers to their effectiveness in dealing with realities existing beyond us and our beliefs.

If our beliefs were only about themselves, and not about independent reality, then practicality wouldn't be an issue: You could step off the top of a tall building, turn into a helicopter, and fly to Capistrano. The fact that it never happens shows that our beliefs are about something beyond themselves -- even in the Braino machine. Beliefs are practical if they work, and they work to the extent that they are consistent with objective reality, whatever it is.

If we ask whether any belief is "as good as" any other, we're asking if any belief is as good as any other for *doing something*, for achieving some worthwhile goal. When we uncover that hidden assumption, then the answer is obviously "no," because we have many different goals and we do many different things.

For designing an airplane, the belief system of physics works well, but the belief system of religious faith doesn't work at all. For finding meaning in life, the situation is reversed: physics tells you to commit suicide now, because according to the Second Law of Thermodynamics (entropy increases), things can only get worse. It's not the encouragement you need for a healthy and happy life. Religious faith can provide that. Of course, it can also do the opposite: just like scientific theories, religious beliefs and belief systems can work well or poorly.

In specific areas of life for specific purposes, truth is not relative at all. Some truths and belief systems work better than others. Some work so badly that it is foolish to use them even if their beliefs are true relative to their own basic descriptions and assumptions. The only exception is the case of beliefs that are simply equivalent ways of describing the same thing, and even then some work better than others -- as in the case of Ptolemaic versus Copernican astronomy. Both work but the latter is better. Even if truth is relative in principle, it's often absolute in practice.

Postmodernism substitutes power for truth

The suggestion that truth is in any sense absolute – or even important -- runs up against the reigning ideology of contemporary academia: postmodernism. If you hold common-sense beliefs about life, society, human nature, or even physical science, postmodernists argue it's because you're ignorant of postmodernist theories. That kind of blind faith has the aroma of a cult: a cult for very smart, highly-educated people to be sure, but a cult nonetheless. Harvard psychologist Steven Pinker argues that postmodernism has severely damaged universities

> "... with its defiant obscurantism, self-refuting relativism, and suffocating political correctness. Many of its luminaries—Nietzsche, Heidegger, Foucault, Lacan, Derrida, the Critical Theorists—are morose cultural pessimists who declare that modernity is odious, all statements are paradoxical, works of art are tools of oppression, liberal democracy is the same as fascism, and Western civilization is circling the drain."[24]

---

[24] Pinker. S. (2018), p. 406.

What postmodernism *asserts* is a little difficult to pin down. Various postmodernist writers make various claims -- and not clearly. Its key texts are obscure. Its sources range from Marxist study groups to writers on art, architecture, and literature.

As a result, any overview of postmodernism will seem over-simplified. Its arguments, concerns, and approaches are so varied that to discuss it fully is to get lost in a thicket of details. However, Its key ideas seem to be:

- **Objective truth doesn't exist.** All truth is relative to the stories we tell and the language we use. There's only "my truth" competing with "your truth." As far as postmodernists are concerned, the idea of "the truth" is a myth -- and they're sure that's the truth.

- **Objective reality doesn't exist.** All reality is shaped by the stories we tell and the language we use. There is "no there, there" to which our stories should conform.

- **Everything is about power.** Stories justify some groups' oppression of others. The idea that stories provide factual and moral guidance, help groups cooperate, or promote human happiness is dismissed as bourgeois propaganda.

The central error of postmodernism is the same as that of most ideologies: It focuses on a few small insights and insists that they're the whole story of everything. It bakes a single grain of truth into a thousand loaves of falsehood. Let's look at its claims.

Claim: Objective truth doesn't exist

Postmodernism's first claim is that objective truth doesn't exist. What does that mean?

People have defined "objective" in various ways. Here, we use it to mean "not depending for its existence on any individual person's set of beliefs." With Thomas Reid and Hilary Putnam (see Chapter 10), we assume that:

- We ourselves exist in some way.

- Other people like us exist in some way.

- We can perceive other people and communicate with them.

Based on those assumptions and our experiences, we deduce that we all perceive a shared "reality" of some kind.[25] It might be the real world or some version of the Braino world. It exists independently of our individual consciousness and beliefs about it. We can and do interpret the world in different ways, but it's the same world.

As previously discussed, truth is always a relation between a belief and "something else." The something else is a system of other beliefs, which can include statements, behaviors, feelings, memories, and other things we can do or experience. But our belief systems are always finite. They don't cover all of reality. Some people know more than other people. Different people's systems cover different things, describe them differently, and often conflict with each other. Sometimes, our belief conflict is only apparent because we define the same words in different ways.

So far, so good. Postmodernism says the same thing. If that's *all* it said, then it would be correct as far as it went. Yale postmodernist Seyla Benhabib writes in *Situating the Self* (1992):

> *"Transcendental guarantees of truth are dead; in the agonal struggle of language games there is no commensurability; there are no criteria of truth transcending local discourses, but only the endless struggle of local narratives vying with one another for legitimation."*

Notice that what she says is still consistent with the existence of objective truth. She's not talking about truth itself: she's talking about "guarantees" and "criteria" of truth. In other words, she's talking about *how we know things* and how certain we can be about them.

She also mentions the fact that words and beliefs have different meanings in different belief networks. Depending on how much overlap there is between the belief networks, the words and beliefs might

---

[25] This is different from Descartes's problem about whether or not anything existed except his mind. With Reid and Putnam, we *assume* that other people exist independently of our own minds. Therefore, if we were trying to solve Descartes's problem, we would have assumed what we wanted to prove, a logical fallacy called "question-begging."

not be "commensurable" -- that is, similar enough in meaning that people with different belief networks are talking about the same things.[26]

So she is correct: We have no absolute guarantees of truth, let alone of transcendental truth. But it's neither a new insight nor unique to postmodernism. One of her predecessors in Yale's Philosophy Department, Brand Blanshard wrote in 1939 that:

> *"The road of history is so thick with discarded certainties as to suggest that any theory which distributes absolute guarantees is touched with charlatanism ... For all the ordinary purposes of life, coherence does not mean coherence with some inaccessible absolute, but with the system of present knowledge."*[27]

But postmodernism doesn't stop there. It goes on to a sweeping and unfounded conclusion: That because different belief systems support different truths, there is no objective truth *at all*. Instead, there are only people's beliefs and the systems ("discourses") that support them.

Apart from its obvious self-contradiction (the claim that "there is no objective truth" is objectively true), the denial of objective truth falls prey to the "jumping off a building" problem.

Suppose that you're looking for your cat. As before, you get down on your hands and knees to look under the bed. You don't see the cat, but in the shadows, you perceive a sweater that you thought you'd lost. "My missing sweater is under the bed:" That's your truth. You reach for the sweater, hear a loud hiss, and get your hand clawed. "I'm what's under the bed:" that's your cat's truth. In this case, your cat's truth is closer to objective reality than yours.

But think about that for a second. If there were no objective truth, only "my truth," "your truth," and "the cat's truth," then your belief about the sweater under the bed would be just as true as the cat's belief that it's not a sweater. You would reach for the sweater, and it would be there.

The same applies to jumping off a building. If the postmodernists' truth that "We won't die" were just as true as my truth that "Sorry, but

---

[26] See the section "Meaning for groups of people" in Chapter 11 of this book.
[27] Blanshard, B., *The Nature of Thought*, Vol. II, pp. 270-271.

you will," then they could step off the building and remain suspended in mid-air. I, on the other hand, would plummet to certain death because that's what "my truth" requires.

Those things don't happen. Even postmodernists know it when they're not making their confused arguments. Even if beliefs are true relative to their systems of belief, objective truth still exists independently of our belief systems. As we test our beliefs by comparing them with new evidence and analysis, our beliefs approach objective truth *asymptotically* -- *i.e*, they get closer and closer to reality but they can never quite reach it because our belief systems are finite and reality isn't.

Even if there are multiple narratives that work (*e.g.*, Ptolemaic vs. Copernican astronomy), we must *choose one* in order to think or do anything. It's like a restaurant menu. The menu might have many acceptable entrees, but to have dinner, you must choose one and not the others. After we choose one, we can compare it to new observations and modify it as needed to fit the new things we've learned about the world.

As different narratives evolve to fit more and more observations, they often start to look more and more alike. In economics, the "classical" approach uses the labor theory of value but had to be modified to recognize the influence of supply and demand. At the same time, the "neoclassical" approach uses supply and demand, but had to be modified to recognize the influence of labor costs and quality. The two approaches end up using different terminology to say increasingly similar things.

Postmodernism says (correctly) that the meanings of words are arbitrary. However, in order to use words, we must choose the specific meanings with which we intend to use them. A particular choice will be more or less helpful, depending on the situation. If we want directions to the Eiffel Tower, we should choose French words; to the Brandenburg Gate, German; likewise for other situations. If we change words' meanings each time we use them, they don't work.

Claim: Objective reality doesn't exist

The flip side of the postmodernists' claim that objective truth doesn't exist is their claim that objective reality doesn't exist.

There's a story about U.S. President Abraham Lincoln (1809-1865) that is probably apocryphal but still instructive. Lincoln was giving a speech and posed a question to his audience:

> *"If you call a tail a leg, then how many legs does a dog have?"*
>
> *"Five!" shouted several people from the audience.*
>
> *"No, it's got four," Lincoln replied. "Calling a tail a leg doesn't make it one."*

That quote from Lincoln, apocryphal or not, highlights the basic error of postmodernists' denial that there is any objective reality.

Like Dr. Pritchett in the quote that begins this chapter, they argue that "nothing is anything." In other words, things have no definite nature that circumscribes what they are and what they do. The opposing claim, "everything is something," is central to the idea of an objective reality that exists and is what it is regardless of our beliefs. As writer Neil deGrasse Tyson succinctly observed:

> *"The good thing about science is that it's true whether or not you believe in it."*

Postmodernism starts with a grain of truth. Our words, concepts, and beliefs *really do* influence how we perceive and talk about the world. However, it's a mistake to leap from that fact to conclude that objective reality doesn't exist, or what amounts to the same thing, that it changes depending on how we talk about it. Our success in life depends on how closely we align our beliefs and our goals with objective reality. If changing our beliefs and goals changed reality, then success would be guaranteed and we'd never fail.

The Sapir-Whorf hypothesis

The Sapir-Whorf hypothesis isn't part of the postmodernist canon, but it might as well be. It declares that "our worldview is determined by the structures of the particular language that we happen to speak."[28] In other words, *what* we see is determined by the words we use. It's not an implausible idea. Consider these pictures. On the left, you can see a fashionable young French woman with her face turned away from the viewer. On the right, you can see a black vase.

If you've seen those pictures before, you know they're a popular example of how we can perceive the same thing in different ways. If you shift your focus a little, the left-side picture shows an older woman, frowning as if she's been beaten down by life. The right-side picture shows the silhouettes of two people facing each other. Whether we describe the pictures in one way or another does seem to affect how we perceive them.

So does the left-side picture show a young woman or an older woman? Does the picture on the right show a vase or two faces? It

---

[28] Cameron, D., in Jackson, S. and Jones, J. (eds), *Contemporary Feminist Theories* (1998), p. 150.

depends on how you look at them. That gives support to the postmodernists' belief that there is no single, objective reality in the pictures and, by extension, in anything else we see.

But that conclusion goes too far. Notice that "What does the picture show?" omits an essential part of the question: "What does the picture show to observer X?" To a blind person, it shows nothing. To someone who had never seen a young woman or a vase, it might show something completely different. "Show" always means "show *to someone*," so it makes a hidden reference to someone's interpretation of what's being shown.

We can interpret each picture in a variety of ways, but that variety has limits. If I described the left-side picture as a vase and the right-side picture as a young woman, you probably couldn't see that no matter how hard you tried. Similarly, you can call a tail a leg if you wish, but a dog still can't walk on it.

The Sapir-Whorf hypothesis is one of those seemingly obvious ideas for which evidence is very hard to find. That's why, over 60 years after its formulation, it's still called a "hypothesis."

In spite of that, two grains of truth make the Sapir-Whorf hypothesis seem plausible. First, its "strong" formulation -- that our language *determines* what we perceive -- is clearly wrong. But Sapir-Whorf also has a weaker version: that our language *influences* what we perceive. That influence exerts itself in two ways.

First, language can make it easier or more difficult to express certain kinds of ideas. In George Orwell's novel *1984*, Newspeak makes it impossible to express ideas about freedom. A variation on the tactic is to require everyone to use terminology that assumes your viewpoint is correct. Canadian psychologist Jordan Peterson has become a minor celebrity by denouncing laws requiring everyone to use such terminology.

Second, belief networks associate words with thoughts and emotions to which they have little or no logical connection. Car commercials, for example, always urge you to "own" a car instead of urging you to "buy" it. "Owning" suggests thoughts of driving a new car and showing it to your friends, with pleasant emotions. "Buying" reminds you that you have to pay for the car. Likewise, car commercials have abandoned the older term "used car" (which reminds you that the car has been driven and possibly damaged) in favor of "pre-owned car" (which suggests that the car might have been sitting in someone's garage so it's in perfect condition). In politics, the smartest thing that gay-marriage advocates ever did was to re-brand their crusade as "marriage equality." Instead of suggesting that they wanted to impose a new institution, gay marriage, their new term implied that they only wanted equal rights. That put it over the top.

So the strong version of the Sapir-Whorf hypothesis is false, but the weaker version is true. The words we use don't control how we think, but they make it easier or more difficult and can influence our emotions. And none of it changes objective reality at all.

That being said, don't get so preoccupied with theory that you forget common sense. If a word annoys your spouse, friends, or co-workers, then don't use it unless there's a good reason that you must. It's not an infringement on your freedom if you choose to exercise courtesy and good judgment. That's one thing you can do to promote social harmony.

"Postmodernism" in 1000 BCE

One thing that postmodernism gets *right* is that our words, concepts, and beliefs play a role in "creating" the world *as we perceive it*. We think that a thing is real when it has a name and we can separate it from other things.

But postmodernists didn't invent the idea. It goes all the way back to the Book of Genesis. Do you remember the first verse of Genesis? It's usually translated "In the beginning, God created the heaven and the earth." The translation suggests that God created the world out of nothing. However, modern Biblical scholars think that this translation is more accurate:

"When God began to create heaven and earth — the earth being unformed and void, with darkness over the surface of the deep and a wind from God sweeping over the water ... "

That translation suggests that something "unformed and void" already existed before God's creative acts. Most people of the Ancient Near East believed that the pre-existing world was made of water, which is interesting because -- even though they didn't know it -- life on earth began in the oceans.

On this reading of Genesis, God didn't create the world out of nothing. Instead, He imposed order on chaos by separating things from each other and giving them names:

> *"God separated the light from the darkness. God called the light day, and the darkness He called night ... God made the firmament, and it separated the water which was below the firmament from the water which was above the firmament ... God called the firmament Sky ... God said, 'Let the water below the sky be gathered into one place, that the dry land may appear.' And it was so. God called the dry land Earth, and the gathering of waters He called Seas." (Genesis 1:4-1:10)*

The translation is also consistent with the other creation stories of the Ancient Near East. As John Walton observes in *Ancient Near Eastern Thought and the Old Testament*:

> *"In the ancient world something came into existence when it was separated out as a distinct entity, given a function, and given a name."*

Postmodernists claim that we create our realities by separating things and naming them -- just as in the first book of the Bible, whose origins date from 3,000 years ago. That idea of theirs is more premodern than postmodern.

Arguing against "essentialism"

Another way that postmodernists deny objective reality is to attack the idea of "essentialism," *i.e.*, the idea that anything has a specific nature that makes it what it is.

The attack on essentialism argues that even if everything is something, it can't be anything specific because most qualities are a matter of degree.

If you took Philosophy 101, you might recognize that argument as "the fallacy of the beard." A clean-shaven man has no (unshaven) whiskers on his face. So how many whiskers does it take to make a beard? One whisker isn't a beard. If you add one more, that's not a beard either. Add another, still no beard. At no point can you say that one more whisker makes it a beard. Thus, goes the argument, there's no such thing as being clean-shaven or having a beard. There's only a continuum of beardedness. The argument is disproven by the simple fact that there are clean-shaven and bearded people.

Zeno's beard

True nerds might recognize the fallacy of the beard as another version of Zeno's paradox. The Greek philosopher Zeno of Elea (490-430 BCE) argued that motion was impossible.

Suppose you want to walk across the room to pick up a book from a table. First, you must walk half the distance to the table. Then you must walk half the remaining distance, half of the rest, and so on. You must take an infinite number of steps to get to the table, so you never arrive at your destination. Zeno's paradox is disproven by the fact that you can walk across the room to pick up a book, just as the fallacy of the beard is disproven by the existence of clean-shaven and bearded people.

Claim: Everything is about power

Postmodernists see almost everything in terms of power. In their view, things like scientific facts and voluntary cooperation are just smokescreens that hide exploitation of some social groups by other social groups.

In a kind of grumpy, unrealistic way, their claim is true, even though they don't believe in truth. No matter how a society is organized, some people will be objectively worse off than other people, and some people will at least *feel* that they are even if they're not.

In addition, every society must explain how and why it's organized in the way that it is. Since every society will have some groups that are better or worse off, then its self-explanation can always be portrayed negatively as an apologetic for "oppressing" some groups. But that applies to every human society that has ever existed or ever will exist. It assumes the possibility of an alternative human society that has no imperfections or complaints. Those don't exist.

Notice that postmodernists' viewpoint is a *philosophical story*. It's a way of interpreting the world and it is in itself neither true nor false. That said, it leads to interpretations that are often beside the point, unhelpful, and downright silly.

Postmodernist luminary Jean-Francis Lyotard, in his book *The Postmodern Condition*, stated frankly his view about the unimportance of truth as compared to power. In Chapter 2, he said that his own analysis "makes no claims of being original, or even true:"

> *"Our hypotheses, therefore, should not be accorded predictive value in relation to reality, but strategic value in relation to [its effects on public power and civil institutions]."*

Equally odd is anthropologist Emily Martin's claim in her article "The Egg and the Sperm" that biological explanations of how human eggs are fertilized:

> *"... imply not only that female biological processes are less worthy than their male counterparts but also that women are less worthy than men."*

Note that neither statement disputes any scientific facts: they just don't like what science says. Of course, odd interpretations of scientific facts do not make a philosophical story false. But they do make it less plausible.

Such claims dovetail with arguments by other postmodernists that since we can use reason to understand and work with ("dominate") nature, rationality is just a tool for dominating *people*. That kind of argument is called a "non-sequitur," meaning its conclusion does not follow from its premises. Its only connection is that you can use the word "dominate" (in different senses) for controlling nature and for coercing people. It's typical of the free-association wordplay that postmodernists offer as a substitute for logical argument.

Why the obsession with power?

What's really behind the postmodernist obsession with power? As usual, there's a grain of truth, baked up into a warehouse full of junk-food snack cakes. You can take almost any description of anything and turn it into a story about how it oppresses someone. Any human interaction can be portrayed as exploitation. But does it make sense to do it? That depends on the situation.

For example, suppose that you're looking for a car. Your neighbor offers to sell you his old car for $5,000. It's more than you want to pay: you'd prefer to get the car for nothing. It's less than your neighbor wants to get: he'd prefer to sell the car for a million dollars. However, after a bit of obligatory haggling, you both agree on the price of $5,000.

On the surface, it looks like a voluntary exchange in which both parties benefit. You could choose not to buy the car, and your neighbor could choose not to sell it. Each of you makes a free choice because you value what you *get* more than what you *give*.

Postmodernists aren't buying any of it: the story, that is, not the car. On their view, the story about voluntary exchange is a "discourse" that hides something nefarious. Somebody must be exploiting somebody because of capitalism, or privilege, or something else. They would want to "interrogate" the situation to find the hidden oppression.

It turns out that you need the car to get to your new job, which starts tomorrow. You don't have time to look around for a better deal. If you have the money, you pretty much have to accept the price that your neighbor offers. Your neighbor is exploiting you to get more money for the car. At the same time, your new salary isn't as high as you'd like. Your new employer is exploiting your need for a job to make you work for less money than you'd like.

On the other hand, your neighbor's wife was just taken to the hospital for emergency surgery. The surgery isn't even over yet, but the bill is already astronomical. Your neighbor desperately needs to get some money. Your new job is at a startup company that is cash-poor. Its founder isn't taking a salary and bought most of the equipment with his personal credit cards. So you are exploiting your neighbor's tragic situation to pay less money, while exploiting your boss's risky business venture to get more money.

The conclusion is simple: if *everything* is exploitation, then *nothing* is exploitation. Postmodernists apply the word so widely and promiscuously that they empty it of meaning. Completely ordinary, wholesome, and necessary human interactions are supposedly all about power and exploitation. Science is a conspiracy to keep down [insert name of oppressed group]. Such reasoning might be politically appealing to its proponents, but it's an inaccurate and unwise guide to action.

Knowledge approaches absolute truth

If objective truth exists but we can never reach it, how do we even know it's there?

First, it helps to distinguish between *absolute* truth, which we can never reach, and *objective* truth, which we *can* reach. They're very different.

Absolute truth cannot be relative to any network of beliefs or set of circumstances. No matter what you assume, what concepts you use, or what situation you're in, it applies and it's true. Otherwise, it's only true *relative* to those factors. Absolute truth needs to cover everything, so it requires infinite knowledge -- which we never have.

Objective truth, as we defined it earlier in the chapter, is truth that doesn't depend on any individual person's set of beliefs. Whether or not you believe it, the speed of light is 186,282 miles per second. A meter is 39.37 inches long. If you step off the top of a tall building, you'll almost certainly die unless Superman swoops in to catch you. And Superman doesn't exist even if you believe that he does, so you would be wise not to step off any tall buildings.

Knowledge = belief divided by ignorance

$$Knowledge = \frac{Belief}{Ignorance}$$

Here's a useful metaphor: a metaphor, not a definition. Think of knowledge as justified belief divided by ignorance: for math nerds, that's $K = B/I$. Ignorance includes both things we don't know and things we believe that aren't objectively true. Then several things can happen:

- As we use observation and reasoning, we remove items of ignorance from I and move them to B. B gets bigger and I gets smaller, so B/I also gets bigger and our knowledge expands.

- If we don't get more ignorant, which has happened occasionally in history, then I either decreases or stays the same. Our knowledge (B/I) either increases or stays the same.

Let's look at a simplified example of how that metaphor might work. Suppose that you hold three justified beliefs:

- Dogs exist.

- Dogs are domesticated carnivorous mammals of the biological species *canis familiaris* that bark, chase cars, and help the Scooby-Doo gang solve mysteries.

- A dog can walk on its legs.

You also hold one false belief ("A tail is a leg"), and there are 2,999 things of which you're unaware. The false belief is grouped with the things of which you're unaware, so you have 3,000 items of ignorance: I = 3,000. Then K (your knowledge) = 3 divided by 3,000 = 0.001, or one-thousandth.

Suppose you do 296 experiments and can never get a dog to use its tail as a leg. Therefore, you decide that your belief "A tail is a leg" is false. You change it to "A tail is not a leg" and move it to the "justified beliefs" group with the 296 beliefs from your experiments. Your knowledge has grown from 3 divided by 3,000 = 0.001 to 300 divided by 2,999 = about 0.1. Quite an increase.

Can the progress go on forever, until we have infinite knowledge and absolute truth? No. There are two reasons. First, we are finite beings with finite intellectual capacities. We cannot achieve infinite knowledge. Second, and I grant it's kind of a math nerd thing, infinite knowledge means we have zero ignorance:

$K = infinity / zero$

and we can't divide by zero. Division doesn't work if we do.[29]

In mathematics, knowledge would be called an "asymptotic function." Our knowledge approaches a limiting value -- in this case, absolute truth -- but it never gets there and it never *can* get there. What we can get are increasingly accurate and comprehensive approximations for absolute truth.

Ignorance can never be zero, but as we learn more and more, it gets closer to zero. As that happens, our knowledge gets closer and closer to reality but it never quite gets there. If it gets close enough for the purpose at hand (that is, if it's a fully or partly objective story instead of a purely subjective story), then it's a good, true story. It's true enough for now, even if we might find a truer story tomorrow.

Situations and purposes with "one truth"

It often makes sense to act as if there is "only one truth." In many standard situations, everyone involved shares the same purpose and the same assumptions for achieving it. Those conditions are so important that they bear repeating. The people involved must share:

- The same purpose, and
- The same assumptions for achieving it.

It's also important for the subject under discussion to have practical implications that can be checked to prove or disprove beliefs about it. Some disagreements are only different ways of interpreting facts that are not themselves in dispute. They are not genuine

---

[29] See "Division by Zero" at http://mathworld.wolfram.com/DivisionbyZero.html.

disagreements, but simply alternative ways of looking at or feeling about the world. We might adopt or change our views on them for emotional, personal, or group reasons, but logical arguments are irrelevant. For subjects with practical implications, however, logic and evidence are relevant.

For example, in a scientific laboratory, we want to discover useful facts about the physical universe. Part of what makes it work is that everyone involved defines the physical universe roughly as "what we can study with the methods of physical science." So they all have the same purpose, accept the same methods, and make the same assumptions about the things they are studying.

Similarly, students in an art history class often share assumptions about what they're studying and what's relevant to it. How did Van Gogh's mental illness affect his style of painting? How did he feel when he painted "Starry Night"? Such questions are irrelevant in physical science: "How did Carl Anderson feel when he discovered the positron?" Nobody cares. That information is not relevant in physical science, but it's very relevant in art history.

Most situations in life are fairly common: Getting to work. Eating lunch. Having a romantic talk with your spouse. Reassuring your child by checking under the bed to make sure there are no monsters lurking.

Just like the situations themselves, the purposes and belief systems we use in them are standard, especially in the same society and social group. They're standard because they've worked for us in those situations in the past, and we don't need to rethink them every time. Yes, the truths we use in such situations are relative and not absolute. Usually, however, it serves no purpose to worry about such things. In principle, truth is relative. In practice, most situations work fine if we assume that the particular truth we're using is absolute -- even though it isn't.

Four seductive fallacies of postmodernism

Certain errors are so common that they merit at least a brief mention. They creep into most debates about social policy and related topics.

They are the moralistic fallacy, the naturalistic fallacy, the rationalistic fallacy, and the existentialist fallacy:

- **Fallacy: morality determines reality.** This fallacy (the moralistic fallacy) assumes that whatever seems morally desirable must be true. If something is undesirable, it must be false. This fallacy is most often committed by the political left.

- **Fallacy: reality determines morality.** This fallacy (the naturalistic fallacy[30]) assumes that whatever seems true must be moral. This fallacy is most often committed by the political right.

- **Fallacy: if it seems to make sense, it's true.** This fallacy (the rationalistic fallacy) assumes that whatever seems to make sense must be true, even if there's no evidence for it. This fallacy is most often committed by college students debating in the dormitory late at night, but many others commit it as well. A joke says if you show economists that something works in practice, they object: "Yes, but does it work in theory?"[31]

- **Fallacy: if you want it to be true, then it is.** This fallacy (the existentialist fallacy) assumes that reality is whatever you want it to be. It is loosely suggested by the philosophy of existentialism, which argues that people must define the meaning of their own lives. It's also a kind of "get out of jail free" card to justify the other fallacies. For example, it enables 52-

---

[30] In academic philosophy, the naturalistic fallacy also means either trying to define moral ideas in terms of non-moral ideas, or trying to deduce moral beliefs from factual beliefs. The versions of the fallacy are obviously related.

[31] Libertarian economist Murray Rothbard gives an admirably candid example of the fallacy in paragraph 2 of his article, "In Defense of Extreme Apriorism," which is available on the web. He argues that because they seem to make sense, his economic analyses are "absolutely true" and "there is consequently no need for empirical testing." It was originally published in *The Southern Economic Journal*, January 1957.

year-old men to claim that they are six-year-old girls and make everyone else pretend to believe it.[32]

When argument can make a difference

If all the truth we can know is relative to foundational concepts and descriptions, then is there any point in arguing about it? If Joe believes in socialism but Jim believes in capitalism, should they agree to disagree, or can they have a reasonable argument in which one of them might convince the other – at least on some points?

The crucial factor is whether or not they share enough concepts, assumptions, and goals for there to be "one truth" that both will accept. Within the same society or civilization, that's very often the case. Even if they disagree about matters of substance, similar people think in similar ways and have similar goals. As Cambridge philosopher and two-time Nobel laureate Bertrand Russell observed:

"Reliance upon reason assumes a certain community of interest between oneself and one's audience. It is true that Mrs. Bond tried it on her ducks when she cried, 'come and be killed, for you must be stuffed and my customers filled'; but in general the appeal to reason is thought ineffective with those whom we mean to devour. Those who believe in eating meat do not attempt to find arguments that would seem valid to a sheep ..."[33]

For example, both Socialist Joe and Capitalist Jim want their society to be fair and prosperous, its citizens to be safe and happy. They disagree about how to accomplish those goals, but both of them accept facts of economics and political science as relevant to their argument. If both of them are more committed to their positive goals than to competitively "winning" the argument, then the facts can lead them to change their opinions. They compare their beliefs with observed facts that they both accept.

They probably also disagree about the meaning of fairness. Resolving that disagreement would require a deeper dive into their

---

[32] Transgender woman leaves wife and 7 kids to live as a 6-year-old girl," *New York Daily News*, Dec. 12, 2015.
[33] "The Ancestry of Fascism," *In Praise of Idleness*, p. 67.

assumptions and moral feelings, but it's at least possible. Each would ask the other to imagine situations in which fairness is relevant, and then to compare his beliefs with his feelings about the example. If Joe or Jim finds that his idea of fairness conflicts with his feelings about some situations, then he'll be more open to changing his mind about it.

Rational disagreement and reasonable argument are possible: they're just difficult. Arguments about morals, politics, and social policies – when reasonable – usually involve these moves:

- Each side starts with its own opinion, call them X and Y.

- Each side argues that the other opinion is inconsistent either with:

    ✓ Factual beliefs on which they agree, or

    ✓ Moral feelings or beliefs on which they agree.

- If one side can convince the other side that its opinion X or Y is inconsistent with agreed-upon factual or moral beliefs, then the other side might change its opinion.

People aren't always rational, but they *can* be if they don't feel threatened or overwhelmed by emotion. A crucial part of productive argument is to stay focused on facts and issues, making it very clear that the argument is not about the people involved. The writer Dale Carnegie offered some wise advice in his best-selling book *How to Win Friends and Influence People*:

> *"A man convinced against his will*
> *Is of the same opinion still."*

Chapter 15:
Why Be Tolerant?

"The first thing to learn in intercourse with others is non-interference with their own peculiar ways of being happy, provided those ways do not assume to interfere by violence with ours ... To dogmatize about them in each other is the root of most human injustices and cruelties, and the trait in human character most likely to make the angels weep."

-- William James

IN EARLIER CHAPTERS, WE LOOKED AT A LOT OF FACTS: about belief, history, biology, religion, meaning, and truth. But facts don't do much good unless we can apply them to improving ourselves, our societies, and our world.

The changes we can make in our societies, in our religions, and even in our own attitudes are limited by the facts of human nature. To have even partial success -- and *partial* success is the best we're going to get -- we must know what we're up against. What is the nature that we have to obey in order to command such a result? What are the facts we must overcome?

We've seen that biological creatures tend to trust, help, and cooperate with those they perceive as their genetic relatives. The degree of such trust, help, and cooperation is in proportion to the nearness of the perceived relation. Genetic competitors tend to provoke the opposite reaction: suspicion, hostility, and attack. Human beings are unique among animal species in that we use not only the same cues as most other animals, but also use cues based on our intellectual and social behaviors -- that is, on our beliefs, languages, traditions, and ritual practices.

As people of goodwill, we want to "command" a goal that is both simple and seemingly impossible: A world of peace. An end to hatred and bloodshed. A cessation of injustice.

In our past efforts to achieve that goal, we've tried ignoring nature or pretending it's something other than what it plainly is.

We've cherry-picked stories about peaceful encounters between people from different groups: usually people who were highly educated, culturally assimilated, and morally pacifistic. We've argued that what applies to a few very unusual people, some of the time, applies to people in general, all of the time. We've seen the results: from Mogadishu, Paris, London, and Ferguson. The results are unacceptable. We have to do better. We *can* do better.

Doing better requires us to answer two questions:

- Why should we be tolerant of beliefs that conflict with our own beliefs?

- How can we build societies that maximize tolerance of different groups and beliefs?

The "why" question is more important than you might think. It's not obvious that we should tolerate beliefs we don't like. Throughout history, most people haven't. Today, most people don't. If we don't know why we should be tolerant, then as soon as we hit a difficulty, our kin selection instincts will kick in and we'll be tempted to start attacking each other again.

The "how" question's importance is clearer. It doesn't do us any good to seek tolerance if we have no idea how to achieve it. If the answer were obvious to everyone, we would have done it by now. The answer isn't rocket science: from reading this book, you know a lot of it already. But we need to transform all that information into action plans to make it happen.

This chapter reviews what we know about why to be tolerant. The next chapter applies what we've learned to show how we can build tolerant societies.

What is tolerance?

Homogeneous societies like 2017 Japan (98.5 percent ethnic Japanese), 2017 China (91.6 percent Han Chinese), and 1965 America (88 percent European-American) have it pretty easy. The vast majority of people tend to perceive others, often accurately, as their genetic kin. They agree about language, customs, religion, culture, and all the important issues of life. They still have conflict, but the majority's overwhelming dominance keeps it at a lower level than it otherwise would be. The resulting social peace will have flaws but will benefit most people.

In a diverse society, on the other hand, tolerance is essential for any social peace at all. It requires at least three things:

- Letting other people live and believe as they wish, as long as they don't harm us or innocent third parties by violence, coercion, or fraud.

- Listening to other people's viewpoints, considering the merits of their arguments, and showing respect for them as people even if we think they're wrong.

- Using violence or coercion only as a last resort, and:
  - ✓ After we have understood and fairly considered objections to our ideas and plans;
  - ✓ Only when the harm avoided by violence far exceeds the harm done by it;
  - ✓ With respect for the costs, feelings, and dignity of people attacked or coerced;
  - ✓ Through public, impersonal, and predictable legal processes wherever possible.

Tolerance isn't the same thing as approval. In fact, if we approve of something, tolerance doesn't make any sense. We don't "tolerate" it if our children get good grades in school, or if a stranger performs an act of kindness. We can only tolerate things we don't like.

Tolerance is also not the same as active support. Requiring people to say or do things that support what they disapprove is intolerant of their right to live and believe as they wish without harming others. Zealots are often confused about that point.

Tolerance has limits

Tolerance does not mean that we must tolerate *everything*, especially if someone is harming other people by violence, coercion, or fraud (or abuse in the case of children). That's the point of the proviso to let others live as they wish *as long as* they don't harm us or innocent third parties.

Sir Charles Napier (1782-1853) told a relevant story about his experience as a British officer in India.

When he and his soldiers arrived at a village, they found the locals preparing to burn a widow alive on her late husband's funeral pyre. The village elders explained that it was their traditional custom to do so. Napier listened respectfully, then replied:

> "Be it so. This burning of widows is your custom; prepare the funeral pile. But my nation has also a custom. When men burn women alive we hang them, and confiscate all their property. My carpenters shall therefore erect gibbets on which to hang all concerned when the widow is consumed. Let us all act according to national customs."[34]

The widow was set free. Today, we might make a similar argument about female genital mutilation (FGM) and other practices of some non-Western migrants in Western countries.

And some limits are conventional

Behavior that clearly harms people is an easy case. Under normal circumstances, it should not be tolerated.

---

[34] Napier, W. (1851), p. 35.

But societies, social groups, and institutions often refuse to tolerate some relatively harmless behavior. Is such intolerance always illegitimate?

It depends on the situation.

All societies, groups, and so forth have customary behaviors that members see as "just how we do things." The obvious function of such behaviors is to distinguish members of the group from non-members. Following the customs also shows respect for the group and its members, since it reinforces their feeling of personal and group security. It makes daily life:

- **Predictable:** Customs enable members to predict how other people will behave in standard situations. That smooths interactions and prevents misunderstanding.

- **Reflective:** Customs reflect the attitudes and beliefs of the group based on its history, purposes, and personalities.

- **Confirming:** Customs confirm the validity of group members' attitudes and beliefs, thereby giving them psychological support and tending to increase their happiness.

- **Unifying:** Customs unify the group by mandating shared behaviors, giving group members visible signs of their shared values and (real or imagined) genetic kinship.

For example, it's illegal almost everywhere in America to walk naked on a city street. It harms no one in any material way, but it makes people uncomfortable because it conflicts with long-established traditions about wearing clothes in public. To flout that convention is to show lack of respect for the society and its people.

In his famous book *On Liberty* (1859), John Stuart Mill identifies the difficult tradeoffs that any society must make between tolerance and conformity:

> *"All that makes life valuable to anyone, depends on the enforcement of restraints upon the actions of other people. Some rules of conduct must be imposed, by law in the first place, and by opinion on many things which are not fit subjects for the operation of law."*

Refusing to behave in customary ways harms the integrity of the group. If we think it's good for the group to continue, then it must be able to enforce such customs by legal or social sanctions. Public nakedness gets you a ticket or a night in jail. Boorish language in inappropriate contexts gets you scolded or shunned.

Because such customs are somewhat arbitrary, they vary between societies and groups. What also varies is the degree to which the societies and groups tolerate deviations. If a custom has social benefits, intolerance of deviation is justified by the custom's benefits. If a custom is neutral or slightly harmful, intolerance of deviation makes less sense.

A fine point: intolerance as the least evil alternative

Our presumption should always be against intolerance, but in some situations, moderate intolerance might be the least harmful of the available choices. A medical analogy is helpful.

In the 18th century, the disease of smallpox was widespread, killing about 30 percent of its victims. However, farm laborers who worked with cows often contracted the disease of cowpox, similar to smallpox but much less harmful. People who'd had cowpox were immune to smallpox. Using pus from infected cows, British physician Edward Jenner (1749-1823) created a vaccine that gave people a mild case of cowpox but made them immune to smallpox. In effect, he gave them a *less* serious illness that protected them from getting a *more* serious illness. That's not an example of intolerance, but it shows how lesser evils can "immunize" people against greater evils.

All societies throughout history have seemed to need scapegoat groups toward which members of the majority can direct the inevitable anger and frustration of their own lives. Sometimes the scapegoats are religious, sometimes ethnic, sometimes chosen by practices such as the use of forbidden drugs. Attempts to create a perfect society without injustice or persecution have ended with even more of the evils they hoped to eliminate, such as the terror and mass slaughter of the French, Russian, and Chinese revolutions.

History supports Voltaire's famous advice: "The perfect is the enemy of the good." Pursuit of a perfect society not only creates worse problems: it also prevents us from embracing practical but imperfect solutions that might be the best we can achieve. Human beings are imperfect, and we can never build a perfect society with imperfect people. Our choice is not between perfect and imperfect, but between the less harmful and the more harmful imperfect.

We need to consider the possibility that some cases of intolerance act as social safety valves. Though evil, they might provide a less destructive social catharsis than the alternatives, just as Jenner showed that cowpox protected people from smallpox. Our presumption must always be against intolerance, but in a small number of cases, it might be our least-evil choice.

Tolerance recognizes our own self-interest

Ayn Rand's novel *Atlas Shrugged* is notoriously a paean to the virtue of selfishness. Of course, it's only "notorious" if you disagree with her premise that selfishness is a good thing.

In fairness, Rand (née Aliza Rosenbaum, born in Russia under Communism) is not talking about mindless selfishness on the order of "Jimmy grabs Sally's ice cream cone because he wants it." She emphasizes that she's talking about *rational* selfishness, which is a different thing. What is really in our self-interest, if we think about it instead of acting impulsively?

One little-noticed feature of *Atlas Shrugged* (and of Rand's earlier novel, *The Fountainhead*) is that its heroes often do things most people would consider unselfish. Before they do, however, the heroes usually make a five-page speech about how what they're doing is *really* in their self-interest even though it seems unselfish. When one character sacrifices his life for another, for example, it's because upholding justice is in his own interest -- even if he gets killed doing it. The routine becomes almost comical: Rand wants her heroes to do heroic things but only for selfish reasons. Their explanations of why their heroism is selfish sometimes get a little farfetched.

That being said, a reasonable person might think that *everyone's* welfare matters. That includes both other people and ourselves. As a result, it's sometimes justified to act in our own interest, sometimes in the interest of other people, and sometimes in the interest of both.

Tolerance falls into the final category: It's in *everyone's* rational self-interest to live in a tolerant society, even if we sometimes have to put up with things and ideas we don't like. As noted in the previous section, if we like things, we don't need to tolerate them: we support them. At the same time, other people who don't like them tolerate *us*.

Tolerance and traffic laws

In some ways, the case for tolerance is the same as the case for traffic laws.

Suppose that it's 8:45pm and you're driving to meet a friend at a coffee shop. The shop closes at 9pm. You arrive at an intersection that has a stop sign. There's no traffic. You looked. There's no police car around. You looked twice. Do you stop for the stop sign, or just ignore it?

If you're like most of us, you're not sure. There's no risk that you'll cause an accident or get a ticket. What's the harm? You're running late. You need to get to the coffee shop before 9pm.

But it might bother you a little. You'd be breaking the law: not an unjust law, but a legitimate law that was enacted for the public good.

Act utilitarianism versus rule utilitarianism

Your moral uneasiness reflects the difference between two theories of morality: act utilitarianism and rule utilitarianism.

Utilitarianism says that you should try to produce the greatest good for the greatest number of people.[35] But what's the most effective way to do that?

---

[35] "Which people count?" is a question that utilitarianism itself doesn't answer. Many political arguments result from answering it in different ways.

Act utilitarianism says that in each situation, you should act in a way that produces the greatest good. If you're an act utilitarian, you ignore the stop sign and drive past it.

Rule utilitarianism says that in each situation, you should act *according to a rule* that produces the greatest good if everyone follows it. If you're a rule utilitarian, you stop for the stop sign. If everyone follows the rules (traffic laws), then there will be fewer automobile accidents.

Politeness is another example. When I walked out of the coffee shop this morning with a briefcase in one hand and a paper cup of coffee in the other, the person in front of me held the door for me. From an act-utilitarian viewpoint, his action produced no net benefit: I got out a little faster and he got out a little slower. But from a rule-utilitarian viewpoint, his action promoted social harmony by showing consideration for another person. He increased the probability not only that I would hold the door for others in similar situations, but that I would treat others with consideration for their welfare and happiness.

When we tolerate other people's behavior or beliefs that we dislike, we do it as rule utilitarians. We accept a little discomfort in the current situation in order to sustain a much greater good: a society where other people tolerate our and each other's beliefs and behaviors that they dislike.

If we want other people to tolerate our beliefs and ways of living, we should start by tolerating theirs, and by promoting tolerance as an important social value. It's in our self-interest to do so.

Tolerating risks

Risk might seem unrelated to tolerance, but it's a tricky problem. The problem is tricky because there's no provable, cookie-cutter answer that applies to everyone and every society.

Every society tolerates some risks and prohibits others. Where they differ is in the risks they tolerate and the risks they prohibit.

For example, in modern America, driving while drunk is against the law. A drunk driver might not harm anyone, but has a greater *risk* of harming someone. Therefore, drunk driving is illegal, and most states outlawed it in the early 20th century. Since the 1980s, when people's perception of the risk has intensified, the legal penalties for drunk driving have become more severe.

That's a clear example of risk. But then we get into murkier issues of belief and free speech. Those are more clearly connected to tolerance.

For example, some college students believe it's too risky to tolerate professors or campus speakers who say things with which they disagree. Such speech makes them "feel unsafe." They believe that violent protest, even violent attacks on speakers and college officials, are justified by the risks of allowing dissent. They don't want to tolerate any ideas they dislike.

It's easy to mock such people as "snowflakes." Their alleged fears have no basis in reality and most of their information – to the extent that they have any – is wrong. However, their argument doesn't differ logically from the argument against drunk driving. Risk is hard to quantify. People's anxiety about risk is subjective. And as Nobel laureate physicist Niels Bohr said, "Prediction is difficult, especially about the future."

Beware of our own psychology

When we dislike things, our minds automatically start looking for reasons to ban them. If an activity doesn't do any harm, we'll unconsciously make up some harm to justify banning it.

And if there really *are* risks of harm, we tend to exaggerate the risks of things we don't like and minimize the risks of things we do like. The 1936 movie "Reefer Madness," which suggests that smoking marijuana turns people into homicidal maniacs, is a famous example. It became a cult classic movie (taken as comedy) because its message about risk was so ludicrously exaggerated.

The things we want to ban are sometimes bad, sometimes debatable, but the main thing is that we just don't like them. Our primary motivation is often not logical, but psychological.

For those reasons, tolerance should be our default attitude toward people, beliefs, and behavior. The burden of proof is on those who want to ban them. Sometimes, the proof is clear. But other times, there isn't any proof of danger: there's only hostility masquerading as self-defense.

Tolerance recognizes the reasons for difference

We differ from each other in many ways: appearance, nationality, language, religion, moral beliefs, and personality are just a few examples. Any of those differences can trigger our kin selection instincts to see other people as genetic competitors who must be either thwarted or destroyed.

For lower animals, that's the end of the story: *Fight or flight.* But we have an ability that lower animals don't have: We can think. We can understand the reasons for our differences. If the differences really mean a "fight or flight" situation, then we can deal with it. But if they're harmless or nearly so, we can reframe them intellectually so we see them for what they *are* instead of what our animal instincts fear they *might* be.

Differences in appearance

People look different for many reasons. In the United States, people tend to obsess about race, but it's only one of many reasons why people look different.

Here's a personal example: I'm not a big fan of tattoos and body piercings, but some people are. One of my friends and colleagues has tattoos all the way up both arms, but he's as smart and sane a person as you'll ever meet. A barista at the local Starbucks has so many tattoos and piercings, including face piercings, that I can barely stand to look at her. Do I think she's a bad person? Of course not. But there's an "ick factor," an involuntary reaction of disgust at her appearance. To deal with the barista, giving her the courtesy she deserves as a human being, I override my ick factor, carefully controlling my voice, expressions, and behavior. That takes concentration and causes stress.

Not all differences in appearance provoke disgust, which makes us avoid people who are disfigured by disease and substances that make us sick, "as an unconscious defense against biological contamination."[36] Other appearance differences provoke hostility to perceived genetic competitors. If you add up the hundreds of millions of such encounters every day, you can see the emotional load on society from some (though obviously not all) kinds of difference in appearance. At best, they cause tension. At worst, they provoke violence.

Almost any difference can hook people's kin selection instincts. Racial appearance plays a role in social conflict, but mainly because it's a clearly visible marker of genetic difference. It's the kind of difference that triggers our kin selection instincts to see people of other races as genetic competitors. Neither the difference nor our instinctive reaction is likely to change. What we *can* change, however, is how we respond to those facts. We should remember that just as we sometimes react negatively to others' unfamiliar or unconventional appearance, they react the same way to our appearance. Usually, no one involved is a villain; we're just human.

Tolerance reflects our commitment to treat people as individuals, with their own individual lives, thoughts, and human dignity, rather than as mere symbols of one group or another.

Differences in belief

Differences in belief affect our appearance and behavior, including our verbal behavior when we declare our support for our beliefs. All of that tends to hook our kin selection instincts to perceive others as genetic competitors.

Even people who know better – *i.e.*, most of us – often interpret differences in belief as a threat and as an indication of moral evil. Occasionally it's true, but usually it isn't.

If someone says that he believes morality is nonsense and that he's entitled to do whatever he wants, that really *is* a warning sign: look up "Leopold and Loeb." But if someone merely says, for instance, "We

---

[36] Steven Pinker, *The Better Angels of Our Nature*, p. 71.

should permit / outlaw abortion," he or she most likely believes it because of:

- A particular foundational description of human beings and the world, such as traditional religion or contemporary secularism.

- Dominant peer group beliefs one way or the other. Living in the wealthier areas of Los Angeles tends to make people see things one way, while living in middle-class areas of Indianapolis tends to make them see things differently.

- Personal experiences, such as knowing a rape victim or seeing an ultrasound of a baby.

What we learn *first* has an especially strong effect on our subsequent beliefs. We interpret new information in terms of what we already believe. We try to fit it into our existing stock of concepts and test its truth partly by comparing it with our existing beliefs. Regardless of the content of our beliefs, we all tend to reason about them in the same ways. And relative to our own foundational descriptions of the world, our conflicting beliefs can all be true.

Finally, our economic interests play a role in forming our beliefs. We don't have to go as far as the 19th-century political economist Karl Marx, who thought that society's material "means of production" determined our beliefs. However, American writer Upton Sinclair struck the right balance when he wrote that:

"It's difficult to get a man to understand something when his salary depends on his not understanding it."

Tolerance recognizes our own limitations

Each of us has a viewpoint limited by our knowledge, experience, biases, and emotions. We can be wrong for the same reasons as other people. If we're reasonably self-aware, we know that we *have* been wrong about many things in the past, and that we're almost certainly wrong about some things now.

That kind of awareness is discouraged by political and moral debates that reward screaming more than logic, self-righteousness more than evidence. When our emotions are enraged, our intelligence tends to go out the window. We stop trying to find the truth and start trying to find an advantage over the people with whom we disagree.

That's not because we're bad people. It's because we're people. We're not passionless robots. Like most things, being human is simultaneously a blessing and -- well, if not a curse, at least a challenge.

When we are tempted by intolerance, to force other people to act or believe as we do, we should always stop and ask: "Could I be wrong?" If we can't give an answer that would satisfy someone who doesn't *already* agree with us, we should err on the side of tolerance.

Welcoming disagreement with our beliefs

Being tolerant of other people's beliefs isn't just a matter of being nice. It's very practical.

As thoughtful people, we recognize that some of our beliefs are wrong. But which ones? How are they wrong? And if they're wrong, then what's right?

The best way to find out is to tolerate disagreement with our beliefs. In fact, we shouldn't just tolerate it: we should *welcome* it. And we should listen to disagreement as fairly as we can.

If someone who disagrees with us proves that our beliefs are illogical, unsupported by evidence, or contradicted by the facts, then he or she has *done us a favor*. As a result, we can replace the incorrect belief with a more correct belief. We understand the world better.

On the other hand, if the other person fails to disprove our belief, that's indirect confirmation that our belief is correct as it stands. We can have more confidence in it.

We make a great mistake if we invest too much of our egos in "always being right." An old co-worker of mine named Tony had worked at Microsoft and was one of the smartest people I've met. Unfortunately, his abrasive personality eventually got him fired. That bothered me, because I'd rather work with abrasive smart people than friendly stupid people.

Tony and I once got into a fairly heated political argument. At the end, it was pretty clear that he was right and I was wrong. Later that week, I bought him lunch. He was surprised because he thought I'd be angry that he'd proven me wrong. I told him exactly what I told you: He had done me a favor by correcting a false belief of mine.

If I had refused to talk to Tony because we disagreed, or if I'd listened to him only with the goal of refuting what he said, I would still hold that mistaken belief.

In a serious argument, as opposed to a political shouting match, the only way to "win" is to *find out the truth*. Tolerance of disagreement is an essential step toward finding it.[37]

The error of Whig history

Most people haven't heard of Whig history, but they believe in it.

The term was coined by Cambridge University historian Herbert Butterfield in a 1931 book *The Whig Interpretation of History*. It's the view that history is inevitably progress, so later eras are always more enlightened than earlier ones.

To some degree, we are all the intellectual prisoners of our own era. The ancient Israelites, arguably among the most enlightened people of their time, slaughtered the Canaanites without mercy. Aristotle considered women to be on about the same level as horses. Spartacus led a slave revolt but didn't oppose slavery on principle; he just didn't want to be a slave himself. A belief that our own time is uniquely wise and morally advanced is a prescription for intolerance.

Knowing history partly frees us from the prison of our era. Ignorance makes us more inclined to believe that history is a steady upward march from barbarism to sophistication. It's not.

Indoor plumbing, antibiotics, printed books, ebooks, and cell phones are undeniable advances, but they are only technological advances. They change the *conditions* in which we live, but not human nature. And it's human nature that shapes society, using whatever technologies are available.

---

[37] Recall from Chapter 13 that even though all the truth we know is relative, it can be treated as "absolute" in standard situations where people share the same goals and enough common assumptions to make argument possible.

People can't see parallels between the United States and the Roman Empire if they know little about the former and nothing about the latter. They can't know that exactly the same political problems and moral dilemmas we face today were already debated, and sometimes solved, in Ancient Athens, Rome, England, and in the early years of the United States. They can't know if 1940s America was better or worse than it is in 2018 because they know hardly anything about either.

Americans in 2018 have socialist Senator Bernie Sanders and the Occupy movement to call for better treatment of the poor. Ancient Romans had the Tribunes of the Plebs (government officials who could veto laws that hurt the poor) and "the struggle of the orders"[38] between the Patricians (the old-money rich) and the Plebians (the working class). The basics don't change; only the details and the technology do.

Of course, sometimes the details and the technology *are* significant. Even if "the poor are always with us," as Jesus advised, technology has reduced extreme poverty all over the world. The poor still have less than the rich, but a much smaller percentage are so poor that they can barely stay alive. And the advent of a computer-connected world is a true game-changer whose ultimate results are unpredictable. So it's not quite true that nothing ever changes.

What doesn't change much, or very fast, is human nature, and human society reflects human nature. Each new generation faces the same kinds of social problems, has the same kinds of debates, and reaches solutions that have usually been tried many times before -- sometimes successfully, sometimes not.

Each generation can learn from previous generations, but only if it *listens* to them through the record of history. And even history doesn't dictate the moral values or political institutions that we should adopt. Often, as with the Baby Boom generation of the 1960s, new values seem to come more from adolescent rebellion against their parents than from any considered rejection on the merits.

---

[38] Sometimes called "the conflict of the orders," if you decide to look it up.

People who know nothing of history are trapped in the present moment. As far as they know, beliefs that are now popular have always been obviously true. Beliefs from 10 years ago are suspect, while beliefs from 50 or 100 years ago are automatically presumed wrong. Ideas that they encountered for the first time on a website this morning seem completely new, never before having been tried and eventually rejected when their defects became obvious.

Let's consider just one example. Americans in 2018 disagree about many basic moral and political values. They argue bitterly and struggle to control the federal government so that they can impose their own values on people with whom they disagree. Whether the issue is prayer in schools, abortion, transgender bathrooms, Islam, or affirmative action, their disagreements are largely regional: people in California and Kentucky might as well be on different planets. You could describe the situation like this:

> *"A zeal for different opinions concerning religion, concerning government, and many other points; an attachment to different leaders ambitiously contending for pre-eminence and power ... have, in turn, divided mankind into parties, inflamed them with mutual animosity, and rendered them much more disposed to vex and oppress each other than to co-operate for their common good."*

Okay, the word "vex" might have tipped you off that the quote didn't come from today's issue of *The New York Times*. It's from Federalist Paper #10 by James Madison, published in 1788. He was one of the architects of the U.S. Constitution. The bitter national dissension we see today is a problem that was solved (as well as it can be) a long time ago. We just forgot the solution.

The American Founders needed to unite the colonies into one nation in spite of their disagreements. They did it with the last article in the U.S. Constitution's Bill of Rights:

> *"The powers not delegated to the United States by the Constitution, nor prohibited by it to the States, are reserved to the States respectively, or to the people." (10th Amendment)*

In Federalist Paper #45, Madison explained the meaning:

"The powers delegated by the proposed Constitution to the federal government are few and defined. Those which are to remain in the State governments are numerous and indefinite. The former will be exercised principally on external objects, as war, peace, negotiation, and foreign commerce ...The powers reserved to the several States will extend to all the objects which, in the ordinary course of affairs, concern the lives, liberties, and properties of the people, and the internal order, improvement, and prosperity of the State."

Federalism has no necessary connection with libertarianism, or indeed with any particular political philosophy. It is most of all a *practical strategy* for uniting a society in which different groups have irresolvable disagreements. Each group, in its own geographical area, can follow its own majority viewpoint as long as it recognizes the same right for other groups in their own areas. The areas cooperate on the "few and defined" issues about which they agree and that affect the country as a whole.

Tolerance recognizes inherent dignity of all people

A lesson of this book is that for good and for ill, we share the animal side of our nature with lower animals. We have many of the same impulses and weaknesses as they do.

But even the most dedicated skeptic knows we are more than that. For one thing, we can *think*, without which skepticism is impossible. We can speculate about our future and dig up artifacts to learn about our past. We can wonder why the world works as it does. We can yearn for some kind of meaning beyond ourselves. We can ask if our lives really matter.

If you have a religious background, it's easy to find your place in the universe. Whether or not you take them literally, you know the foundational beliefs of your own tradition. Jews, Christians, and Muslims all look to Genesis 1:27:

"So God created man in his own image, in the image of God created He him; male and female created He them."

If you believe it or even half-believe it, it's a good answer. Every human life is sacred because every person is created in the image of

God. Even skeptics draw inspiration from it, as did Pico della Mirandola (1463-1494) in his *Oration on the Dignity of Man*:

> *"We have made you a creature neither of heaven nor of earth, neither mortal nor immortal, in order that you may, as the free and proud shaper of your own being, fashion yourself in the form you may prefer. It will be in your power to descend to the lower, brutish forms of life; you will be able, through your own decision, to rise again to the superior orders whose life is Divine."*

American novelist Mark Twain had a similar view. In his book *Letters from the Earth* (published posthumously because Twain knew it would cause an uproar), Twain tells how Satan was exiled from heaven and sent to earth. Satan wrote to the other archangels to tell them about humanity:

> *"Man is a marvelous curiosity. When he is at his very best he is a sort of low grade nickel-plated angel; at his worst he is unspeakable, unimaginable; and first and last and all the time he is a sarcasm. Yet he blandly and in all sincerity calls himself the 'noblest work of God.' This is the truth I am telling you. And this is not a new idea with him, he has talked it through the ages, and believed it. Believed it, and found nobody among all his race to laugh at it."*

What if you're neither believer, half-believer, nor even a sympathetic skeptic? "Praise Jesus," if you'll pardon the expression, there's still hope for you. There's a purely secular explanation for why everyone's life matters, deserving respect and tolerance. Human beings have inalienable value because they are self-aware.

Goodness and self-awareness

In Chapter 11, we discussed why meaning depends on consciousness. Meaning is connection. In a lifeless world, marks on paper wouldn't mean anything. To someone who didn't understand the language in which they were written, marks on paper wouldn't mean anything. It's only to a mind that things can have meaning. Consciousness bestows meaning on what was previously meaningless.

Likewise, *goodness* depends on consciousness. However we define goodness, it depends on a mind that connects it with something else. Exercise is good because it promotes health; health is good because it enables us to achieve our other goals and suffer less pain. Achieving our goals is good because it fulfills our abilities and gives us pleasure. And pleasure is good, while pain is bad, because (according to many people) they are intrinsically so.

As far as we can tell, all animals feel pleasure and pain. In a different way, even plants seem to feel them. But humans not only feel pleasure and pain, they can be *aware of themselves* feeling pleasure and pain. They not only see, but can be *aware* they are seeing. They not only think, but – just like Descartes – they can realize "I am thinking."

The crucial difference between humans and lower animals is that humans can be aware of their own existence, lives, and consciousness. That higher-level awareness means they can bestow value on themselves. In other words, they can value their own lives whether or not anyone else values them.

Like God, human beings are self-aware. In philosophical jargon (in case you want to impress people at a party), they are simultaneously the subject and object of their own consciousness. As a result, they have *reflexive self-value*. Their value, dignity, and rights are independent of what anyone else thinks about them. As long as they are alive and capable of self-awareness, they can value themselves. They have reflexive self-value of which no one else can deprive them. In the words of the Declaration of Independence, their value as people is "unalienable."

Whatever we think about other people's beliefs or ways of life, their inherent and unalienable value restricts what we can morally do to them. Some things such as murder are always off-limits: even in extreme cases that have some justification, they are still wrong. Other things such as intolerance are presumed wrong unless proven otherwise: the burden of proof is on the people who want to restrict others or inflict suffering on them because of their beliefs.

Tolerance is essential not just for a good human society, but for a good human life.

Recognizing the inherent value and dignity in all people is a necessary part of being a decent person and a good citizen.

Chapter 16:
Building Tolerant Societies

"Nature, to be commanded, must be obeyed."

-- Francis Bacon

THE QUOTE THAT INTRODUCES THIS CHAPTER makes an important point: To live successfully, we must pay attention to facts and natural laws. Ignorance, whether accidental or willful, is a prescription for failure. Wishful thinking about politics and social policy is a prescription for failure.

Nowhere is that more true than in dealing with human nature. It's easy to say nice words about tolerance, and most people do. It's very easy to say nice words about peace, and most people do. Books are full of it. How much good has it done? To judge by each day's news, not much.

Uttering platitudes is easy. That's why people do it so much. It's more daunting to arrange social relations in a way that maximizes tolerance and peace while minimizing hatred and bloodshed.

This chapter explores how to create such social arrangements. There's a lot we can do. It's also important to know what we *can't* do, or not very well, or without much likelihood of success.

Choose the achievable imperfect

The first thing we can't do is create a perfect society. Unless human nature changes, there can *never* be a perfect society. Accepting that fact is the first step to making society better in ways that are possible instead of dreamy and utopian. Tolerance is very much on the agenda, but it won't be perfect and some people won't think it's enough.

A perfect society is impossible for three reasons.

First, human beings are imperfect. We are capable of intelligent thought and moral nobility, but not always or even most of the time. Too often, we are selfish, narrow-minded, impatient, cruel, and thoughtless. We want what we want, and we don't care about others or the common good. We easily rationalize whatever sins we can't deny. Alexander Pope (1688-1744) described it in his *Essay on Man*:

> *"Virtuous and vicious every man must be,*
> *Few in the extreme, but all in the degree;*
> *The rogue and fool by fits is fair and wise;*
> *And even the best by fits what they despise."*

Second, social perfection is subjective. What we consider a "perfect society" depends on our life experience, emotional makeup, moral values, and settled beliefs. Even people who have a lot in common often disagree about the details of a good society. Any large society has many groups of people with little in common, so it has many such disagreements. Those who disagree are all right, and they're all wrong. There's no provable definition of a perfect society because it's only partly dependent on facts. The rest depends on the people defining it.

In order to survive, a society needs a majority population who agree on *enough* to work together for the common good and see each other as members of the same in-group. It also needs some general agreement about what the common good *is*.

Third, no matter how fortunate people are, they are never satisfied with what they have. Smart people want to be popular. Popular people want to be smart. Poor people wish they had money. Rich people fondly recall the simplicity of their lives when they were broke. Young people want to be older, older people want to be younger.

Single people yearn for the security of marriage, while married people yearn for the freedom of being single. Wherever we are, we always seem to think there's a better place just over the horizon. As Pope later observed in the same poem:

"Hope springs eternal in the human brest;
Man never is, but always to be, blest."

If society were totally peaceful and loving, with everyone having enough and no one suffering injustice, we'd *still* find reasons to complain about it. The Harvard philosopher William James (1842-1910) once visited a utopian community in Chautauqua, New York that came as close to a perfect society as any ever has. He described it in his essay "What Makes a Life Significant?"

"I went in curiosity for a day. I stayed for a week, spellbound by the charm and ease of everything, by the middle-class paradise, without a sin, without a victim, without a blot, without a tear."

The surprise came when he departed from the society of humanity's highest ideals:

"What was my own astonishment, on emerging into the dark and wicked world again, to catch myself saying: 'What a relief! Now for something primordial and savage, even though it were as bad as an Armenian massacre, to set the balance straight again. This order is too tame, this culture too second-rate, this goodness too uninspiring. This drama without a villain, this atrocious harmlessness of all things -- I cannot abide with it. Let me take my chances again in the big outside worldly wilderness with all its sins and sufferings.'"

Amazingly, imperfection is like a vitamin

"Perfection" is impossible in human society because it is *imperfection* that motivates us and helps give meaning to our lives. Like the utopian community James described, a perfect society would be too tame, too second-rate, and too uninspiring. We are not merely thinking machines. We are full-blooded human beings, with energy, drives, and passions that we need to exercise on meeting challenges and solving problems. Without them, we stagnate in mediocrity.

That's why many people in prosperous countries react to trivial problems as if they were earth-shaking, life-or-death struggles. They *have* no life-or-death struggles, but they need them: it's part of being human. We need to feel that our lives have a significance beyond our span of years. We hope that we'll achieve some great good to survive us and to remind the world that we were here.[39] But when the worst social problems of which we have first-hand knowledge are who gets to use which bathroom or who used the wrong pronoun, we feel bereft. Where is the great challenge we can overcome, the invincible monster we can defeat, the intolerable wrong we can set right? Where is our chance to make a mark on the world: to be remembered, even if only by a few?

We cannot achieve perfection, but in striving to improve what we can, we make our societies and ourselves the best they can be. That's how we make our mark. And that's good enough.

Understand the social possibilities frontier

We also need to set realistic expectations about what we can accomplish. The possibilities for any society are limited not only by human nature but also by the history, customs, institutions, and dominant populations of the society. Those create a "social possibilities frontier"[40] beyond which a society cannot progress without prior improvements in its social resources.

For example, if some group of people has always lived under despotic government, then that experience formed their foundational beliefs about freedom, rights, and the rule of law. If you tell them that democratic government is better, they will evaluate what you say in terms of what they already believe, so they won't believe you. It's *outside* of their social possibilities frontier.

Similarly, you cannot take an illiterate population that believes in magic instead of science, give it some computers, and expect it to

---

[39] It's not a new thing. The ancient Greeks called it *kleos*, usually translated as "glory." It was the desire to do something important enough to be remembered by future generations.

[40] Analogous to the "production possibilities frontier" concept in economics.

sustain an advanced technological society. That's *outside* of its social possibilities frontier.

Education and cultural evolution can move the social possibilities frontier and change a society, but that takes generations and creates conflict. We must balance the possible future good it might achieve against the guaranteed present evils that it causes. British political philosopher Michael Oakeshott explains in his book *Rationalism in Politics*:

> ""*Innovation entails certain loss and possible gain. Therefore, the burden of proof, to show that the proposed change will be on the whole beneficial, is with the would-be innovator."*

Understand the second law of social dynamics

As far as I know, nobody has stated a second law of social dynamics, but there is one. It's the reason for Oakeshott's caution about the risks of innovation.

The corresponding law in physical science is the Second Law of Thermodynamics. It says that in a closed system, disorder (entropy) increases over time. That's why cars eventually fall apart, and it's part of the reason for human aging.

Disorder increases because there are more ways for things to be chaotic than for them to be organized in useful ways. As a result, the probability of disorder is greater than the probability of order.

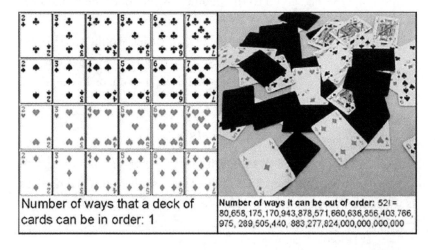

Number of ways that a deck of cards can be in order: 1	Number of ways it can be out of order: 52! = 80,658,175,170,943,878,571,660,636,856,403,766, 975, 289,505,440, 883,277,824,000,000,000,000

Suppose that you throw a deck of cards on the floor. There is only one way for the cards to fall so that they're in order, but there are 52! ways for them to fall out of order.[41] Therefore, it's much more likely they will fall out of order (see figure).

Applied to human society, it means that there are many more ways for things to go *wrong* than for them to go *right*. That implies three important points:

- Other things being equal, the overall result of any social change is more likely to be bad than to be good. The overall result includes not only the intended result, but also all the other results that nobody expected or considered.

- Therefore, it's important to make any social changes slowly and carefully, allowing time to evaluate their results before taking them any further. Evaluation includes considering the social consensus about the results, not merely their abstract merits or demerits.

- Social improvements are not permanent. Unless they are sustained by continuous effort and proper education of each new generation, they disappear. Taking their place will be new "improvements" that will probably make things worse.

American Founder Benjamin Franklin alluded to the second law of social dynamics when a woman asked what the Constitutional Convention of 1787 had given to the people. "A republic," he replied, "if you can keep it."

Franklin knew that as time passed, disorder would start to eat away at America's Constitutional system of government. Constant work would be needed to keep it from falling into chaos like a pile of playing cards on the floor.

Understand that benefits have costs

The second law of social dynamics implies something that it's easy to forget: benefits have costs. That applies just as much to social policies as it does to buying a car. In order to *get* one thing, societies usually

---

[41] That's "52 factorial," if you want to look it up.

must *give up* something else. Social groups disagree about whether the new thing is worth the cost. It's often because the people who get the benefits are different from the people who pay the costs. For example:

- Supporters of medical licensing argue that it reduces the risk of incompetent doctors. Critics of licensing (including Nobel laureate economist Milton Friedman) argue that it increases the cost of medical care. Both sides are right, but they disagree about whether it's more important to reduce risks or reduce costs.

- Gay marriage supporters argue that equal treatment under the law requires devoutly Christian bakers to create wedding cakes for gay couples even if they have religious objections. Devout Christians argue that it infringes on their freedom of religion. Both sides are right, but they disagree about which principle is more important.[42]

There is no perfect way to resolve such zero-sum disputes. The best of the imperfect ways is to decide them locally through the democratic process at the lowest practical level of government, such as states or provinces.

Understand variation in empathy

Social theorists often make a deadly mistake: they assume that people are all alike. In some ways, that's true: they all share a common nature with the same basic rights and human dignity. But in other ways, it's false. Empathy is one of the ways it's false.

Empathy is our ability to care about, imagine, and understand how other people feel. Lack of empathy increases the risk of conflict. We don't naturally feel empathy for those we see as outsiders, but society can do things to encourage such feelings. Even if we feel like attacking each other, empathy can stop us from doing it. Empathy requires that:

---

[42] On June 4, 2018, the U.S. Supreme Court decided by a vote of 7 to 2 that religious freedom was more important (Masterpiece Cake Shop v. Colorado Civil Rights Commission).

- We *perceive* what other people feel.
- We *feel* what we think other people feel.
- We *care about* what other people feel.

All three of those factors are lessened when we confront people who differ from us:

- We find it harder to perceive what they're feeling because different cultures have different conventional expressions and behaviors to indicate emotion.

- We find it harder to feel what they feel because kin selection makes us perceive them as "other." We don't identify with them emotionally.

- We find it harder to care about what they feel because we have no instinctive emotional investment in their welfare.

Like most human traits, empathy also varies within populations. Some people (16 percent) naturally have a lot of empathy, some (16 percent) have very little, and most (68 percent) have a medium amount.[43] People's natural empathy can be damaged by trauma such as war, violence, or abuse, especially in childhood.

Adding the high-empathy and medium-empathy groups means that 84 percent of people either aren't likely to harm others or can be talked out of it by appeals to conscience. The low-empathy 16 percent can't be talked out of it. If they want to harm others, they will unless they're deterred by the threat of punishment. Offenses must be defined as clearly as possible by the law, and the punishments of those found guilty must be severe, swift, and certain.

Make Tolerance Easier

We aren't machines. Our ability to tolerate difference has limits. The more strongly we disapprove of something, the harder it is for us to tolerate it. That's why tolerance requires at least some common ground, some shared beliefs, shared loyalty, or shared commitment to

---

[43] If you want to look it up, those percentages are what the science of statistics calls a "normal distribution."

the common good. In his 1993 book *Political Liberalism*, the Harvard philosopher John Rawls wondered:

> *"How is it possible for there to exist over time a just and stable society of free and equal citizens, who remain profoundly divided by reasonable religious, philosophical, and moral doctrines?"*

And Rawls concluded:

> *"In fact, historical experience suggests that it rarely is."*

Every society will have divisions: urban versus rural, political parties, religions, and so forth. The problem arises not if society is divided, because that's inevitable. The problem arises when it is, as Rawls said, *profoundly* divided, to the extent that people feel they have no common ground: that people who disagree with them are "other." In that situation, people's emotions start supplying them with reasons to attack each other.

For example, consider two societies. Society #1 has X as its dominant culture, which could be Christianity, Judaism, Islam, or secular materialism: it almost doesn't matter what it is. Society #2 has *no* dominant culture, but has a dozen or more incompatible cultures.

Because Society #1 has a dominant culture, most people in the society will either agree with the mainstream or be fairly close to it. That means three important things:

- Their shared beliefs bias them to perceive other people as genetic relatives.

- Their individual beliefs usually won't stray too far from the mainstream.

- They are less likely to express beliefs that enrage other people to the point of violence.

Remember: we don't expect perfection. It's impossible to eliminate violence and intolerance. Even in a dominant-culture society, there will still be strong disagreements and sometimes there will be violence. Our goal is to improve the odds.

On the other hand, society #2 has multiple non-dominant cultures. Most people only agree with members of their own small segment of the population. That means three important things:

- Their different beliefs bias them to perceive unbelievers as genetic competitors.

- Their individual beliefs sometimes stray far, far away from those of other groups.

- They are *more* likely to express beliefs that enrage other people to the point of violence.

When we talk about beliefs enraging people to the point of violence, it's important to recall that we're not talking about polite disagreements at the Harvard Club. Those certainly exist, but they are not the rule.

Yes, people with vastly different cultures and belief systems *can* get along. It does happen. But the opposite is much more common. As Dutch Foreign Minister Stef Blok observed in a talk to representatives of international organizations:

> *"'I have asked my ministry this and I will pose the question here as well. Give me an example of a multi-ethnic or multi-cultural society in which the original population still lives, and where there is a peaceful cohabitation. I don't know of one.'*
>
> *The minister went further and said it might be all fun and games to go to a 'Turkish bakery on Sunday' if you live in a well-off part of the city, but 'a number of side effects' promptly become tangible if one lives in a migrant-packed neighborhood. 'You very quickly reach the limits of what a society can take,' Blok stated."*[44]

Tolerance is most easily achieved in societies that have a dominant culture held by an overwhelming majority of the population. Other cultures, religions, and the like should certainly be allowed, not legally persecuted, but also not encouraged.

The larger point is: If you've got social division, then deal with it as well as you can. Avoid doing anything that would make the situation *worse* by creating even more social division. Manage the problems you have, but don't go looking for more of them.

---

[44] "Peaceful multicultural societies don't exist, Dutch FM says in explosive leaked speech," RT News, July 18, 2018.

Use federalism to reduce conflict

Even in a society with a dominant majority population and culture, there will still be some strong disagreements. Those lead to zero-sum situations where if one side wins, the other loses. Such situations cause harm both to individuals (unhappiness) and to society (division and distrust).

If such situations are unavoidable, then we can't do anything about them. However, if beliefs differ geographically, then federalism can help minimize the harm they cause. Federalism has three main components:

- Limiting the national government to decisions that affect the entire country, such as international trade, foreign policy, national defense, and basic human rights.

- Leaving all other decisions to lower-level authorities, such as state governments, local governments, or even (in innocuous cases) to social groups and peer pressure.

- A willingness to "live and let live" if people in other regions, states, or communities follow beliefs and practices with which we disagree.

"Live and let live" is hard for most people to accept, which leads them to reject the first two components as well. People dominated by emotion instead of reason are convinced of their right to control what everyone does anywhere in their country or even the entire world. When they get the power, they go on wild binges of coercion. They don't imagine that other people might legitimately disagree with them. Nor do they pause to think that they might someday lose power and fall victim to coercion or revenge by those they formerly coerced -- as happens fairly often in history.

Arbitrary power seems like a great idea when you're the one who has it. When it's wielded by someone with whom you disagree, it suddenly becomes much less attractive.

Follow stare decisis

Stare decisis ("to stand by things decided") is a crucial legal doctrine. It tells courts that if an issue has previously been decided, then they should abide by the earlier decision unless there are overwhelmingly important reasons to overturn it.

The doctrine comes from one of the main purposes of law: to make social life *predictable* so people can plan their actions rationally. The law needs to make it very clear what is allowed, what is forbidden, and what people can legitimately expect in various situations.

For example, suppose you're buying a used car. The seller knows there is something wrong with it that you won't discover until later. Is the seller required to tell you about it? Do you have a right to expect such a warning? Based on established law and custom, you might or might not.

That highlights another purpose of law beyond mere prediction: enabling people to know what they are morally entitled to *expect* in certain situations. If they don't get what they expect, they feel frustrated and angry. They think that their rights have been violated because past practice says someone must do X but he did Y instead.

A third goal of law is to foster peaceful and harmonious societies, so stare decisis supports all three goals: to make life predictable, to set moral expectations, and to support social peace.

Therefore, government and society should follow settled law and custom unless there is an overwhelmingly important reason to overturn them.

Sometimes, there really *is* such a reason. The U.S. Supreme Court's 1857 Dred Scott decision held that African-Americans could not be U.S. citizens and that slaves living in states where slavery was outlawed were still slaves. Even at the time, the decision was widely condemned. Later, in 1865, the U.S. Constitution's 13th Amendment set aside stare decisis to outlaw slavery in the United States. The issue was important enough to insist on a change from past practice.

Even in our own time, stare decisis controls – and should control – important decisions in law and social policy. For example, a legally scrupulous judge in 2008 would rule against gay marriage because it was opposed by existing law and past court decisions, not to mention the statements of both major parties' presidential candidates. However, the *same* judge in 2018 would rule in favor of gay marriage because the Supreme Court's 2015 decision in Obergefell v. Hodges settled the issue and declared that gay marriage is a Constitutional right.

The bottom line is that people form beliefs about their rights partly by their expectations based on past law and custom. To frustrate those expectations causes individual unhappiness and threatens social peace. Unless there is an overwhelmingly important reason to change past law or practice – and we're really *sure* about the result, per the second law of social dynamics – we should "stand by things decided" and follow stare decisis. In other words:

- If it ain't broke, don't fix it.
- If it *is* broke, then decide if it's important enough to fix. Not everything is.

  Remember that the perfect is the enemy of the good. Just because a situation is imperfect does not mean that it can or should be fixed. Some imperfection is inevitable, and when we try to correct one imperfection, we are likely to cause others. Our only choice is which imperfections we accept and which we try to correct.
- If you fix it, then do it slowly and carefully so you don't make the situation worse.

Encourage civil and respectful behavior

We all tend to see our cherished beliefs as part of *who we are*. In other words, we identify our beliefs with ourselves. The same applies to our important symbols, texts, and relationships. We tend to perceive criticisms of them as attacks on us. We react instinctively with hostility and "counter-attack," as if we were in physical danger.

That's why civil and respectful behavior are important, especially in debates over emotionally-charged issues. We need to show from the outset that we are focused on the issues and not on the people with whom we disagree.

That's why, for example, politicians debating legislation used to refer to each other by terms such as "my honorable colleague." Even if they hated each other's guts, it was (and still is) counter-productive to bring that into the discussion. Such customs focus attention away from people and onto issues. They help resolve disputes both peacefully and more efficiently than would otherwise be possible.

So how can we put those ideas to work for a more harmonious society? That's the tough part because it requires sensible leadership and changed social expectations:

- Social and political leaders should set a good example by civil and respectful behavior in their public statements and activities.

- News media should report facts objectively and with minimal emotionalism, particularly in covering events or issues about which emotions already run hot.

- Entertainment media should portray positive role models with protagonists who act rationally and responsibly.

- Individuals and private associations should enforce social sanctions against those who violate norms of civil and respectful behavior.

Encourage stable social roles

As discussed in Chapter 15, some forms of intolerance are socially beneficial. However, they also limit individual freedom. For that reason, intolerance should be avoided when possible and minimized when necessary.

Customary social roles are a case of intolerance that limits individual autonomy but that can be socially beneficial. It *can* be, though it's not always.

In Chapter 11, we saw how general words and concepts make thinking more efficient by letting us group things together. In a similar way, social roles make thinking, acting, and social interactions more efficient. Whether they are a good thing or a bad thing depends on the tradeoff: How much individual freedom is surrendered in exchange for how much individual and social good?

Paradoxically, social roles can benefit individuals as well as society at large. As Harvard law professor Cass Sunstein observed:

> *"Are social roles an obstacle to freedom? In a way, the answer is yes, since people would often like to do things that their role forbids. But this would be a far too simple conclusion. Without roles, life would be very hard to negotiate. Like social norms, social roles are facilitating as well as constraining ... In fact, norms make freedom possible. Social life is not possible -- not even imaginable -- without them ... In the absence of social norms, we would be unable to understand each other."[45]*

There's the paradox: "Norms make freedom possible." In other words, limitations on freedom make freedom possible. It seems like a contradiction. How can that be?

Consider an example. You go to a restaurant for dinner. The server arrives and asks what you want. When you request a menu, the server says there are no menus. You are completely free to order anything you wish. Your choices are not limited to those on a menu. Water? Would you like spring water from Pennsylvania, Ohio, Switzerland, Iceland or elsewhere? Tap water? From where? In a bottle? What kind of bottle: plastic, glass, ceramic, wood, leather? Should the bottle be large or small, tall or short? How tall or short? What temperature should the water be? When do you want it? Where should the server put it?

You spend so much time trying to get a glass of water that you starve to death before you can ever order dinner. And even if you survive the "trial by water," you face the same process when you try to get your food.

A restaurant menu limits your freedom. Your choices are limited to those on the menu. Even if you can order something that's not on the menu, the server will impose social sanctions (giving you an

---

[45] Sunstein, C., "Social Roles and Social Norms." University of Chicago Program in Law and Economics Working Paper No. 36, 1996.

annoyed look, expecting a larger tip) as a cost of your behavior. Every restaurant tries to have things on its menu that will satisfy most of its customers: if it didn't, it would quickly go out of business. To get your dinner efficiently, you sacrifice a little freedom but are still mostly happy with the result.

Of course, it matters *how* individual freedom is limited. If it's limited only by social sanctions (an annoyed look from the server), then it can meet a lower standard than if it's limited by coercion (you go to jail if you don't order from the menu).

Roles that are enforced by social sanctions can be violated by determined people. The great French mathematician Sophie Germain (1776-1831) defied her parents, French society, and French universities to study mathematics. Women weren't allowed to attend university lectures, so she listened from outside lecture halls and borrowed notes from male students. She wrote most of her work under a male pseudonym and earned the respect of Carl Friedrich Gauss, the greatest mathematician of her era.

The important questions to ask about social roles are:

- Are they enforced by social sanctions or by coercion?

  Roles enforced by coercion must have more justification than roles enforced only by social sanctions.

- Do they match the needs and desires of most people in the society?

  Just as a restaurant goes out of business if most people dislike its menu items, a society suffers if most people dislike their social roles. Remember that "the perfect is the enemy of the good." No set of social roles will satisfy everyone, and few roles will satisfy anyone completely: "Man never is, but always to be, blest."

- Do they match human nature?

  Postmodernists deny the existence of human nature because it seems to limit the autonomy of groups they consider oppressed. Even so, humans show regular patterns of biology and behavior that can be considered their "nature." Roles that match human nature make most people happy, while those that conflict with it make them unhappy.

- Do they support a peaceful, happy, and successful society?

Roles affect society as well as individuals. For example, Western societies now face a "birth dearth" as they fail to produce enough children to sustain their populations.[46] Feminism broke down arbitrary limits on women's freedom, and that was a good thing -- but it had a cost. Post-feminist women marry later, if at all, and have fewer children than women in earlier eras and in traditional societies. As a result, Western populations are shrinking. In that case, we looked at the tradeoff between individual freedom and social good, and we decided in favor of freedom. Our population deficit is being remedied by immigrants who believe neither in freedom *nor* feminism. The results are not entirely predictable.

Mitigate kin selection hostilities

What are some things that a society can do to reduce irrational hostility, division, and violence?

Use visual cues to override instinctive hostility

Physical appearance is one of the main factors by which animals, including humans, identify potential allies or enemies. When people look like us, it inclines us to feel that they are genetic relatives to whom we should give trust and cooperation. Conversely, when they look different from us, it inclines us to feel that they are genetic competitors who pose a threat, thus inspiring fear and hostility. Racial differences and discord are a prime example of this problem.

Our reaction to such visual cues is instantaneous and unconscious. We feel before we think, which in this case is a tragic riff on Mark Twain's joke that "a lie can travel halfway around the world while the

---

[46] Demographer Ben Wattenberg discussed the problem in his books *The Birth Dearth* (1987) and *Fewer: How the New Demography of Depopulation Will Shape Our Future* (2005).

truth is putting on its shoes." We need to slow down the lie or speed up the truth.

Fortunately, we can do both: not perfectly, nor always, but often enough to make a difference. The strategy is twofold:

- Distract people's attention away from the visual cues that cause hostility and harm.
- Attract people's attention to a visual marker of in-group membership.

Various experiments have shown this strategy can be effective. In one experiment, psychologist Robert Kurzban had people watch videos of arguments between two mixed-race basketball teams. In the absence of any other visual cues, people's reactions were biased by the race of the players making the arguments. However, in the second phase of the experiment, Kurzban gave the players colorful t-shirts that clearly marked them as belonging to one team or the other. That minor change caused his test subjects to ignore the race of the players and to focus instead on their team membership.[47]

Would it have worked just as well if Kurzban had simply *told* his test subjects which teams had which players? No. The test subjects' instant emotional reaction was based on what they *saw*. By the time they could think about team membership, they had already reacted emotionally. The key to the remedy was that Kurzban provided a clear, attention-grabbing visual cue to which the people could also react instantly. That blocked the simultaneous racial reaction and redirected the test subjects to a harmless reaction instead.

Government and social leaders should identify which visual cues most often lead to hatred and violence. Then, they should encourage or mandate use of alternate visual cues that can block reaction to the harmful cues. Such cues are already used in many contexts:

- **Military:** Uniforms show the wearer's tribe (Army, Navy, etc.), family (infantry, legal, etc.), identity (name), and position in the hierarchy (rank). They imply that the wearer's primary and important identity is as a member of the military,

---

[47] Greene, J., *Moral Tribes*, p. 52.

not as a member of a racial or sexual group. It's an imperfect solution but has been used for millennia in societies around the world. History has proven that it works.

- **Business:** Identification badges show the wearer's tribe (company), identity (name and photo), and provide access to company facilities (buildings, computers, etc.).

- **Education:** School uniforms show the wearer's tribe (school) and other information (class rank, club memberships, etc.). Some schools go even further: One high school in Osaka, Japan requires students who do not have black hair to dye it black.[48]

In some cases, mandated clothing or behaviors do even more than just distract from divisive visual cues: they replace them with cues that support cooperation. Uniforms replace clothing that might cause division within the group. Mandated behaviors, to some extent, work similarly: If you're doing one thing, you're probably not doing another at the same time.

Such cues also reassure the wearers themselves by giving visual confirmation of their identity and membership in a group to which they give their loyalty. If troubled by existential questions like "who am I?", they can simply check their name badges and uniforms.

The alternative cues point either to membership in the viewer's own group, or to membership in another group with which authorities have defined and cultivated an innocuous rivalry. The latter step is necessary because people will always divide themselves into groups. Divisions can't be eliminated, but we can trick human nature by substituting less harmful for more harmful ones.

Use the power of distraction

If you're skeptical about the ability of t-shirts to distract people from racial differences, here's a striking example that might convince you.

---

[48] "Japan teen 'forced to dye hair black' for school," BBC News, October 27, 2017.

The Smithsonian Magazine reports that psychologists have run experiments in which plainly-visible things are "invisible" because people's attention is focused elsewhere:

> *"We showed people a video and asked them to count how many times three basketball players wearing white shirts passed a ball. After about 30 seconds, a woman in a gorilla suit sauntered into the scene, faced the camera, thumped her chest and walked away. Half the viewers missed her. In fact, some people looked right at the gorilla and did not see it."*[49]

People see what they *want* to see, *expect* to see, or are *trying* to see. They tend to ignore other things. It's one reason, as in the title of this book, why sane people believe "crazy" things. You and other people can look at the same situation -- such a riot on campus, or a police shooting of a criminal suspect -- but see different things and reach different conclusions. Neither of you is necessarily evil or stupid: You're just human.

Evolution has shaped our minds to pay attention to the most important aspects of situations. In the wilderness, facing a hungry pack of wolves, the choice of what's most important is simple: run. In a complex society, with a thousand different facts that might be relevant, what we see as most important is influenced by our emotions, preconceived ideas, and personal life experience. The surprise is not that we sometimes disagree; the surprise is that we agree as often as we do.

Provide less-harmful controlled rivalries

Recall a suggestion from earlier in the chapter: We are not merely thinking machines, but are full-blooded human beings with energy, drives, and passions we need to exercise on meeting challenges and solving problems.

As harmful as it can be, social division also serves a purpose. In order to have an in-group, people need an out-group. We define ourselves not merely by what we *are*, but also by what we *are not*. Socially

---

[49] "Did You See the Gorilla? The Problem with Inattentional Blindness." *Smithsonian Magazine*, September 2012.

and individually, we need at least some difference and division. The problem is to find a middle way: *enough* difference and division for a healthy society, but not so much that it becomes destructive.

Social and political leaders should identify the separate groups that already exist, then decide which group divisions cause the most harm and the least harm. Relatively harmless divisions can be encouraged and remade (imperfectly, but enough) into relatively harmless rivalries by:

- Visual cues of the kind discussed in the previous section.

- Persuasion campaigns that encourage each group to take pride in its own customs, members, and achievements without denigrating those of other groups.

- Media and entertainment storylines that show constructive, positive examples of how different groups can compete peacefully.

If there aren't enough relatively harmless group divisions, government and social leaders can create them. Such new divisions have the advantage of not carrying historical animosities. Left to their own devices, without socially-supplied divisions, people will make up their own. And the divisions they make up might cause much more harm than those deliberately designed. Harvard biologist E.O. Wilson observed in *The Social Conquest of Earth* (2012) that:

> *"Experiments conducted over many years by social psychologists revealed how swiftly and decisively people divide into groups, then discriminate in favor of the one to which they belong. Even when experimenters created the groups arbitrarily ... participants always ranked the out-group below the in-group. They judged their 'opponents' to be less likable, less fair, less trustworthy, less competent."*

The same methods can work to de-emphasize divisions that are excessively harmful. The key, as always, is to work *with* nature as much as possible. Any new divisions should be created as much as possible along already-existing lines and public preferences. Where real differences or intractable disagreements exist, leaders should only try to downplay them instead of eliminating them. Attempted changes that clash too starkly with realities "on the ground" are doomed to fail.

Provide rational leadership

Providing rational leadership is easier to suggest than to accomplish. It faces a number of hurdles:

- Those who seek high political office are often motivated by a desire for personal power and enrichment, not by a desire to serve the public good. That's always been true. The ancient Greek philosopher Plato suggested that those most fit to rule would have to be forced to take the job.

- Empathy and conscience vary like other human traits. People who lack empathy and conscience feel no guilt or remorse about doing "whatever it takes" to win. Therefore, they have an advantage over competitors whose actions are limited by moral concerns. People who don't want power -- like Plato's ideal rulers who don't want the job -- are less likely to get it than people who do want power and don't care how they get it.

- Politicians and other social leaders can often acquire power and increase their own influence by vilifying their rivals. That divides a society into hostile factions between which compromise and cooperation are much more difficult.

- People disagree about what the public good *is* and how to achieve it. Should leaders represent the interests of a country's majority, or prioritize the welfare of disadvantaged groups at the expense of the majority? Should they act for the welfare of "the world," or just of their own country? Short-term welfare or long-term? How is welfare defined? Cultural homogeneity makes it easier to answer such questions, but doesn't by itself provide the answers.

To some degree, rational leadership is a matter of luck. We can't know in advance who will be the next Marcus Aurelius, George Washington, or Winston Churchill. Nor can most people have much influence over who ascends to positions of leadership. However, by supporting those who act constructively and form coalitions for the common good, we can do what's possible.

Minimize interactions between hostile groups

Even more important is the creation of safe spaces for different groups. When we encounter people whom we perceive as genetic competitors, biology inclines both them and us to attack or run away. Such encounters are an obvious aggression trigger.

Human groups that can't stop killing each other should be *physically separated* from each other and their interactions carefully controlled. That minimizes both their impulses to harm each other and their opportunities to do so. In his book *The Meaning of Human Existence*, E.O. Wilson identifies the problem:

> "*All things being equal (fortunately things are seldom equal, not exactly), people prefer to be with others who look like them, speak the same dialect, and hold the same beliefs. An amplification of this evidently inborn predisposition leads with frightening ease to racism and religious bigotry. Then, also with frightening ease, good people do bad things.*"

Create Positive Experiences of Cooperation

A final step is to create positive experiences of cooperation when possible. If social adversaries work together on areas where they agree — even projects like getting roads repaired — they begin to see each other less as "the dangerous other" and more as fellow human beings who have needs, interests, and points of view. That decreases their aggressive impulses and increases their empathy.

Use the power of beliefs

Most people in Western countries think it's none of the government's business to promote or discourage beliefs, at least in general. When it comes to beliefs that they support or despise, of course, it's another matter. They're quite happy to have government "on their side" in political, moral, or religious disputes.

And of course, governments *do* take sides although we usually pretend that they don't. Even in the aggressively secular culture of 2018, American currency still bears the motto "In God we trust." In Britain, public criticism of Islam brings a visit from the police, who even arrested one political candidate for quoting a criticism of Islam by former British Prime Minister Winston Churchill.[50] In Germany, Sweden, China, Russia, and other countries that have no historical traditions of free speech, government control is even stricter.

Legal restrictions are only one way that government and institutional leaders shape belief. People tend to believe what they see, or what they hear repeated over and over by different sources. Those beliefs can be helpful, harmful, both, or neutral. For example:

- Television commercials for shaving cream always show men using about 10 times more shaving cream than needed. Many boys never see their fathers shave, so when they grow up, they buy much more shaving cream. Nobody needs a pound of shaving cream to shave, but they absorbed that image as children and never gave it any thought. It's a profitable belief for the sellers and relatively innocuous as beliefs go.

- A 1990s American television series, "Melrose Place," had main characters who were either insane, criminal, or despicable. There was only one exception: Matt Fielding, a gay character, was so sane and saintly that he was almost unlikeable. That was one step on a path from the 1950s, when gays were stigmatized as immoral, to our era when gays are celebrated and almost nobody cares about the issue anymore. Government worked with entertainment and news media to alter belief in a more humane direction.

- Chinese and Japanese television series, on the other hand, promote traditional values and behaviors. Patriotism is encouraged. Female characters often have positions of authority (Mafia boss, executive, etc.) but are sweet and feminine, while male characters have similarly varied roles but are

---

[50] "Arrested for quoting Winston Churchill," *The Daily Mail*, April 28, 2014.

strong and masculine. Dating is chaste and sex is assumed to be only for marriage. Neither men nor women disparage the other sex.

- The German television sitcom "Türkisch für Anfänger" (Turkish for Beginners) promotes German viewers' acceptance of mass migration from Turkey and other Islamic countries.

The power to shape beliefs is a dangerous one, used as often to promote harmful beliefs as helpful ones. In "An Outline of Intellectual Rubbish," the British philosopher and two-time Nobel laureate Bertrand Russell (1872-1970) explained:

"Give me an adequate army with more pay and better food than the average man, and I will undertake, within thirty years, to make the majority of the population believe that two and two are three, that water freezes when it gets hot and boils when it gets cold, or any other nonsense that might seem to serve the interest of the State ...

Any verbal denial of the mystic doctrine would be made illegal, and obstinate heretics would be 'frozen' at the stake. No person who did not accept the official doctrine would be allowed to teach or to have any position of power. Only the very highest officials, in their cups, would whisper to each other what rubbish it all is; then they would laugh and drink again."

The parallels with contemporary society are obvious. Certain beliefs are grounds for firing, public shaming, harassment, and even arrest. The social function of such beliefs is to show membership in the society's in-group for cooperation and trust, just as denying the beliefs marks people as being members of the out-group to be resisted or destroyed. That applies whether the beliefs are true or false, morally helpful or harmful, though of course it's better if they are factually true and morally helpful. There is no way to guarantee that leaders will be moral and that they will promote helpful beliefs. The best of the imperfect remedies is to have democratic and open government if it's possible.

Government, institutions, and social leaders should try to reach informal consensus about the set of helpful beliefs that they will promote. They can then work together to promote them and avoid confusing the population with mixed or inconsistent messages.

Encourage helpful foundation myths

Especially important are "foundation myths" that illustrate morally desirable behavior and confer legitimacy on the social order. Note that "myths" are not necessarily false. Most foundation myths combine fact with legend. Examples are:

- The story mentioned in Chapter 1 of John Hancock's signature on the Declaration of Independence. The British had issued a death warrant for Hancock, so he signed extra large to show his defiance. That demonstrates courage.

- Saul and David, who were kings of Israel, were chosen by God. The story implies that the foundation of the nation of Israel was endorsed by the Creator of the universe, and thereby adds to its moral and political legitimacy.

At a minimum, foundation myths should teach that:

- The society and its history are basically good even if not completely so.

- The social order is worthy of support, though any flaws should be corrected.

- Members of the society follow (or at least should follow) generally accepted moral principles such as honesty, loyalty, obedience to law, and help to the needy.

- Members of the society are all partners who cooperate for the common good while respecting each other's individual rights and identities.

Foundation myths are sometimes based in historical events, but strict historical accuracy is irrelevant to them. Their main job is to encourage moral behavior and to legitimize the social order. Attacks on the foundation myths are socially harmful, even if motivated by concerns of historical accuracy. Government and social leaders should discourage such attacks.

Some intellectuals argue that myths legitimize power relations, define mores, and suggest social roles. And they usually do. But those results are only bad if they lead to less happiness and more suffering than the practical alternatives. Human societies are by nature hierarchical: a ship with 1,000 captains is unlikely to go anywhere. If a hierarchy promotes the welfare of most people without imposing avoidable and unacceptable suffering on other people, then it's a good thing, and so are myths that support it. As always, our only choice is between the better imperfect and the worse.

Discourage harmful beliefs

The flip side of encouraging helpful beliefs is to *discourage* beliefs that are harmful or risky. Even if we decide that it's justified to suppress such beliefs, it's a dangerous path to tread. The path is all the more dangerous because we can't discuss it openly. If we discuss openly whether or not we should suppress some beliefs, then we *admit* openly that we think the beliefs are -- or might be -- factually true. Such an admission makes it impossible publicly to condemn them as false.

Of course, what is helpful or harmful depends on the goals to be achieved. In warfare, it is sometimes helpful to believe that "the enemy" consists of homicidal monsters with whom reasoning or compromise are impossible, so we must destroy them before they destroy us. However, warfare is not the model we want for our societies -- or for our world, given a choice. Reasonable goals are to make our societies peaceful, tolerant, and happy, as well as minimize violent conflict between societies.

But those goals sometimes have a cost. They must be balanced against other things that are *also* valuable, such as truth and freedom of thought.

Human happiness and social harmony are valuable. So is our freedom to speak the truth, or even to state our sincere opinions whether or not they're true. In the real world, we often must give up some of one good thing in order to get another good thing that we value. It's a judgment that different people and societies will make in different ways.

Some beliefs are risky or hurtful enough that it's at least open to debate that they should be suppressed, preferably by social rather than legal sanctions. If such beliefs divide society, or cause harm in spite of having social benefits, then reasonable people will often make different judgments about them.

One example of a risky belief is eugenics, the idea that the human race can and should be improved by encouraging "superior" people to have children and discouraging or preventing "inferior" people from having children.

Although people in 2018 identify eugenics mainly with the Nazis' program of genocide against groups they deemed inferior, the Nazis got a lot of ideas from mainstream science and opinion in the United States. Former *New York Times* science writer Nicholas Wade observed in his book *A Troublesome Inheritance* that:

> "Many of the elements in the [Nazis'] eugenics program could be found in the American eugenics program ... Nordic supremacy, purity of the blood, condemnation of intermarriage, sterilization of the unfit—all these were ideas embraced by American eugenicists ... ideas about race are **dangerous** when linked to political agendas." [my emphasis]

As a result, Western scientists and social leaders are now wary of any beliefs (true or not) that might lead to such horrible results.

Suppressing potentially harmful beliefs is highly debatable but not obviously crazy. However, it can also backfire, causing even worse results than if the beliefs had not been suppressed. That can happen in two ways.

First, if the beliefs are factually true, then suppressing them prevents people from basing their actions on truth and forces them to base their actions on falsehood. The costs might be high or they might be low.

For example, the Soviet Union (the Russian Empire) of the 20th century suppressed scientific knowledge of genetics in favor of its official Marxist theory of Lysenkoism.[51] The results were disastrous for Soviet agriculture. The country also tried to socially engineer its people so they would have no culture, nationality, or ethnicity except for the official versions.[52] That, too, was a disaster.

Second, as psychologist Steven Pinker observed in a December 11, 2017 forum at Harvard, suppression of true beliefs can cause an angry backlash when people discover that they have been deceived:

> *"When they are exposed for the first time to true statements that have never been voiced on college campuses, in The New York Times, or in respectable media, it's like a bacillus to which they have no immunity. They are infected both with a feeling of outrage that these truths are unsayable, and no defense against taking them to rather repellant conclusions."[53]*

For those reasons, the presumption should always be *against* suppression of beliefs, especially beliefs for which there is factual evidence. The costs, benefits, and risks must be carefully considered before attempting such suppression. Two less-risky alternatives are:

- Surround the beliefs with a smokescreen of obfuscation.

  As U.S. President Dwight D. Eisenhower (1890-1969) once said prior to a news conference with questions he didn't want to answer, "If I can't dazzle them with brilliance, I'll baffle them them with bullfeathers."

- Reformulate the beliefs in terms less likely to cause harm. This alternative is both more honest and less risky.

  For example, discussing genetic contributions to intelligence is risky because racists might exploit the data to foment hatred and discrimination. Writing in *Slate*, William Saletan suggested parsing the data in a way that is truthful but safer: "You can talk about the genetics of race. You can talk about the

---

[51] For information about Lysenkoism, see Martin Gardner's book *Fads & Fallacies in the Name of Science*.

[52] They referred to their desired type of person as "the new Soviet man," if you want to look it up. The oft-repeated claim that Americans have no nationality or culture of their own is obviously similar to the Soviet doctrine.

[53] "Harvard Professor Steven Pinker Points Out How Political Correctness Drives The Alt-Right," *The Daily Wire*, January 11, 2018.

genetics of intelligence. But stop implying they're the same thing. Connecting intelligence to race adds nothing useful. It overextends the science you're defending, and it engulfs the whole debate in moral flames." ("Stop Talking About Race and IQ," April 27, 2018)[54]

Require specific assimilations to the dominant culture

The word "culture" comes from the Latin *cultus*, meaning the shared religious cult of a society. Culture is a set of shared beliefs, stories, attitudes, behaviors, and customs. Like law, it helps to make life predictable, sets moral expectations, and supports social peace.

It's reasonable for a society to require all citizens or permanent residents to assimilate to the dominant culture in at least some ways. Different societies make different decisions about which ways, how many ways, and how intrusive the ways are going to be. Those decisions will usually be made by social and political leaders in concert with the democratic process. Two principles should guide assimilation requirements:

- Only public appearance and behavior affect society, so assimilation should be required only in public aspects of life. What people do in their homes or private group spaces, as long as it is not criminal, should be left to their own beliefs, preferences, and identities.

- Assimilation requirements should be limited to those that are clearly helpful, should be small in number, and should be as unintrusive as possible. They limit people's freedom to engage in non-aggressive activities of their choice. We want to minimize such limitations and maximize the sphere of individual freedom.

Examples of such requirements are to use an official national language for government and business, celebrate national holidays, and

---

[54] See also my article about "Genetic Explanations of Poverty" in *The Encyclopedia of World Poverty*, Sage Publications, 2006.

show respect for national symbols such as the flag. Depending on the case, sanctions might be legal or only social.

For example, in Iran, laws prohibit undesirable speech (mofsed-e-filarz, "spreading corruption on the earth") whose penalties range from imprisonment to torture and execution.[55]

Western countries walk a murkier line between legal and social punishments, often calling undesirable speech "hate speech" to suggest it lacks the legal protection given to "free speech" that doesn't offend anyone considered important.[56] Spain has gone so far as to jail people for a puppet show.[57] Anyone employed by a large corporation knows that even mildly dissenting beliefs can get them fired, as in the case of former Google software engineer James Damore.[58]

In all such cases, the good of society must be balanced against the harm of coercing people to act in ways they do not want. Different people and societies will balance them differently.

---

[55] "National Laws on Blasphemy: Iran," Berkeley Center for Religion, Peace, and World Affairs, Georgetown University.

[56] "Europe's Free-Speech Apocalypse is Already Here," *Foreign Policy*, March 17, 2016.

[57] "Two jailed over 'terrorist' glove puppet show at Madrid Carnival," *The Telegraph*, February 9, 2016.

[58] "Silicon Valley's Ultimate Diversity Problem is Ideological," *Reason.com*, March 29, 2018.

It all begins with you ...

There's an old saying:

"Pressure makes diamonds."

It's meant as encouragement, but it doubles as a warning. Pressure makes diamonds, but it can also make dust.

What tips the scale between diamonds and dust? Heat. For diamonds, at least 2,000 degrees Fahrenheit. Adding intense heat to immense pressure gives you one of earth's most beautiful and valuable stones.

You, too, are under pressure. You have limited abilities, limited resources, and limited *time* to make a difference with your life:

"Dust thou art, and to dust thou shalt return." (Genesis 3:19)

If you let it, the weight of that pressure will crush you to dust long before you take your final breath. But it doesn't have to be that way. Your life can matter. As a thinking being, you can bring the heat that transforms your life from dust into diamond.

This book gave you some of that heat, as knowledge and understanding. But what happens between the dust of dawn and the dust of dusk is up to you.

If you falter, if you give in to fear or indifference, you're already dust.

If you bring the heat of your own courage, compassion, and clarity, you can be a diamond that shines light through the darkness.

Then at the end, when you finally return to the dust, you can do it with no regrets.

Make the world better.

Be a diamond.

Appendix A:
Why "Modest Foundationalism" is Circular Reasoning

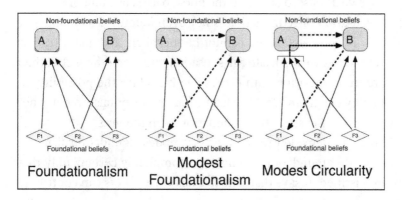

THIS APPENDIX IS FOR READERS interested in details about one of foundationalism's problems. The material is not required for understanding the rest of the book.

Foundationalism divides beliefs into two groups:

- Foundational beliefs that are self-justifying.
- Non-foundational beliefs that are justified by reference to foundational beliefs.

Non-foundational beliefs can get extra justification from other non-foundational beliefs, but the latter get *their* justification from foundational beliefs. Therefore, all the justification ultimately comes from foundational beliefs. There is no other source.

Though terminology varies, traditional theories assert that foundational beliefs are completely certain. No additional evidence can make them more certain or more justified. In his article "The Foundation of Knowledge," Moritz Schlick gives the principle with unusual clarity and frankness. Foundational beliefs are:

> "... statements which express the facts with absolute simplicity, without any moulding, alteration, or addition, in whose elaboration every science consists, and which precede all knowing, every judgment regarding the world."

Since Schlick's time, much of the writing about foundationalism has served to obfuscate that basic idea, but the problem remains: *No such foundational statements exist, or can exist.*

As we've discussed earlier in the book, bare sensations are not beliefs. A sensation of redness that is not even identified as redness or as a color is not a statement, cannot be mistaken, and is not true or false. As soon as we associate the sensation with something else, then compare the association with others, we introduce the possibility of conflict between them. That is what becomes true or false, but it is not foundational in the sense that foundationalism requires.

Those problems led to the idea of "modest foundationalism." It claims not that foundational beliefs are completely certain, only that they are justified. It says that non-foundational beliefs can contribute to their certainty and justification. Non-foundational beliefs can also contribute to each other's certainty.

On the left, the diagram shows the original idea of foundationalism. Foundational beliefs are self-justifying and neither get nor need any justification beyond that. Non-foundational beliefs are justified entirely by their reliance on foundational beliefs.

In the middle, the diagram shows modest foundationalism. Foundational beliefs are still self-justifying, but they can receive additional justification from non-foundational beliefs. Belief B provides additional support to foundational belief F1, while Belief A provides additional support to Belief B.

On the right, the diagram shows the flaw in modest foundational-ism. Belief B gets direct support from foundational beliefs F2 and F3, as well as from Belief A. It then provides additional support for foun-dational belief F1. But Belief A also gets support from F1, which it then provides to Belief B. The support from F1 to B is hidden because it passes through Belief A.

You can call it "justification laundering," after the organized crime practice of laundering money through legal businesses to hide its origin. Hidden or not, it's still circular reasoning. F1 is partly justified by B, which is partly justified by F1.

Note that the problem arises because foundationalism says foun-dational beliefs are ultimately the only source of belief justification. Unless they can be traced back to foundational beliefs, any non-foun-dational beliefs have no justification.

This book advocates a non-foundationalist theory of knowledge. Every belief has some initial presumption in its favor: not enough to justify it, but enough to be considered as *possibly true*. Justification comes from the network of support between multiple beliefs. If A sup-ports B and B supports A, that strengthens the claim of both, but it's still not by itself enough to justify A or B. Additional supporting con-nections to other things are needed to justify both. Justification grows as the network grows, with more support between different kinds of beliefs.

Bibliography

Alcock, J. (2001), *The Triumph of Sociobiology*. Oxford University Press, Oxford, UK.

Anscombe, G.E.M. translator (1953), *Philosophical Investigations* by Ludwig Wittgenstein. Macmillan, New York.

Aquinas, T. (2014), *The Summa Theologica*. Catholic Way Publishing, New York.

Barrett, J. (2011), *Cognitive Science, Religion, and Theology: From Human Minds to Divine Minds*. Templeton Press, West Conshohocken, PA.

Bear, M.F. et al (2007), *Neuroscience: Exploring the Brain*. Lippincott, Williams, & Wilkins, Baltimore, MD.

Bennett, M. et al (2003), *Neuroscience and Philosophy: Brain, Mind, and Language*. Columbia University Press, New York.

Blackburn, S. and Simmons, K., editors (1999), *Truth*. Oxford University Press, Oxford.

Blanshard, Brand (1939), *The Nature of Thought*. George Allen & Unwin Ltd., London.

Bosanquet, B. (1888), *Logic, or the Morphology of Knowledge*. Oxford University Press, Oxford, UK.

Brettler, M. et al (2014), *The Jewish Study Bible*, second edition. Oxford University Press, Oxford, UK.

Chavel, C.B. translator (1967), *Maimonides's The Commandments*. Soncino Press, London.

Clifford, W.K. (1999), *The Ethics of Belief and Other Essays*. Prometheus Books, Amherst, NY.

Cottingham, J. translator (1996), *Meditations on First Philosophy by Rene Descartes*. Cambridge University Press, Cambridge, UK.

Crowe, M.J. (2001), *Theories of the World from Antiquity to the Copernican Revolution*. Dover Publications, Mineola, NY.

Damasio, A. (1994), *Descartes' Error: Emotion, Reason, and the Human Brain*. Penguin Books, New York.

De Selincourt, A., translator (2005), *Livy: The Early History of Rome, Books 1-5*. Penguin Books, New York.

Duggan, T., editor (1970), *An Inquiry into the Human Mind by Thomas Reid*. University of Chicago Press, Chicago.

Edwards, J. et al (2005), *Sinners in the Hands of an Angry God and Other Puritan Sermons*. Dover Books, Mineola, NY.

Fox, M. (1990), *Interpreting Maimonides: Studies in Methodology, Metaphysics, and Moral Philosophy*. University of Chicago Press, Chicago.

Firestone, R. (2008), *Who Are the Real Chosen People?* Skylight Paths Publishing, Woodstock, VT.

Frankfort, H. et al (1946), *The Intellectual Adventure of Ancient Man: An Essay on Speculative Thought in the Ancient Near East*. University of Chicago Press, Chicago. Kindle edition.

Gottlieb, M., editor (2011), *Moses Mendelssohn: Writings on Judaism, Christianity, and the Bible*. Brandeis University Press, Waltham, MA.

Grayling, A.C. (1997), *An Introduction to Philosophical Logic*. Blackwell Publishing, Oxford, UK.

Graziano, M.S.A. (2013), *Consciousness and the Social Brain*. Oxford University Press, Oxford, UK.

Greene, J. (2013), *Moral Tribes: Emotion, Reason, and the Gap Between Us and Them*. Penguin Books, New York.

Grunfeld, I., translator (1962), *Horeb* by Samson Raphael Hirsch. Soncino Press, New York.

Haidt, J. (2012), *The Righteous Mind: Why Good People Are Divided by Politics and Religion*. Pantheon Books, New York.

Halbertal, M. (1997), *People of the Book*. Harvard University Press, Cambridge, MA. Kindle edition.

Heschel, A.J. (1976), *God in Search of Man: A Philosophy of Judaism*. Farrar, Straus, and Giroux, New York.

Holland, T., translator (2013), *Herodotus: The Histories*. Penguin Books, New York.

Hughes, G.E. and Cresswell, M.J. (1968), *An Introduction to Modal Logic*. Methuen & Co., London, UK.

Israel, J., editor (2007) *Theological-Political Treatise*. Cambridge University Press, Cambridge, UK.

Jacobson, S., editor (1995), *Toward a Meaningful Life: The Wisdom of Rebbe Menachem Mendel Schneerson*. HarperCollins, New York.

Jardine, L. and Silverthorne, M., editors (2000), *The New Organon by Francis Bacon*. Cambridge University Press, Cambridge, UK.

Jewish Publication Society (1985), *Tanakh: The Holy Scriptures*. Jewish Publication Society, Jerusalem.

Kellner, Menachem (2006), *Must a Jew Believe Anything?* second edition. Littman Library of Jewish Civilization, Oxford, UK.

Kim, J. (2010), *Philosophy of Mind*. Westview Press, Boulder, CO. Kindle edition.

Kreisel, H. (2017), "Were Maimonides and Some of His Followers Orthoprax?" TheTorah.com, http://thetorah.com/were-maimonides-and-some-of-his-followers-orthoprax/.

Lynch, M. (2012), *In Praise of Reason*. M.I.T. Press, Cambridge, MA.

Lewy, H. et al (2006), *3 Jewish Philosophers*. Toby Press, London, UK. Kindle edition.

Melville, R. translator (1997), *On the Nature of the Universe by Lucretius*. Oxford University Press, Oxford, UK.

Menand, L. (2002), *The Metaphysical Club*. New York: Farrar, Straus, and Giroux.

Muffs, Y. (2011), *The Personhood of God*. Jewish Lights Publishing, Woodstock, VT. Kindle edition.

Nadler, S. (2006), *Spinoza's Ethics: An Introduction*. Cambridge University Press, Cambridge, UK.

Napier, W. (1851), *History of General Sir Charles Napier's Administration of Scinde*. Chapman and Hall, London.

Nash, R. (1969), *The Light of the Mind: St. Augustine's Theory of Knowledge*. Louisville: University Press of Kentucky.

Natoli, J. and Hutcheon, L. (1993), *A Postmodern Reader*. State University of New York Press, Albany, NY.

Nilsson, N. (2014), *Understanding Beliefs*. Cambridge: Massachusetts Institute of Technology Press. Kindle edition.

Pines, S. translator (1963), *The Guide of the Perplexed*, Volume 1 and Volume 2. University of Chicago Press, Chicago.

Pinker, S. (2007), *The Language Instinct: How the Mind Creates Language*. Harper Perennial, New York.

Pinker, S. (2011), *The Better Angels of Our Nature: Why Violence Has Declined*. Penguin Books, New York.

Pinker, S. (2018), *Enlightenment Now: The Case for Reason, Science, Humanism, and Progress*. Penguin Books, New York.

Plantinga, A. (2015), *Knowledge and Christian Belief*. Cambridge: Eerdmans Publishing Co.

Postgate, J. (1896), *Semantics: Studies in the Science of Meaning*. Henry Holt Publishing, New York.

Prager, D. (1995), *Think a Second Time*. Harper Collins, New York.

Putnam, H. (2008), *Jewish Philosophy as a Guide to Life*. Indiana University Press, Bloomington, IN.

Putnam, R. (2000), *Bowling Alone: The Collapse and Revival of American Community*. Simon & Schuster, New York.

Rawls, J. (1993), *Political Liberalism*. New York: Columbia University Press. Kindle edition.

Rescher, N. (1973), *The Coherence Theory of Truth*. Oxford University Press, Oxford.

Rosenblatt, S., translator (1947), *Saadia Gaon: The Book of Beliefs and Opinions*. Yale University Press, New Haven.

Russell, Bertrand (1948), *Human Knowledge: Its Scope and Limits*. Simon & Schuster Publishing, New York.

Russell, Bertrand (1935), *In Praise of Idleness*. Unwin Hyman Ltd., London.

Russell, Bertrand (1961), *The Basic Writings of Bertrand Russell*. George Allen & Unwin, London, UK.

Schilpp, P.A., ed. (1980), *The Philosophy of Brand Blanshard*. Open Court Publishing, LaSalle, IL.

Schimmel, S. (2008), *The Tenacity of Unreasonable Beliefs*. Oxford University Press, Oxford, UK. Kindle edition.

Shirley, S. translator (2011), *The Ethics by Baruch de Spinoza*. Hackett Publishing, Indianapolis, IN.

Singer. A. (2008), *The Outsider's Guide to Orthodox Judaism*. Self-published by Rabbi Arnie Singer, www.arniesinger.com, New York.

Slater, P.J. et al (1994), *Behaviour and Evolution*. Cambridge University Press, Cambridge, UK.

Slone, D. Jason (2004), *Theological Incorrectness: Why Religious People Believe What They Shouldn't*. Oxford University Press, Oxford, UK.

Sproul, Barbara C. (2013), *Primal Myths*. HarperOne Publishing, New York.

Telushkin, J. (2008), *Jewish Literacy*. Harper Collins, New York.

Twersky, I. editor (1972), *A Maimonides Reader*. Behrman House, Inc., Springfield, New Jersey.

Vermes, G. (2004), *The Complete Dead Sea Scrolls in English*. Penguin Books, New York. Kindle edition.

Wilson, E.O. (2012), *The Social Conquest of Earth*. Norton Publishing, New York.

Workman, L. et al (2014), *Evolutionary Psychology*. Cambridge University Press, Cambridge, UK.